Maverick Investing *with* Doug Fabian

Mission Possible:
Control Your Future,
Seize Opportunities,
and Invest in Your Dreams

McGraw-Hill

A Division of The **McGraw·Hill** *Companies*

Copyright © 2002 by Doug Fabian. All rights reserved. Printed in the United States of America. Except as permitted under the United States Copyright Act of 1976, no part of this publication may be reproduced or distributed in any form or by any means, or stored in a data base or retrieval system, without the prior written permission of the publisher.

1 2 3 4 5 6 7 8 9 0   DOC/DOC   0 9 8 7 6 5 4 3 2 1

ISBN 0-07-137562-7

This book was set in Times New Roman by North Market Street Graphics.

Printed and bound by R. R. Donnelley & Sons Company.

McGraw-Hill books are available at special quantity discounts to use as premiums and sales promotions, or for use in corporate training programs. For more information, please write to the Director of Special Sales, McGraw-Hill Professional, Two Penn Plaza, New York, NY 10121-2298. Or contact your local bookstore.

This book is printed on recycled, acid-free paper containing a minimum of 50% recycled de-inked fiber.

Contents

Part 3   Maverick Investing Techniques

Part 4   Maverick Advances in the World of Investing

Annotated Contents

Acknowledgments

I have not been alone in the development of the Maverick Investing Lifestyle. There have been significant contributions by others to this work and to my success in the financial leadership field. It is only appropriate to acknowledge the contribution of others.

The most significant contribution to the Maverick Lifestyle has come from my dad, Dick Fabian. His first book, *How to Be Your Own Investment Counselor,* set in stone how individuals can take control of their financial lives. His invitation for me to join him on his quest to empower the individual investor was the opportunity of a lifetime. His coaching, wisdom, experience, and passion to bring a unique message to the public have earned him the title of the "Original Maverick Investor." To my dad, I cannot say thank you enough for all that you have done for me.

This work started as an idea, much like my Maverick Investing radio talk show. The individual who pushed and prodded me to start the ball rolling was Michael Tomlinson (aka MT), the executive producer of the show.

The challenge of a project like this is in successfully encompassing the vast scope of the material that must be presented. The depth, detail, and entertaining prose were a direct result of my colleague and on-air sidekick Gary Gordon, also known as the "Gee Man." His writing, research, and ideas have been invaluable to this book.

To Jennifer Shammamy, our head of research at Maverick Central, a huge thank you. To Darlene March, my public relations manager, I could not have done this without you. To my Sunday morning surf buddies Buck Kimball and Jim Rock, thanks for putting up with my Maverick moments and lectures "on the boards."

To my kids, David, Michael, Morgan, and Jordan, thanks for allowing me to complete this project and for giving me the support that you did. And finally to my wife, Karen, Thank You for the support, the space, and the encouragement to bring the Maverick message to the audience worldwide. I am truly blessed to have you as a partner in this life.

Introduction

Have you ever kicked yourself for not being more aggressive in the stock market?

Or in light of the Nasdaq meltdown of 2000, do you wish that you hadn't been quite so heavy on technology?

Has anyone ever made you feel stupid for asking questions about your money? Have you ever felt like you were at the mercy of the big brokerage firms? Did you ever curse yourself for buying a stock fund straight out of a magazine?

Are money woes—recent losses, or anxiety about college tuitions or retirement—causing disharmony at home?

Have you ever said to yourself, "I want to take more responsibility for my financial future"?

Or, conversely, do you ever find yourself thinking, "Life is short . . . I don't want to spend my time worrying about hot IPOs, about daily fluctuations in the S&P 500, or about how thick Alan Greenspan's briefcase is today"?

If you answered "yes" to any of these questions, then this book is for you. This book can help you make yourself rich. Notice that I didn't say "get rich quick." This book isn't about tricks, gimmicks, or shortcuts. It's about wealth-building a different way. Anybody can do it. And everybody *should* do it.

It doesn't matter how much money you have today. It doesn't matter whether it's $250 in a checking account, or $250,000 in a 401(k) portfolio. You can build enormous wealth. Let me say that again, with an emphasis on "you": *You* can build enormous wealth. And although time is your friend—as we'll see in later chapters—getting started late doesn't prevent you from building substantial wealth. In this book, I'll show you a flexible approach to investing that will get you that new house you've been dreaming about, pay those tuition bills, or enable you to retire when you want to. (*You* decide.)

How are you feeling about your financial situation? Does it feel like your broker sold you down the river? Are you kicking yourself because you missed a certain boomlet, or didn't predict the bursting of that particular bubble? Well, if you're tired of beating yourself up, or of banging your head against the Wall—as in "Wall Street"—this book will put you on track. It will provide you with all of the habits, attitudes, values, and practices you need to create your fortune.

Maybe you've had some bad experiences in trying to learn the ropes on your own. Or perhaps you've enjoyed some growth on your portfolio, but you've still fallen far short of your high expectations. First, I'd say, "Congratulations for having those high expectations! That's a key part of the puzzle!" And second, I'd say, "Put all those fears to rest." Why? Because this book will give you what you haven't been able to find anywhere else: a simple and rewarding *investing lifestyle.*

This gives me the chance to work in one of my other favorite words: *maverick.* I was surprised to find that there really *was* a Maverick, although the television series and the movie got a lot of the details wrong. The real Maverick was Samuel A. Maverick, a rancher in the West in the 1870s who refused to brand his cattle. His name has come to stand for someone who is an independent thinker, and who refuses to go along with the thinking or habits of his group.

In this book, I want to help you transform yourself into a modern-day maverick. When we succeed at that, we'll help secure your financial future.

MYTH VERSUS MAVERICK

Let's look at five conventional nuggets of financial "wisdom" that you've probably already been exposed to a dozen times, or maybe a hundred times, or maybe a thousand times.

I'll refer to them as "myths," because to the maverick, that's exactly what they are.

And I'll provide the maverick antidote to these five myths. You should begin to see just how different we mavericks really are from the average cattle-brander.

Myth Number 1: *Buying and holding your stocks for the long-term is the key to investing success. Buy and hold! Buy and hold!*

The Maverick Antidote: The key to investing success is understanding both when to buy and when to sell.

"Buy and hold" has been called the ultimate investment strategy. But even as everyone on Wall Street shouts "buy and hold" from the rooftops, the question they never address is, buy and hold *what?* Buy and hold the S&P 500? Buy and hold the Jacobs Internet Fund? Buy and hold Lucent, Qualcomm, AT&T, or Xerox? Especially after the 2000–2001 bear market, nobody can answer *what* to buy and hold.

Well, there's no longer any such thing as a "buy, hold, and forget-about-it" stock investment. Period, stop: No such thing. If there ever was such a day, that day is over. Extraordinary wealth makers like us understand that selling eliminates excessive losses, and creates new opportunities.

Myth Number 2: *Spreading your assets across stocks, bonds, and cash is the best way to invest. Diversify!*

The Maverick Antidote: Getting 100 percent of your money in stocks (at the right times in the cycle, of course) is the smart way to achieve wealth.

Investors have been force-fed the idea that the best way to minimize market risk is to diversify across the three asset classes. Extraordinary wealth-makers know that there are many ways to minimize the downside risk of stocks, while still aiming for the unequaled rewards of a 100 percent stock solution.

Myth Number 3: *Paying attention to stock market volatility provokes unnecessary fear, and consumes too much time.*

The Maverick Antidote: Spending as little as five minutes a week can keep you in touch with the stock market, increase your knowledge, help you manage downside risk, and identify new opportunities.

Let's face it: If you're breathing, talking with neighbors or coworkers, or ingesting even a little dose of the media every day, you're already living with stock-market volatility. It's part of every news program, drives (and makes money for) a couple of cable TV networks, and provides grist for the Hollywood mill—TV series, movies, and so on. So you're already following the plot line—and if you're an investor, you're a player in the drama. So your job is not to wish it all away, and let Wall Street worry about it. Your job is to filter out the noise, find the quality resources that are already out there for portfolio tracking and assessing the current market environment, and *act*.

Myth Number 4: *Brokers and planners can manage your money better than you can.*

The Maverick Antidote: Nope. Nobody else cares as much about your money as you do. You can manage your money better than they can.

Ordinary investors let others tell them what to do. Extraordinary wealth-makers take *complete responsibility* for their attitudes and actions, even if they only oversee a portion of their money. Do you let other people make decisions regarding your children's education or manage your household finances? Some things are too important to delegate. You have more passion to build wealth for yourself than anyone else has. *Use* that passion!

Myth Number 5: *Reducing your stock exposure as you near the age of retirement is a good strategy, because it reduces the risk of losing capital.*

The Maverick Antidote: Perhaps, but there is *another* risk that is just as real—the risk of outliving your money.

It doesn't quite add up, does it? You're told throughout your peak earning years that you have to buy 'n hold through any market conditions, as if downside risk didn't exist. But when you get closer to retirement age, you start hearing that the stock market is suddenly too dangerous a neighborhood to hang around in.

Mavericks understand that people in the United States are living longer—well past their sixties and seventies, and into their eighties and nineties. So a reasonably healthy 55-year-old person today has *every reason* to adopt a 30-year time horizon for his or her stock portfolio. As a maverick, you can commit to growth in stocks for *your entire life*.

INVEST IN YOUR DREAMS—TODAY!

When you change the way you invest, along the lines laid out in this book, you will boost your net worth, promote your self-confidence, and enhance the way you live. Make no mistake about it: If you're willing to modify what hasn't worked, while capitalizing on the things that *have* worked, you will grow richer than you ever imagined.

In my experience, most people are eager to achieve more, and to go farther. The problem is, they don't know where to turn for help. Personal finance books are cold, confusing, or fad-oriented. Brokers are *selling* more than they're *telling*. Financial advisors seem inclined to recommend only the products that their companies sell. And who can make tails or heads out of the absolute torrent of conflicting info on the Internet—all those Web sites, e-mail lists, user groups, chat rooms, and message boards?

But what if there were a clear path to personal wealth? Let's conjure up a surfing metaphor. (I'm from California, and yes, I've always loved surfing.) Suppose there really was a "perfect wave" out there, and all you had to do was spot it, catch it, and ride it. Wouldn't you start taking the steps necessary to make that happen?

If you could catch a wave to financial security—or better yet, create your own wave—wouldn't you start investing in your dreams this very minute?

If the answer is "yes," then you've picked up the right book. Welcome to the uniquely rewarding world of maverick investing!

WHO'S DOUG FABIAN?

It's time to give you a little background about myself, and about my family, so that you can decide for yourself whether my background qualifies me to give you helpful advice.

First things first: I'm no relation to Fabian, the teen singing idol and heart-throb from the 1950s. His real name was Fabian Forte, so again, no relation. In fact, I'm only in my forties, so I'm too young to have paid much attention to Fabian in his prime. But since I get asked that question all the time—Are you related to *the* Fabian?—I've come to realize that Mr. Forte had a big impact on the generation ahead of mine.

If you switch the focus to a very different line of work, however, I *am* related to "the" Fabian. His name is Dick Fabian, and he's my dad. Dick Fabian sold real estate in the Los Angeles area in the 1960s. He was always interested in the stock market, and when I was in grade school, our TV set was more or less constantly tuned in to the local Los Angeles stock market channel.

My father became a stockbroker in the early 1970s, just in time to go through the devastation of the 1973–1974 bear market. He didn't escape that devastation. In 1974, the year I graduated from high school, my dad found himself flat broke and out of work. It was by far the most difficult period in his life. I give him enormous credit for sucking it up, regrouping, and getting back into the game. A lot of people wouldn't have had that kind of resilience, or that kind of courage.

Briefly, he went back to selling real estate, but he was already looking for a way to apply his hard-won lessons in wealth-building. In 1976 he wrote a book—*How to Be Your Own Investment Counselor*—with the notion of selling it for $10 a copy. At that price, he was mainly hoping to get the word out. But then he realized that it probably wasn't going to be good enough just to put his ideas out in the marketplace and hope for the best. He decided to publish a newsletter that would provide guidance to subscribers on a continuing basis.

The result was *The Telephone Switch Newsletter,* a title that reflected a revolutionary new tool that had recently become available to mutual fund investors: the ability to switch resources from one fund to another over the phone. A quarter-century later, we investors take this kind of thing for granted. But back then, the telephone switch was a *big deal.* It was the crack in the dam of control that had been exercised by Wall Street since forever. It gave Little Guys—like you and me, for example—a chance to start controlling our own financial destiny.

Except that I wasn't paying too much attention at the time. I had finished high school, gone to college, knocked around, done my share of surfing, and eventually opened a cabinet shop. This satisfied me for a while, and earned me a decent living. But one day, I woke up and realized that there had to be more to life than cutting wood for interior designers. So I asked my father if he had any career advice for me, and he said, "Hey— your mom and I could use some help with this newsletter business. Why don't you come work for me?"

So I did. That was the summer of 1979. My first job for the family business—which is what the newsletter business had just turned into, to everyone's surprise—was doing library research. I spent many hours crunching numbers by hand, plotting price movements, and charting the recent history of the stock market. Today, there are software programs that do this stuff more or less automatically, and many of the analyses I was producing back then are readily available through the Web today, if you know where to look. But back then, I felt like I was an explorer in unknown territory. I fell in love with numbers, with the stock market and its history, and with investing, and I looked for new ways to deepen my knowledge and make our newsletter even more helpful.

After a few years of this, in 1983, my dad brought me in as coeditor of the newsletter. Eventually, he devoted himself full-time to the money-management business, and I took over the publishing business. This proved to be a good division of labor, and it helped us head off some of the difficult dynamics that often crop up in the family-business setting.

The Telephone Switch Newsletter (by this time called *The Fabian Investment Resource*) more or less made its own friends. My father's investment philosophies—which, along with my own ideas, infuse the pages of this book—helped the newsletter grow steadily throughout the 1980s. Then something happened that interrupted our trendline of steady but modest growth. We sent out a "sell" signal just prior to the stock market crash of 1987. (I'll return to the subject of word choices, like "crash" and "panic," in later chapters. Wall Street doesn't like these words.) The news of our good advice got around quickly, and our business doubled in size in 1988. By the early 1990s, our subscriber base had grown to 45,000. Many of our subscribers had been with us for two decades, quietly and steadily building wealth according to the Fabian principles. Then came the big stock market boom of the 1990s. It became easy to make money—or so it seemed. Our subscription base tapered off gently. For the next half-decade or so, people didn't need much encouragement from us to *get into the game.* They got in it, and got in *deep.* (Judging from developments at the end of the decade, though, it appears that many of them got into it without a clear set of goals, or a structured way to achieve those goals.) Meanwhile, we Fabians stuck to our disciplines, as did tens of thousands of people who believed in our principles of long-term wealth building. I will weave some of their personal stories into the pages of this book.

Then two more interesting things happened. In March of 1999, on the first FM talk station in Los Angeles, I started a radio broadcast called *Maverick Investing with Doug Fabian.* This was something I had always wanted to do, because it seemed like yet another way to do what the Fabians had always tried to do—build relationships with people, and help them achieve their wealth-building goals. Among other things, I wanted to speak to younger people. To reach them, I decided to talk about serious subjects in a not-so-serious way. Combining tongue-in-cheek themes ("The Seven Deadly Sins of Wall Street") with phone calls from listeners and snippets of rock music, my colleagues and I created a new kind of financially oriented talk show.

Today, we're broadcasting nationwide, and *Maverick Investing* is the fastest-growing financial talk show in America, with more than 100,000 listeners weekly. Several thousand more join us each week on the Web at www.fabianlive.com.

And then came the Nasdaq Meltdown of 2000. Suddenly, investing seemed *tough* again. We started gaining a thousand new newsletter subscribers a month. When people decide they need help, our circulation soars. We're a little bit like those guys you see selling umbrellas on city street corners on a rainy day—except that come boom or bust, we're *always* there with the umbrellas. And also with sunglasses and sunscreen, to make the metaphor a little more accurate. (We help you through all kinds of financial weather.)

In 2000, my father published another important book: *The Mutual Fund Wealth Builder.* He told me he wrote it mainly for his grandchildren, of whom he has 15 (at last count). If I can be allowed to speak for all humankind, we're very lucky he did. In some cultures, they believe that when an elder dies, it's like a library burning down. Now my father has put his life lessons between two covers, and the library is safe.

In this book, I want to carry the family tradition forward. I firmly believe in the magic of compounded growth, which Albert Einstein once referred to as the greatest mathematical discovery of all time, and which is at the heart of my father's investment strategy. And while my father focuses exclusively on the world of mutual funds, I believe that many of the principles that we have refined and espoused over the years can be applied to a whole range of investment vehicles.

Here's a statement that may surprise you: I don't purchase individual stocks. I've always bought mutual funds. And I was no Boy Wonder when it came to mutual funds, either. I didn't buy my first mutual fund shares until I was 23 years old.

I *was* a financial genius once, when I played the options market. I received a windfall of $35,000 in 1991. I decided to plunge into the exotic world of options. On my first trade, I tripled my money. Turned $6000 into $18,000. I had always *suspected* I might be some kind of financial genius; now I *knew* it. (Evidence of genius: always a bad sign!) All I had to do was double my money a half-dozen more times over the next few years, and I'd be set for life.

So over the next six months, trading options on the indexes, I lost *every penny.* I lost the whole $12,000 profit. I lost my original $35,000 stake. In so doing, I not only created the kind of marital disharmony I referred to at the beginning of this chapter, I also joined the vast majority of options traders—something like 80 percent—who wind up losing money in that particular game. I learned from this experience that in fact, I'm *not* a financial genius.

So that's my best answer to the question, "Who's Doug Fabian?" For more than 20 years, I've been helping self-directed investors just like you realize their potential. I've shared what I've learned, from my father and others, so that people who followed the Fabian principles would be able to turn small amounts of cash into huge sums of money. And though I may be a little farther down the maverick road, I want exactly what you want—the very best for me and my family.

I invite you to read the rest of this Introduction, and Chapter 1, and then decide for yourself whether Doug Fabian and maverick investing make sense for you.

TWO TOOLS AND A MINDSET

I'm going to help you change the way you invest your time and money. That's an ambitious goal, I realize. But I'm a passionate person. And I'm committed to helping you acquire all of the skills you need to make the most of the twenty-first century.

I want you to understand how the wealth-building process works, and how to put that knowledge to use for your portfolio.

To do this, you need two tools:

1. *The Internet.* The Web is sitting out there, 24/7, serving up quick quotes, speedy searches, customized charts, and instant info. If you don't have a good enough PC, scrape the money together and buy one—*now.* And within your budget, get the fastest possible connection to the Web, too. (A slow-moving Internet connection will drive you crazy, and is a false economy.) Beg, borrow, barter—but get connected! In later chapters, I'll tell you how to find the best pages for financial news, stock/fund screening, and portfolio tracking. Which leads me naturally to tool number 2:

2. *Your Money . . . Online!* There's no substitute for executing trades and tracking your assets online. A Web-based account offers low fees, easy access, and viable member resources.

And finally, you also need a mindset: *a maverick approach.* I love knowledge. Understanding how things work is the foundation on which we'll build our financial futures. But the media bombards you with useless, breathless, and scary info on a daily basis. You need to be able to swim in the river of data without getting panicked (or drowned!). You need a perspective, an attitude, an *approach* to lend structure to your wealth-building. The one I like is the maverick approach.

HOW THIS BOOK WILL HELP YOU

I'll make sure that you get all of the tips, concepts, secrets, and principles to make your investing lifestyle sizzle. Keep in mind that most of the ideas herein are so unconventional that you'll have to get rid of preconceived notions. So what? After some initial discomfort, nothing feels better than unloading outdated ideas.

My aim is to give it to you straight—without any attitude, or obscure financial jargon. You will not have to study technical descriptions of the Producer Price Index, market capitalizations, or long bond yields. (To all that, I say, "*Blecch!*") I spell out every technique in plain, easy-to-comprehend English. I give you what you need, and *only* what you need, to prosper.

Part One of *Maverick Investing* helps you to take charge of your money and strengthen your understanding of the maverick investing lifestyle.

Part Two gives you insights into the stock market itself—the players, the playing field, and the emotions that tend to distract and hurt investors—so that you'll be able to get 100 percent of your money into stocks (when that's the right place to be).

Part Three shows you how to put maverick tools and techniques to use for your investment portfolio—increasing your profit potential while managing the downside dangers.

Part Four opens the door to advancements in the world of investing, including sectors, ETFs, EIFs, VULs, VAs, and what I call the maverick road to financial freedom.

HERE'S HOW WE'RE GOING TO DO IT TOGETHER

Time for another sports metaphor. In maverick investing, *you're* the star. Me? I'm your success coach. And like most committed coaches, I'm going to be *in your face.* When you read (and reread) the chapters of this book, I'm going to be right alongside you. When you turn on your car radio, or that radio in the kitchen, you're going to *hear* my distinctive voice. And when you log on, you're going to find me—and maverick investing sites— all over the Web. You're going to feel like I've got you surrounded.

And that's a good thing! We're a team.

Specifically, here's how we're going to do it together:

1. **We'll capitalize on new opportunities.** For instance, you'll be able to buy baskets of stocks in the utilities, health care, and technology sectors through exchange-traded funds (ETFs). An ETF gives you the flexibility of an individual stock and the simplicity of an index fund— all wrapped into one!

2. **We'll focus on what matters most to you.** For example, we'll hone in on techniques for getting more aggressive with your 401(k). You'll know exactly how to get the biggest bang from those limited choices— going after the best stock fund with the strongest momentum!

3. **We'll tame the "greedies."** It's not about choosing the one fund that's going to rise 300 percent this year. (If anybody tells you they can do that for you, clamp your hand on your wallet!) It's not about getting in on the hottest IPO. Hitting home runs seems cool, but winning in this game is more about hitting singles.

4. **We'll make sure it's fun.** Why should investing bore you sense-less? If this stuff can be fun—and it can—then it *should* be fun. Not just unboring, or unpainful. *Fun.* Especially when your money keeps growing, and growing, and growing. . . .

5. **We'll let you be you.** The maverick way is not only fun and finan-cially rewarding, it's also an individualist's dream. It's a lifestyle, and because you're the one who designs it, it's *your* lifestyle.

I won't lie to you. This maverick stuff isn't for everybody. Some people don't want to *know* when they're in danger of being hustled. Others derive comfort from sticking to their well-established patterns, even when the results aren't all that great. Still others can't handle hearing that there is any downside risk, but simply choose to buy and hope for the best.

But as I see it, maverick investing is for anyone who (1) honestly wants to achieve a greater piece of the American dream, and (2) is willing to change the way he or she thinks about the stock market. Yeah, it may be a little bit of a struggle at first. But all good things require effort. And some-times, it's that struggle, that extra effort, that makes the difference between living the life you want and wanting the life you're not yet living.

Let's go maverick!

MISSION POSSIBLE OVERVIEW

- The key to creating extraordinary wealth is affirming an *investing lifestyle.*
- The twenty-first century demands that you use technological advances to your advantage. You'll need high-speed access to the Internet, an online brokerage account, and familiarity with a very select set of Web sites.
- Wall Street encourages conformity. Unless you question what Wall Street's agents tell you—and question them intelligently—you'll get burned. Poke holes in myths using maverick logic.
- You define your goals. They're *yours.* But getting to your goals will require investing 100 percent of your money in stocks. This requires an understanding of your own values and emotions, and a clear picture of how the stock market works. I'll take care of that last piece.
- We're going to do this together. We're going to make it fun. And we're going to start achieving your dreams.
- In fact, we've already started.

PART 1

Take Charge of Your Money

1

What is a Maverick?

Inquisitive, flexible, assertive, upbeat, and independent. These are a few of the qualities that mavericks possess—and a few of the traits that will help you embark on a new investing path.

You must be inquisitive enough to question traditional mindsets and conventional wisdom. You must be open-minded enough to accept the possibility that most of what you've heard about investing is wrong. (*You* weren't wrong. *They* were wrong.)

Mavericks are assertive. We demand excellence from our investments, as well as from our brokerage-house relationships. We always know how our 401(k) selections are performing. And we're not afraid to exercise the trade option (in the sports sense) when our superstars start dogging it.

Mavericks are "glass-half-full" thinkers. We see opportunities, not shortfalls. We make goals, not excuses. We thrive on the emotional high of our accomplishments. And we believe in our hearts that we can become wealthy.

Last, but definitely not least, mavericks are fiercely independent. We are rugged individualists who (1) discover how to grow rich, (2) become resolved to achieve that goal, (3) keep learning constantly, and (4) incorporate what we learn into a personal blueprint for prosperity.

3

Not everyone can be a maverick. Not every investor will take control of the stock reins, find the (minimal) time needed to track his or her investment choices, set aggressive goals, and question authority. But many will!

I'm looking for those individuals who want to invest differently from the herd. I'm looking for those who are curious by nature, and who are avid believers in what Thomas Jefferson called the "pursuit of happiness."

LIFE, LIBERTY, AND THE FREEDOM TO GROW RICH!

What did the old red-headed revolutionary mean by that memorable phrase in the Declaration of Independence? I think he meant that you have the natural-born right to seek your "fortune," broadly defined. Male, female, old, young, dark skin, light skin—it doesn't matter. You're free to define and pursue your personal ambitions.

When the Founding Fathers got around to writing a constitution for the country they were trying to create, they got more specific about the rights that the government would not be permitted to infringe upon. One of my personal favorites in the Bill of Rights is the Fifth Amendment, which says that Congress may not deprive anyone of "life, liberty, or property without due process of law."

Now, *that's* freedom! As an American, your right to own property is sacrosanct. Back in the eighteenth century, that meant that no king with a powdered wig (or his red-coated representatives) could steal your stuff. Today, it means that you have the freedom—unrivalled anywhere in the world—to create the wealth you desire. Add to that the remarkable political stability of the United States, and you have an astounding opportunity as an investor.

So why are some of us so reluctant to take up this opportunity? What keeps us from plunging in, and building wealth for ourselves?

TOO MUCH SALESMANSHIP, TOO MUCH INFO, NOT ENOUGH TIME

I think there are a couple of reasons, starting with the fact that people today are stressed out. That's one of the first things that people from other countries notice about Americans: We work our keyboard fingers to the fingertip bones. (Sorry; no time for lunch!) And we volunteer for a zillion things in the community. And of course, most important, we love up our kids as much as we can—feeding them, clothing them, getting them to and from the soccer games, reading them stories, and getting them to bed.

So we've got a ton of stuff going on. It's not surprising that many of us have placed this "investing thing" on the back burner. And there are still other factors that discourage us from pursuing wealth in a systematic way.

Too Much Info, Not Enough Time

Did you know there are more than *25,000* investment choices? There are at least 11,000 mutual funds, 5000 Nasdaq stocks, 3000 NYSE stocks, a wide variety of exchange-traded vehicles, annuities, bonds, variable life options, currencies, commodities, and fixed-income products. It's enough to make your head spin.

Equally frustrating is the sheer volume of financial data coming over the airwaves and streaming over the Internet. I've seen estimates that there are more than 25,000 investment-related Web sites—meaning that there are more virtual places to go get advice from than there are places to put your money!

Take heart! As a maverick, you don't need to worry about every bit and byte on the Web. Most likely, as I'll explain in subsequent chapters, you should start by focusing on the relatively few growth-oriented choices within your employer's 401(k) plan. In many instances, there are just seven or eight to choose from, only two or three of which turn out to be worthwhile choices. (I'll tell you how to figure out which is which.)

Nor do you have to be a financial whiz to track the choices in your IRA. You just have to build 5 to 10 minutes of Web time into your weekly routine. Instead of having that second cup of coffee on Saturday morning at the kitchen table, in front of your newspaper, have it in front of your computer. After all: If you knew *for certain* that regularly tracking your investments *guaranteed* a multimillion dollar future, wouldn't you find the precious few seconds you needed to get ahead?

Sure you would.

Too Much Hype, Too Little Help

Here's another reason why people shy away from taking charge of their financial future: too much hype out there. Think about the last time you went out car-shopping. Sure, it's exciting to think about driving that new car home. But who enjoys all the hype that you have to put up with from the salespeople on the floor?

The same stuff goes on in the financial arena, but it's worse there because there's so much mumbo-jumbo involved, and the product is so much more intangible. (Can I test-drive that mutual fund, please?) Think back: Have you ever felt that a financial advisor got the better of you, even though he or she is supposed to be on your side? Have you had that sneaking suspicion that a planner has slipped you into an investment that you didn't really need? Have you ever dealt with a broker who excused himself or herself for losses in your account—losses that he or she somehow wasn't responsible for?

Don't feel bad if you have to answer "yes" to any or all of these questions. Everybody who sticks more than their big toe into the investment game gets bad advice, at some point, and has to deal with the hype that goes along with that bad advice—before, during, or after. What I'm arguing here is that your response shouldn't be to throw in the towel. Your response should be to *get maverick* on all those commission-driven brokers.

And then there's that bad feeling that arises when you realize that even though you're paying good money for help with your investments, you're not necessarily *getting* any help. Consider e-mail that I received recently from a *Maverick Investing* radio show listener, whom I'll call Cynthia:

> I have $50,000 with my brokerage firm and, thanks to you, Doug, I realize I'm only making $500 a year with my four mutual funds. That's only 1 percent. I put the numbers into your Web site calculator, and if my money compounded at 20 percent, I'd have $5 million in 25 years.

At first glance, one might be tempted to state the obvious: Cynthia's holding the wrong mutual funds. But wait a minute: Why hasn't she been able to talk to someone at her full-service firm about this problem? (You're absolutely right, Cynthia; 1 percent is a *problem*.) Or going a step further: Why hasn't somebody from the brokerage house called her, and suggested a new strategy? Hasn't she already *paid* to get the best advice of a financial professional?

I congratulated Cynthia on taking responsibility, and advised her to reevaluate her brokerage house relationship. I said to ask the tough questions. How are they getting paid? How, exactly, is *she* benefiting from the "front-end loads," or sales charges, that the brokers have been deducting from her investments? And most important, why isn't she receiving the guidance needed to achieve a higher rate of return?

Cynthia's rude awakening isn't all that unusual. (I help people have them almost every day.) What's important is how you *react* to the bad news. Sometimes people respond to a bad experience by saying, "Oh, the hell with it. The game is rigged against me, anyway. I'll just take what they give me." Or worse: "I'll just give up on the whole idea of accumulating wealth."

Wrong reactions! You have to *take control* of your assets, and by extension, your life. When you do, you'll begin to feel good about your financial future, and you'll pursue happiness successfully.

You need to exercise your right to be rich. It's your money. The goals are yours. Your dreams are yours. Take the bull by the horns and decide once and for all that you are going to win at this investing game—and do it!

THE LIFESTYLE OF CHAMPIONS

In fact, one of the most important reasons to invest like a maverick is that it will make you feel *good* about yourself—after you get over that first fear of the unknown. Many compare this experience to modifying their levels of physical activity. At first, you may not love the exercise—you may shy away from getting in the water for a few laps, or hopping on a bike for a three-mile ride. But ask any jogger, mountain biker, swimmer, or surfer, and they'll tell you: There's no better way to develop a sense of pride, accomplishment, and well-being than getting your body in shape.

You'll get the same kind of emotional high when you take the maverick investing lifestyle to heart. It may take a few scrapes—a trial here, a tribulation there—but you'll love the results. Imagine how it will feel to select winners consistently. Imagine how it will feel to get out of the market early enough to protect your gains. And imagine how it will feel to make sensational gains, year after year.

As with our bodies, you can't work on every muscle all at once. But let's take a look at the essential ingredients of this radically different approach.

THE FINE POINTS OF PLANNING

Success is 80 percent planning, 20 percent doing.—Anonymous

If one does not know to which port one is sailing, no wind is favorable.—Seneca

What is the use of running if we're not on the right road?—German proverb

If you don't know where you're going, any road will do.—Dick Fabian

Sometimes people tell me that I could save myself a lot of work if I would just sell everyone a list of stocks and funds that I think will do well in the next 5 to 10 years. Easy, right?

Wrong. First of all, as I'll reiterate throughout this book, I want you to be an independent thinker. Relying on someone else to do your homework is the wrong attitude. It's what gets most people ordinary returns and into trouble.

And just as important: Mavericks know that winning the investment game requires (1) goals, (2) a strategy to reach those goals, and (3) a *plan* for implementing that strategy. The chances that a "Fabian List" (or *any* list) would fit your specific needs are too small to measure.

Let's look at the subject of planning. What is the essence of your investing plan? Do you *have* an investing plan?

Here's my prescription for effective planning:

- **Spell out your aspirations.**   I hope you're picking up on one of my key messages by now: that *your needs are not the same as any other investor's needs.* We already touched on your right to define the "pursuit of happiness" for yourself. You're an individual. You have very specific dreams. So make them real with your own numbers. Create your treasure map with goals that have personal meaning. House, plane, train, auto, college—mavericks spell it out!
- **Go for extraordinary growth every year.**   This is one that almost always gets people's attention. Why? Because conventional planners have been telling them for years that they should hope for a compounded growth of 8 percent. So anybody who talks about 20 percent must be nuts, right? Well, no. There were a grand total of 84 stock mutual funds that compounded at 20 percent per year during the 1990s. Put it this way: Do you think you'll do better aspiring to 8 percent, or 20 percent? Here's an incentive: If you do achieve an average of 20 percent—and many people who follow our principles do—your assets will double every four years. (See Figure 1-1.)
- **Take charge of the stock reins.**   Nobody's as passionate about your money as you are. So *manage your own assets.* Assume responsibility for your success. If you choose to pay for some expert advice along the way, fine, but always maintain some element of control and accountability. That's the only way to know what's going on, and to know if you're on track to meet your goals.
- **Know the right questions to ask.**   Questions like, "Why should I buy this stock fund? When would I ever sell it? What are the fees, expenses, commissions, and/or transaction costs?" When you ask the smart questions, you'll always profit from the answers!

FIGURE 1-1   20% Annualized Compounded Growth Table

Lump Sum Deposit	5 Years	10 Years	15 Years	20 Years	25 Years
$10,000	$24,833	$61,917	$154,070	$383,376	$953,962
$25,000	$62,208	$154,793	$385,176	$958,440	$2,384,905
$50,000	$124,416	$309,587	$770,351	$1,916,880	$4,769,811
$100,000	$248,832	$619,174	$1,540,702	$3,833,760	$9,539,622
$250,000	$622,080	$1,547,934	$3,851,755	$9,584,400	$23,849,054

FIGURE 1-2   Stocks versus Bonds by Decade

Time Period	1971–1980	1981–1990	1991–2000
Stocks	8.44%	13.93%	17.5%
Bonds	3.9%	13.75%	10.3%

- **Just say "no" to bonds.**   Bonds are inferior to stocks in both upside gain (see Figure 1-2) and relative risk. Just say NO to bonds, bond funds, and any investments that do not allow for growth. By sticking to equities (stocks) alone, you'll retire quicker, happier, and richer!

- **Give most of your attention to your tax-deferred dollars.**   When your money grows in an IRA or 401(k) plan, it grows fast. And you never have to worry about taxes when you buy or sell. When you keep your tax-deferred plans in the front of your mind, you create wealth faster!

- **Commit to the stock market for life.**   Common wisdom says that investors should hold a little bit of everything—a handful of stocks, a fist-ful of bonds, and a pocketful of cash. This is called "asset allocating," and it's exactly how to wind up with that 8 percent rate of return. It's not for you! Asset allocation gets ordinary results, whereas Mavericks demand *extraordinary* results. I'm not saying that you're going to be in the market 100 percent all of the time. Far from it! I'm saying that you need to know when it's time to be in—and when it *is* time, you need to be in 100 per-cent. And this prescription doesn't change as you get older. Stay true to the stock market throughout your lifespan!

MAKING PROGRESS, REALIZING YOUR POTENTIAL

Franklin D. Roosevelt said, "There are many ways of going forward, but only one way of standing still." You can do all the preparation and planning exercises in the world, but if you don't take action, your determination will erode and your dreams will fade.

Here are some of the "action" components of the maverick lifestyle.

- **Fire underachievers and overchargers.**   If a broker does not pro-vide the service you demand, show him or her the door. (Be polite, but be fast and firm!) If a fund family sells you a lemon, sell it back to them, and then go find another provider. Exercise your rights. Build high-value relationships. And never allow yourself to be sucked in, or intimidated, by Wall Street snobbery.

- **Ignore pop media.**   Which do you think magazine columnists and financial pundits on the tube have more of: inside knowledge, or deadlines? The answer, of course, is "deadlines." More often than not, pop-media types are behind the trends, giving you advice only after the markets have already moved. The truth is, you have as much access to essential industry info as they do. (And if you have broadband or DSL-speed access to the Internet, you can probably get it faster than they can.)

- **Acquire emotional intelligence.**   Bull markets tend to pump up investors—first with confidence, and then with giddiness and greed. Bear markets, on the other hand, tend to demoralize investors and fill them full of fear and despair. These are *emotional* reactions. We're only human, and we'll never get rid of our emotions (thank goodness). But I counsel you to *use your emotions* intelligently. And that means, *keep them about a million miles away from the decision-making process.* By all means—get excited! But focus your excitement and passion on having what you want at a precise point in the future.

- **Avoid the bear trap.**   Wall Street brokers money on you whether the market is up or down—as long as you leave your money with them. That's why they continue to push the buy-'n'-hold mantra. But mavericks understand the carnage a bear can cause (see Figure 1-3). We know that, sometimes, we're going to step aside!

- **Lock in profits.**   "Sell" may be a four-letter word, but there's nothing dirty about it. You get to lock in your gains. You get to take brand-new steps with your money. What's more, you protect against downside risk.

- **Track your assets and your choices regularly.**   No stock, no fund, no index, no investment will be right for you forever. That's why you need to use technology to stay in touch with the stock market—viewing your portfolio monthly, and checking in on all of your options quarterly. It's a breeze with the Worldwide Web!

- **Invest more in your winners.**   It's common practice for people to rebalance their portfolios. They sell portions of their winners, add to their losers, and reestablish their "diversified" position. That's exactly the wrong way to do it. If you had car that worked and another that didn't, which one would you get rid of? Mavericks go with the momentum. We sell losers, and add to the winners!

WHY THE MAVERICK LIFESTYLE WORKS!

My dad taught me one of the fundamental truths of investing discipline: People will stick to a plan if it's simple. To that I'd add, they'll also stick

FIGURE 1-3   Bear Market Math

Percentage Models		Effects of Bear Market on $100,0000 Value	
If you have a loss of . . .	Then you need a gain of . . .	If you now have . . .	Then you need a gain of . . .
−90.00%	900%	$10,000	$90,000
−70.00%	233%	$30,000	$70,000
−50.00%	100%	$50,000	$50,000
−45.00%	82%	$55,000	$45,000
−40.00%	67%	$60,000	$40,000
−35.00%	54%	$65,000	$35,000
−30.00%	43%	$70,000	$30,000
−25.00%	33%	$75,000	$25,000
−20.00%	25%	$80,000	$20,000
−15.00%	18%	$85,000	$15,000
−10.00%	11%	$90,000	$10,000
−5.00%	5%	$95,000	$5,000

to a plan that *makes sense*. When we can easily grasp something and it "feels right," we're more likely to be disciplined about carrying out that plan.

Can a financial plan—a plan for changing the whole future of your life—be simple?

Absolutely! No, you can't jump right on the maverick train without risking a few bumps and bruises. (You're likely to learn some unpleasant things about the current state of your affairs, for example.) And "simple" doesn't mean precooked and shrink-wrapped. Even a simple plan will require you to think for yourself, make tough choices, and accept change. Most people will go to great lengths to avoid change. Mavericks know they don't have that luxury.

Research reveals that a large percentage of Americans are overweight. Do you think it's because they don't know that they should exercise regularly and eat properly? No. Most of us already know what's good for us. If we get overweight and stay overweight, it's because we haven't made a decisive, no-holds-barred commitment to *change*.

So, "simple?" Yes. "Painless?" Probably not, especially on the front end. But the Maverick approach becomes a way of life for many people because it *works*. It makes you feel better about yourself while it steers you toward financial security. It promotes both emotional and financial well-being. All you have to do is make the all-important decision to get out of your old patterns, and embrace the beauty and simplicity of the maverick investing lifestyle.

TWO MAVERICK SUCCESS STORIES

Tired of hearing Doug toot his own horn? Here's some unsolicited testimony that came in the form of letters from Maverick investors Mark Isenberg and Warren Engle.

"My first exposure to maverick investing began after the Persian Gulf War period. Like most Americans who were investing for their future, I had experienced the 1987 Crash, the Gulf War, and the emotional ups and downs that accompanied that time. I had just learned of the *Fabian Plan,* and I made the commitment to implement the approach shortly thereafter.

"This commitment has served my family and me well. The plan has been priceless. It has removed the majority of anxiety and emotion from investing for the future. Unlike other investors, I have been able to sleep nights during periods of market turmoil.

"More importantly, I made a second commitment to myself: to expose my children to Maverick investing for the rest of their lives. My daughter, Julia, started her IRA at age nine. In each of the last six years, she has contributed modest amounts of earned income—in fact, never even coming close to the maximum allowable yearly contribution. This is solely comprised of baby-sitting money. The results? Julia has just turned 15, and has a five-figure Roth IRA. My son Ross started his Roth IRA two years ago and is also well on his way to securing his financial future."

—*Mark Isenberg*

"I retired from the sporting goods industry with no retirement income from my company and no plan for generating enough income on which to live in our retirement years. I have followed the Fabian Plan to a letter with no contributions to our beginning cash, and we have done almost exactly as the compounding plan shows.

"Eleven years ago, we lived off 12 percent of our nest egg or $43,000 per year; this year it will be $60,000. Our $300,000 has grown to $500,000. Most importantly, our living standard has gone up instead of down since retirement."

—*Warren Engle*

2

Living with Your Money

Here's an interesting experiment you can try: Whistle up an Internet search engine and type in the word "casablanca." You're pretty likely to run into the 1944 Oscar winner for Best Picture, starring Humphrey Bogart, Ingrid Bergman, Claude Rains, and the rest of the now-legendary gang. If you dig a little deeper, you can even find a video clip of Bogie giving a non-Maverick explanation of why he wound up in Casablanca: "*I was misinformed.*"

Now type in "raging bull." In the spring of 1981, Robert DeNiro was named Best Actor for his role as a hard-hitting boxer with volatile mood swings. (In the last chapter, I wrote about the importance of discipline: DeNiro first gained and then lost 40 pounds to make his character more convincing. Now *that's* discipline!) That movie was called *Raging Bull.* But Internet search engines don't usually pull up references to DeNiro's masterpiece. Why? Because the raging bull that most people wanted to talk about throughout the 1990s was the U.S. stock market.

Why are we as a nation so obsessed with stocks? Because they've given so many people hope that they'll enjoy a wealthier tomorrow. That's an exciting prospect for individuals in every walk and phase of life—long-time shareholders, first-time investors, middle-class families, college graduates, small-business owners, even foreign investors with Ameritrade accounts.

I think it's *great* to have hope. But I also think that informed hope is far better than blind hope. Think of all those people who derive their hope from buying lottery tickets, where the deck is deeply, hopelessly stacked against them.

A lot of stock market investors are almost as oblivious to the challenges that lie ahead of them. Switching to a railroad metaphor: Many of them hopped on the first train that pulled into the station, with little thought about its destination. Others hopped aboard knowing that the train's destination wasn't necessarily where they wanted to go, but were afraid to contradict (or even question) those guys who were running the train. So they took their seats, and let the brokers and the Wall Street gurus run the railroad.

Mavericks, by contrast, don't get stampeded. They don't climb aboard someone else's train (unless, of course, it happens to be going exactly where they want to go). They think smarter and execute more intelligently than the ordinary investor. They earmark their money—their savings, pretax dollars, and hard-earned greenbacks—for specific life goals. They even turn short-term obstacles into midrange milestones and long-term opportunities.

That's what living with your money is all about—accepting challenges and taking responsibility for the results.

MAVERICKS MEET CHALLENGES HEAD-ON

The ordinary investor shies away from challenges; the maverick meets them head-on. Like what, for example? Here are three challenges that mavericks will have to pay close attention to in the early years of the twenty-first century:

1. Maybe you're not sitting on huge gains for the 1990s.   If you were fortunate enough to build a large nest egg in the 1990s—only to see it deflate 30 to 50 percent in the 2000–2001 bear market, you are ready for a safer way to invest. On the other hand, if you have been saving for years and years and now are finally ready to start putting this money to work, your view of this bear market (from the sidelines) has you worried about becoming 100 percent invested. Those who missed the bull run of the 1990s must do two things that pull in different directions: (1) protect their principal, and (2) place that money at risk for growth.

2. The solutions that worked well last year WON'T work as well next year.   In 1998, it was the S&P 500 index funds. In 1999, it was the Nasdaq's astonishing jump of 85 percent. In 2000, a money market fund outperformed all major indexes. Those who arrived late in 1998, 1999, and 2000 must change their approach by understanding that the market is like the weather: It's constantly changing.

3. You CAN'T rely on your broker for the goods.   Many financial planners are as overwhelmed by 25,000 choices as you are. Worse yet, they may not represent the high performers and the heavy hitting investments you demand. Fortunately, you can take your business anywhere, at any time. It's your money!

MAVERICKS DETERMINE THEIR OWN FINANCIAL FATE
Did you know that Medicare is expected to go broke in the not-too-distant future, and Social Security a decade or two after that? (Sorry to be vague, but this is a football that the politicians kick around almost every year.)

Are you aware that some corporations (perhaps including your own) have all but abandoned pension plans?

Do you expect to live securely in your retirement on some version of a universal health care system?

My point in raising these questions should be clear: Not only *can* you be the master of your own destiny—the captain of your own financial ship—but you *must* be. You can't stick your head in the sand, because there's nowhere to hide. The future will come looking for you.

Maybe the idea of having to invest for yourself and your future scares you. Or maybe this is just the wake-up call you've been waiting for. I'm saying, once again, that you *must* rise to the occasion. You must take control of your financial future, if you hope to reap the rewards of your efforts and participate in the new American Dream.

Here's the gist of a phone call I recently received from a radio listener named Jeffrey:

> I am 40 years old, married, and haven't saved a dime for my retirement. However, I know that if I don't start now, I'm going to be working until the day I die. I don't want to do that! I want to be a maverick. Can you show a rookie directions on how to get started?

Jeffrey's plea for help—and hope—is very similar to the e-mails and calls I receive from thousands of "newbies" every month. There's the fear of starting, and there's the fear of *not* starting!

But what if Jeff knew, in his heart of hearts, that the future wealth he desires would come to him, on a precise schedule, if he committed himself to a relatively painless discipline? Would he take the very first steps toward change?

I tried to steer him in that direction. I explained to him that if he saved $5.50 each day for an IRA, he would have accumulated more than **$500,000** by his 61st birthday (see Figure 2-1). On his 65th birthday, he would have **$1,132,755.** And if his wife put away $5.50 each day as well, their combined net worth at age 65 would be **$2,265,510.**

But for Jeff to realize his financial potential, he has to *take control.* He must contribute $2,000 a year to his individual retirement account (IRA), and he must pursue a course that will earn 20 percent annual growth. And his first step—his very first step—must be to grab hold of the stock reins.

Here's an e-mail I received from a newsletter subscriber named Jason:

> I would like to get out of the rat race and retire at 50. My wife and I are both 30, but we only have $20,000 in my former company's pension. My uncle likes Vanguard 500, Wellington, and Windsor stock funds. So does my accountant. What do you think?

I gave Jason the good news—no, the *great* news. If he and his wife start taking charge of their investments immediately, they will have **$1,662,854** at 50 (see Figure 2-2). Even better, they will have **$4,173,434** at the age of 55. What's the secret? You guessed it: adding $2000 per person every year, and achieving 20 percent annual growth. That's it!

The other thing I tried to tell Jason, without being too rude about it, was that if he persists in clinging to his collection of advisers, he almost certainly *won't* reach his destination of financial independence. If he continues to rely on his uncle, or his accountant, or anybody other than himself, he won't become a multimillionaire. Jason has to assume responsibility for his successes and failures. He must decide to invest on his own two feet.

FIGURE 2-1   Jeffrey's Projected Wealth

$2000 Annual Investment at 20% Compounded Interest

Age	Total Invested	Result
40	$2000	$2200
45	$10,000	$17,860
50	$20,000	$62,301
55	$30,000	$172,884
60	$40,000	$448,051
65	$50,000	$1,132,755

FIGURE 2-2   Jason's Projected Wealth

$20,000 Initial Investment with a $4000 Annual Investment at 20%

Age	Total Invested	Result
30	$24,000	$28,800
35	$28,000	$85,486
40	$32,000	$248,436
45	$36,000	$653,909
50	$40,000	$1,662,854
55	$44,000	$4,173,434
60	$48,000	$10,420,558

That's what mavericks do: They *invest upright.* This doesn't mean that you can't ask for help. On the contrary! Self-reliant individuals are particularly skilled at knowing the questions to ask—of a planner, of a brokerage house, or even of a 401(k) administrator.

It's about asking, "Should I roll over money from my former company's pension to a Roth?" Or, "How much should I add to my IRA every year?" And, "What rate of return will I need to get out of the rat race when I'm 50?"

Sometimes, newly hatched mavericks have to climb out of a deep hole. Take the case of Elizabeth, who phoned our radio show fairly recently:

> I racked up $35,000 on credit cards to buy furniture and stuff for our new home. So last month I borrowed $15,000 against my 401(k). My question is, how can I pay off the $20,000 left on high-interest credit cards and still invest for my retirement?

The big positive here, of course, is that Elizabeth is demonstrating maverick commitment to overcoming debt. That's an important first step—you have to focus your eyes on the prize.

On the other hand, you don't want a debt reduction path that hurts your greatest wealth-building asset—your 401(k). For example, at a maverick growth rate of 20 percent, the $15,000 that Elizabeth borrowed is worth **$1.4 million** in 25 years (see Figure 2-3). And that's without any contributions!

Obviously, Elizabeth needs to pay this 401(k) loan back ASAP. But what can she do to pay off those high-interest cards? A home equity loan.

FIGURE 2-3   Elizabeth's Projected 401(k) Wealth

$15,000 Lump Sum Investment at 20% for 25 Years

Years	Result
5	$37,325
10	$92,876
15	$231,105
20	$575,064
25	$1,430,943

For one thing, 9 percent is far more favorable than 18 percent. Plus, most people can deduct mortgage interest from their taxes.

Granted, Elizabeth must make sure she has the cash flow to take on a higher monthly mortgage; she must also learn to live within her means. But if her commitment is genuine—if she really wants to get out of credit card hell, and start investing for that **$1.4 million**—she has to take ownership of her financial future.

It's not about luck. There are no excuses. If you recognize the power of self-determination, of believing that you can control your own financial fate, then you will attain the wealth you need.

MAVERICKS COMPETE

Here are some interesting statistics: Monday Night Football's viewership in 2000 fell 20 percent from the previous year. Interest in, and viewership of the 2000 Sydney Olympics plummeted from 1996 levels. And according to Neilson Media Research, something like 33 percent fewer fans tuned in to watch Shaquille O'Neal's Los Angeles Lakers take the NBA championship in 2000 than watched Michael Jordan's Chicago Bulls win the same championship two years earlier.

Different people have different theories about why football, basketball, and other pastimes have been in decline. Yes, Sydney suffered from being awake while the rest of the world was asleep, and yes, Shaq isn't Air Jordan. But I see a more compelling explanation: *Investing is the new American sport.*

Consider these facts. CNBC's highly touted *Business Center* grew 47 percent between July 1999 and the end of March 2000. And in July 2000, CNBC, the premier provider of "round-the-clock" trading coverage, surpassed CNN as the highest-rated news and information network on cable. (Of course, it suffered correspondingly during the bear market of 2000–2001.)

What does it all mean? It means that you had better step up to the plate and compete. There's a new game in your town, and the way you play it will shape your financial future.

As a maverick, you have to find reasons to achieve the goals you're most passionate about. You have to break away from bad advisers, cut off lousy fund families, and tame emotional reactions.

These are the things that mavericks do—we compete! We accept challenges. And we fight for our right to become extraordinarily wealthy.

BEFORE YOU PLAY BALL

Before you take up a new sport or game—Monopoly, blackjack, golf, whatever—you need to know a few key things about that activity. In tennis, for example, you need to understand what the court is all about. (The white lines tell you what's in bounds, and what's out of bounds.)

You also need to know the rules. For instance, you get two chances per point to accurately serve the ball to your opponent. You need to learn to use the language, like "15-love," "deuce," and "add in." You need to get hold of some equipment—such as shoes, racquets, and balls—that will help you play this game.

Drilling down a little deeper, you eventually need to understand how various forces work for and against you. For example, there are different playing surfaces, including clay, grass, and cement. There are sunny and windy weather conditions that will affect different players' games differently. (Pity the server with the high toss on a windy day!) This means that it's better to know something about your opponent than to be completely in the dark.

And if you haven't learned this in some other context, you'll surely learn it now: Your emotions—anger, frustration, fear—will absolutely affect your performance. Almost always, they'll make you play worse.

Like tennis, investing requires knowledge about how the game is played and won. It requires an awareness of the playing field, the equipment, the lingo, the rules of the game, and the players. That's why I've devoted the entire next section of this book—"The Maverick Perspective"—to sharpening your understanding of the stock market game.

Here in Part I, though, we need to focus on getting a feel for the *winning lifestyle.* You need to understand your dreams, goals, and emotions: the building-blocks of *you.* You also need to understand the values, attitudes, and principles that can make you a remarkable success.

THE BROKER MADE ME DO IT!

A guiding principle for mavericks is the notion that you can take back control of your financial life and do this "investing thing" on your own. But you need to be aware that many brokers, planners, and advisers don't want you to think for yourself—and you need to understand *why* they have that priority.

In his 1999 bestseller, *The Roaring 2000s Investor,* Harry Dent suggests that if you haven't beaten the S&P 500 over the past 5 or 10 years, you should employ a "very good financial adviser." What Mr. Dent *doesn't* point out is that 86 percent of professional money managers didn't beat the S&P in the 1990s. What's more, he implies that you shouldn't invest on your own two feet unless you've been doing so for a decade—and, of course, doing it better than almost all the pros.

My point is that without a doubt *you are the most qualified person to represent your own financial interests.*

Not sure? Ask yourself these questions:

- Who is more passionate about making me wealthy—me, or my broker?
- Who values my future more—me, or my financial planner?
- Who understands better what is going on in my life—me, or my broker?
- Who is more likely to position me in a high quality, *commission-free* investment—me, or my adviser?

As I see it, there are five immense, Everest-like reasons why a broker won't make you rich:

1. He/she often recommends only those things he/she makes money on.   Insurance specialist, accountant, registered rep, or commission broker—it doesn't matter what they call themselves. Even when they are honestly trying to get your money to grow, *your needs are secondary.* They make money on what they recommend—whether your stock goes up or goes down.

2. They never tell you what's in it for them.   More often than not, there's more at stake than the commission. Brokers get bonuses, perks, and vacations that are directly tied to getting more money into a very specific investment.

3. They often don't know more than their own product lines.   It's not desirable (or even possible) to keep track of everything on Planet Wall Street. People sell what they know—even if what they know is a small group of load funds with greater risks than rewards.

4. They have no idea when to sell.   They'll tell you that stocks always bounce back. They'll say that you won't make money with short-term thinking. They'll scare you off with tax consequences. The truth behind the talk? They have *no idea* when to get you out with a profit. (But they do know that the longer their company controls your assets, the better their careers.)

5. Their advice is permanently bullish.   When you strip away all the smoke and mirrors, their job is to get you to buy, and buy, and buy some more. Ever noticed this phenomenon? When a stock drops 10 percent, he'll tell you to buy the dips. When the stock loses 20 percent, he'll call it a fabulous buying opportunity. When the stock plunges to 50 percent lower than your purchase price, he'll insist that you won't want to realize the loss—that *of course* the stock will rebound . . . someday.

THE ALTERNATIVE

Yes, I'm going to say it again: You *must* represent yourself. When you take charge, you bring more desire to the table, you can commit more time to the challenge, and you can create more good choices for yourself. You have access to the *same info and knowledge* that a broker has access to. (Like I said earlier: It's all on the Net!)

Bottom line? Mavericks take complete responsibility for their investment attitudes and actions, while ordinary investors let others tell them what to do.

Be a maverick! Grab the captain's hat, and put your hands on the wheel! Meet the challenges of living with your money—of owning your performance—and you will achieve the wealth you desire.

MAVERICK LESSONS FOR LIVING WITH YOUR MONEY

- **Meet challenges head-on.**   You may be coping with limited cash flow, or you may be reeling from mistakes you've made in the past. But now's not the time to shy away from the fast balls. Step up to the plate. Seize control of your financial future, and make the changes that make the difference.
- **Decide to own your financial destiny.**   Are you 25, and up to your Adam's apple in debt? Are you 30, and dying to get out of the rat race at 50? Are you 40, and just getting started? Doesn't matter: *You can achieve financial independence.* You can achieve any goal—buy your dream house, pay for college, start your own business—once you've made the decision to become independently wealthy.

- **Discover your competitive spirit.** We're only human, and winning (or trying to win) is part of everything we do. Sports, careers, negotiation, debates, "win-win" agreements—you name it, each of us tries in myriad ways to improve his or her lot in life. Mavericks are scrappy, rebellious, and assertive, as they seek to improve their financial standing. Oh, yes: They're also ethical and intelligent, as they set out to secure their self-interest.
- **Question authority.** We mavericks refuse to let others pull the wool over our eyes. We examine whether a broker does or does not have the knowledge to take our portfolios higher. We explore the motivation of others who tell us what may or may not be in our best interest. And we question fixed mindsets.

Boy, do we question those mindsets!

3

What Are
the Maverick Principles?

Have you ever taken financial advice from a friend, a cousin, or maybe even that smart guy with the locker next to yours at the racquet club—and then found yourself regretting it later?

Have you ever paid good money to a financial planner who, at the end of the day, really didn't provide the advice or the performance you expected?

Do you sometimes wonder if the entire investment game is rigged against you?

If you've been down any of these roads, you're not alone. Every investor, myself included, has had his or her share of frustrations and disappointments.

At the same time, you can learn from your mistakes. In fact, by embracing a principled investing lifestyle—one that you can believe in, and one that makes things happen—you can create a remarkably exciting and financially rewarding future.

That's what maverick investing does—it creates a wealthier tomorrow. But to get there, you need to change the way you invest today. You need to *take charge*. You need to grab hold of your financial future.

TAKING CHARGE: 10 PRINCIPLES THAT WILL EMPOWER YOU FOR LIFE!

The way to take charge is to embrace a set of key principles that you can live with for years to come. I've identified 10 maverick principles—10 guidelines that enable mavericks to thrive as stock market winners:

1. I take full responsibility for my financial future.
2. I invest for clear-cut, attainable goals.
3. I strive for extraordinary portfolio.
4. I maximize all of my tax-deferred investing opportunities.
5. I put 100 percent of my money into stocks.
6. I track the performance of the stock market, my holdings, and my alternative choices.
7. I know when to buy and when to sell every asset in my portfolio.
8. I pursue growth in stocks throughout my entire life.
9. I never predict the direction of stock prices.
10. I capitalize on market change and investment innovation.

Let's examine each one of these principles in context. In other words, let's look at some real-life applications of each.

Principle Number 1: I Take Full Responsibility for My Financial Future

If you want to improve your investing performance, take a look in the mirror first. Don't blame your broker or your brother. Don't rely on your company or the federal government. This is *your* money. These are *your* dreams, and if you leave the task of achieving them to someone else, you'll regret it later.

If you choose a full-service brokerage like Smith Barney or Merrill Lynch, for example, you've chosen more than a place to house your money; you've selected a *relationship*. And if it's not working out—in terms of service, performance, fees—then you owe it to yourself to end that relationship.

At the other end of the spectrum, if you establish a relationship with a major discounter—Schwab, Fidelity, Ameritrade, E-Trade—you'll take full responsibility for which stocks and funds to buy or sell. The choices you'll make will be yours, and yours alone.

This is a totally maverick way to invest. Not only are you taking charge, you're eliminating pricey sales commissions and costly conflicts of interest at the full-service firms. That goes a long way toward improving the bottom line.

Picking the right investments is relatively easy (and in subsequent chapters, I'll show you how). The hard part is making the commitment to own your personal performance. Start with an account relationship that encourages, rather than discourages, individual involvement and decision making.

Principle Number 2: I Invest for Clear-Cut, Attainable Goals

Do you know why you are investing? Do you let the media, friends, or relatives tell you what you should or shouldn't be doing with your money? Are you eavesdropping on a potential high flyer at the coffee house, rather than concentrating on the choices you have within your own 401(k) plan?

Ordinary investors lose their focus. Or worse, they never establish clear-cut, attainable goals in the first place—goals toward which they can measure their progress. "Getting rich someday" isn't a goal; it's a pipe dream. Mavericks set real goals for themselves. We don't talk in hazy terms about financial independence; we decide where, when, how much, and *why.* A 35-year-old "mav" might write, for example, "I will have $2.7 million in my 401(k) when I turn 55, so that I can begin living on the interest and smack golf balls five days a week."

Maybe you read that particular goal statement and said, "Ugh—I can't imagine anything more boring!" Well, great. That kind of reaction probably means that you have strong ideas about how you'd rather spend your time at age 55 and how much you will need. My point is that there's nothing wishy-washy about "$2.7 million." There's no uncertainty about "55 years of age," or the focus on a 401(k) account. These are clear-cut goals. You can make progress toward them, and you can *measure* that progress.

Other guidelines related to goals? Display them prominently. Make sure they affect you (and *reflect* you) personally, and on a regular basis. Check to see that they are practical, precise, positive, and focused on growth. Why? Because the more genuine a goal is, the more likely you are to establish a plan to attain it—and then *do* it!

Principle Number 3: I Strive for Extraordinary Portfolio Growth

Remember: We're aiming for the extraordinary. The only way you're going to achieve 20 percent compounded growth—extraordinary by any long-term standard—is to invest exclusively in vehicles that can get you there. Stocks and stock funds can get you there; bonds and bond funds cannot.

This means that you have to look at your investment choices carefully, and weed out the turkeys. Some products have names that sound promising enough—for example, "Putnam Growth and Income." To the untrained ear, both "growth" and "income" sound pretty good. The problem is, the word "income" implies some sort of bond allocation—as high as 10 to 20 percent. Other products have names that don't tell you anything at all.

Does "Vanguard Wellington" sound good? Does it still sound good after I tell you it's a "balanced" fund? Yes? Well, does it *still* sound good when I tell you that "balanced" funds like Wellington invest 60 percent in stocks, with the other 40 percent going into bonds? If you look at the track records for Wellington and Putnam Growth & Income—which by the way aren't particularly better or worse than others in their peer group—you'll see that there hasn't been a sustained period during bull markets where they returned 20 percent. That's true for most balanced funds and income-oriented investments, because the bonds drag down their performance. Just say no to bonds.

Again: You have to seek vehicles that give you an opportunity to pursue your growth goal. My aggressive growth goal is 20 percent. Maybe you'll decide on a different number. In any case: Looking at anything that gives you a *zero* chance to achieve *your* aggressive growth goal would be an "unmaverick" way to invest.

Principle Number 4: I Maximize All of My Tax-Deferred Investing Opportunities

401(k), 403(b) 457, IRA, Roth IRA, SEP, Keogh, Simple. The money in these accounts is the most important money you will ever manage.

Why? Consider the difference between the dollars you place in a taxable account versus those in a tax-deferred plan (see Figure 3-1). For instance, $2000 at 20 percent per year for 25 years in a taxable account (assuming a 28 percent tax rate) comes to **$443,039.** However, $2000 at 20 percent for 25 years in a tax-deferred plan is **$1,134,755!**

I like the big, seven-figure number a whole lot better than the little six-figure number. Tax-deferred can make a huge difference in determining your retirement future.

Ordinary investors often overlook the ravaging effects of taxation. They focus their attention on winning the lottery—on hitting one out of the park in their online stock account. Well, hitting a home run this way is great, but remember, it's *real hard* to do, and it's only two-thirds as good as it looks. That's because home run–oriented investors give back at least a third of their gains in taxes each and every year.

Meanwhile, we mavericks are just salting it away. It's a little bit like the old story of the tortoise and the hare—except that we "tortoises" aren't just plodding at a steady pace; we're *accelerating.* Tax-deferred dollars *grow fast.* And that's why we "max" our tax-deferred dollars first.

FIGURE 3-1   Taxable versus Tax-Deferred Growth

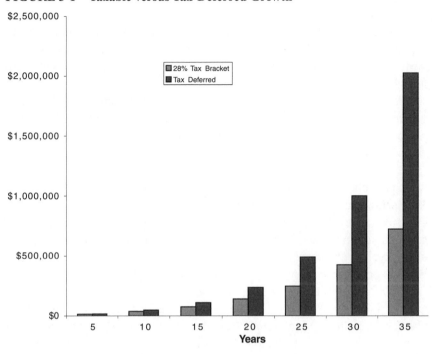

Let the foolish investor waste energy on next-wave, next-generation stocks. *You* concentrate on getting 20 percent in your 401(k). *You* focus on growing the money that the IRS can't touch yet.

Principle Number 5: I Put 100 Percent of My Money into Stocks

As we moved into the twenty-first century, we witnessed a number of remarkable achievements. The Dow traded above 11,000. The Nasdaq climbed above 5000. And stocks demonstrated an ability to appreciate 300 percent across recent 10-year time spans.

For the last 70 years, in fact, the Bull has commanded 78 percent of the trading days. Since 1977, that number becomes 88 percent.

Without question, it makes sense to look for ways to *get 100 percent of your assets into stocks.* You owe it to yourself and your family to create the most wealth possible by investing 100 percent in stocks during every bull market.

Yeah, yeah, I know. Conventional wisdom will tell you that it's "too risky" to put so much of your money into stocks. We've already talked about this particular bit of irony. These are the same folks who insist that you buy 'n' hold through every down cycle, and settle for a meager 8 percent or less per year.

Mavericks are well aware that allocating 100 percent of your money to stock assets entails far more risk than investors who include bonds in their portfolios. But that risk is entirely manageable, as long as you have a plan for when to sell your holdings.

As a maverick, you'll always be prepared for the ravenous Bear. But you're also going to strive for full participation in stocks four-fifths (78 percent) of the time. That's how mavericks outperform the more passive "buy-'n'-hopers."

Principle Number 6: I Track the Performance of the Stock Market, My Holdings, and My Alternative Choices

The stock market is psychological, not logical. Crowd psychology dominates the major trends. Everybody and their brother loves stocks at the top of the cycle, and everybody hates stocks at the bottom of the bear market. But it is possible to identify long-term uptrends and downtrends.

Think about the momentum in a football game. The place is hot. The joint is jumping. When the home team scores a touchdown, the crowd reaches fever pitch! Momentum! But when the visitors kill the home team's momentum by intercepting the ball on the 3-yard line—or worse, when the hometown heroes get down by a large margin—the stadium gets brutally quiet. Little Mo? No Mo?

Momentum is important. In the investing realm, there are a number of indexes that reveal the upward or downward momentum for large-, mid-, small-caps, and even the tech sector. For instance, by looking at the current price of the Russell 2000, and checking how far it is above or below its trend line (200-day average), you can gauge whether to add money to the small-cap arena (see Figure 3-2).

No, you can't predict the outcome of the market, any more than you can predict the outcome of a football game, and you shouldn't even try. But you *can* measure momentum. You want to be 100 percent committed when that trend is up; conversely, you want to be 100 percent at home base—in your money market account—when the market is stone-temple cold.

Principle Number 7: I Know When to Buy and When to Sell Every Asset in My Portfolio

I'm betting that not a lot of my readers are Las Vegas high rollers. (I'm not, either.) So maybe you don't know how high-rollers are treated in Las Vegas. I'm told that many of them get flown in at the casino's expense. Most get

FIGURE 3-2   Russell 2000 Trendline Chart

free or reduced-rate rooms, complimentary food and drink, free entertainment, and so forth. Why? Because statistically speaking, these high rollers don't know when to cash out. They may get ahead of the house at the blackjack table on any given night—but based on their past history, they're almost certain to stay at the table until they lose everything. That explains the "free" tickets, rooms, meals, and so on.

When it comes to investing, mavericks know when to leave the table. Mavericks ensure their success by deciding, *in advance,* the conditions under which they'll give this stock, or that stock fund, the axe. Maybe the guideline is a decline in value. (How much? What percent?) If the stock is below water, maybe it's "hold until I break even." On the upside, maybe it's "sell when I've doubled my money."

You might decide that as soon as an individual stock drops 15 percent from its highest point, you'll lock in your profits. Similarly, you might decide that when the S&P 500 falls below its long-term trendline and signals a potential down cycle in stocks, you'll move your 401(k) stock fund holdings into the safety of a money-market account.

The most important aspect of your investing lifestyle is to know what you're going to do ahead of time. Literally: *You know when you're going to sell before you buy.* This may be one of the most difficult lessons for any investor, but it is of immense importance in determining your future.

Unless you know the conditions under which you will "exit" an investment, you should not get into it in the first place.

Principle Number 8: I Pursue Growth in Stocks Throughout My Entire Life

Ordinary investors say that they will participate in stocks until they retire. But those who follow this old guideline and stop working between ages 55 and 65 are likely to find themselves in a bind. Not only will their standard of living decrease over their retirement years, but the 6 to 8 percent they might realize from bonds and cash won't sustain them for three more decades.

Don't forget: On average, we're living longer than ever before. And since stocks are essential to continuous wealth-building, we need to discover ways to *stay involved in the market at every age.*

But not "every day at every age," of course. Mavericks are in when it makes sense to be in; they're out when they have to be. And when they have to be out of the market, they use their money-market accounts as home base.

I love the sound of that phrase: *home base.* It's not a baseball analogy; I think it's a holdover from childhood—from all those games like hide-and-seek that cast home base as a place of safety, rest, and regrouping for the next round of fun. Especially if you're starting small, "home base" (e.g., a money-market account) is where you're most likely to start investing. I have no qualms about going back to home base when circumstances demand it, and you shouldn't either. Need to sell your equity positions to sidestep a downtrend? Great! Sell, and go to home base for a while. It's the best place to relax and contemplate your next maverick move.

And conversely, you don't want to hang out at home base forever. As soon as the stock market starts to trend higher, we take the steps necessary to participate in that growth. In other words, money accounts are a nice place to visit, but we wouldn't want to live there. The key is paying attention to the trends and not being afraid to return to home base when the situation warrants it.

Principle Number 9: I Never Predict the Direction of Stock Prices

Have you ever been convinced that a correction in the Nasdaq was an excellent buying opportunity? Have you ever found yourself just *itching* to "buy the dips?" Have you ever looked at new 52-week lows of once-popular dot.coms and thought, "Well, heck, they *surely* can't go any lower than this"?

Before letting a (seemingly) low price spur you into an action you might come to regret, review and then *re-review* your strategy. How much do you really know about the company's prospects? Have you read its annual report, income statement, and balance sheet? Are you sure it corresponds to some kind of reality? What about all those footnotes in the annual report? Are the patents really all that rock solid? Are you really comfortable with that sky-high P/E ratio? (What? No earnings yet?)

Be honest: Exactly what do you have to go on, besides intuition, to call which way the Nasdaq is going to move?

Consider Lucy's story. (Lucy is now one of our newsletter subscribers; she wasn't when this story played out.) She purchased 20 shares of a biotech stock she knew nothing about. Why? Well, she just convinced herself that this sector would continue performing much better than older, more established stocks. Turns out that she got this somewhat hazy idea from the media.

Well, despite the media's affection, Science & Technology funds quickly corrected 15 percent downward. Buried in that bad news was even worse news for Lucy. Her biotech pick had pulled back 40 percent, which isn't all that uncommon for individual companies. And yet, Lucy still believed that her price would eventually go higher. It *had* to! After all: Hadn't she read somewhere that this company was part of the "New Economy"?

It wasn't until Lucy spotted the name of her company in an online article, "Dot Trouble," that she got nervous. In fact, predicting that her stock was now a loser, she sold her position at a 60 percent loss.

Really painful footnote: One month later, the same biotech stock charged forward to an all-time high.

Predictions usually end in disaster. Mavericks just say "no" to predictions. Instead, we let the market trends tell us where our money needs to be. Take a lesson from Lucy's story and don't be pulled in by the hype. Even the most responsible programs and publications can confuse most investors.

Principle Number 10: I Capitalize on Market Change and Investment Innovation

If you've spent even a few years around the stock market, you know one thing. The environment can flip from bullish to bearish to bullish with lightning speed.

Remember back in 1998, when you couldn't get away from the media's embarrassing love affair with S&P index funds? These funds were being billed as the ultimate investment. (They aren't.) One year later, the New Economy was ballyhooed as being invincible. (It wasn't.) And when large-cap growth started falling down the tech mountain in 2000, Old Economy advocates started cheering their "value" stocks and beaten-down sectors.

Mavericks understand that change in the stock market is constant, and that pundits see best in hindsight. That's why we cherish the freedom to move our money—to prosper from changes in the market environment and/or protect our assets from undue risk. We know that what's *hot* today will *not* be hot tomorrow.

Mavericks are adept at recognizing useful investment-related innovations, and quickly capitalizing on them. Here are three absolutely *huge* innovations that you need to embrace, if you haven't already:

1. The Internet. No, no, I'm not talking about buying dot.com stocks. I'm talking about the Internet's impact on the way we invest. Online accounts from leading on-line brokerages let you access critical info instantly, execute buys and sells quickly, confirm your trades promptly, track your progress regularly, and invest inexpensively. Most Web sites give you access to stock charts, historical analyses, etc. Get wired! Before the Internet, only professionals had access to this much information. Now it's available free to all investors, 24 hours a day, 7 days a week.

2. Funds that trade like stocks. Lower annual expenses, intraday trading, active indexing, AND diversification by style, company size, or industry sector: These are just a handful of the benefits that exchange-traded funds (ETFs) offer. And this universe extends well beyond ETFs. There are other "baskets" that now let individuals customize their own personal stock funds at exceptionally reasonable prices.

3. $50, $5, $0 Investing. Innovative technology, coupled with investor need, has put an end to the "I can't afford to get started" excuse (see Figure 3-3). There are more than 250 mutual funds that let you invest $50 or less. There are several companies that let you invest $5—in other words, whenever you have even minimal moola combined with the urge to save. And one venture even lets rebates from online shopping go directly into your investment account!

FLYING IN THE FACE OF CONVENTION

Are you tired of following the herd? Does conventional investing seem old-fashioned or obsolete to you? Do you like the idea of bucking the system and coming out ahead?

Maverick investing is like that electronic game that your six-year-old is so obsessed with: Each maverick principle is another powerful weapon in your personal arsenal. Each principle differs markedly from the plain-

FIGURE 3-3   Some "Get Started" Mutual Funds (Fund Families with Low Minimum Entrance Requirements)

$50/month–automatic withdrawal investment plan
    Fidelity Destiny Funds
    T. Rowe Price
    Invesco
    Scudder
    Transamerica

$250.00 Minimum
    Strong IRAs
    Transamerica IRAs
    Warburg-Pincus IRAs

$500.00 Minimum
    Fidelity IRA
    Janus IRA

vanilla concepts you get from Wall Street. In fact, most of the maverick principles run directly counter to conventional wisdom. (And that's a good thing).

Here are just a few point/counterpoint examples of the Word from Wall Street versus the Maverick philosophy. Which approach sounds right to *you?*

- **Wall Street.**   "Investment and wealth building, although very simple in principle, are almost as complex as health care and medicine. . . . Would you want to go to a discount doctor or a discount surgeon if you had a serious heart problem?"—*Harry Dent, "Why You May Need a Financial Advisor," Roaring 2000s Investor.*

    Maverick Principle Number 1.   Investment and wealth building are easy when you make them part of your investing lifestyle. Take ownership of your performance, and you can be your own investment counselor.

- **Wall Street.**   "Stocks as measured by the S&P 500 returned 11.2 percent between 1925 and 1998. Large-cap stocks should produce a median return of 11.6 percent between 1999 and 2025."—*Ibbotson Associates Research.*

    Maverick Principle Number 3.   There are many extended periods of time when stock mutual funds have compounded at an annual rate of 20 percent or more. Extraordinary investors take advantage of these bull market opportunities and avoid holding through bearish down cycles.

- **Wall Street.** "So when you set up your portfolio, you must stretch it across different asset classes and then be prepared to sit tight. When one class outperforms, you will have that in your portfolio. You'll have the one that underperforms as well. But they will balance each other out." *Mary Rowland, The New Common Sense Guide to Mutual Funds, Bloomberg Press.*

  Maverick Principle Number 5. The best way to achieve your goals is to put 100 percent of your money in stock assets. They out-performed the other asset classes—bonds, cash—in every 20-year time period and in eight out of nine decades in the twentieth century. (Bonds did outperform stocks in the 1970s.)

- **Wall Street.** "You can choose either a managed fund or an index fund; and with dollar cost averaging the beauty is that when the mar-ket goes down, you'll simply be able to buy more shares. So don't be afraid. You have plenty of time to let that money sit. Buy, too, when the market is up, because next month—who knows?—it might be up even more. Just buy, each and every month."—*Suze Orman, The 9 Steps to Financial Freedom.*

  Maverick Principle Number 7. You've got to know *when* to buy, and—just as important—when to sell everything in your portfo-lio. The idea that you should buy whether the market heads up or down is a prescription for ordinary in the best of times, and a recipe for disaster in the worst of times.

- **Wall Street.** "Gruntal's Joseph Battipaglia is slashing his year-end outlook for the Nasdaq to a more moderate 4300 from an outlandishly optimistic 5500. And Credit Suisse First Boston's Thomas Galvin is cutting his 12-month target . . . to 4500 from 5300." *The Big Flip-Flop, Smart Money.com, 10/17/00.* (Nasdaq at 3171.)

  Maverick Principle Number 9. Let the market tell you what direction it's heading, ignore pundit prognostications, and never pre-dict the direction of stock prices.

THE MAVERICK PRINCIPLES

Once again, these are the 10 rules that enable mavericks to thrive as stock-market winners:

1. **I take full responsibility for my financial future.** It's mine; I own it; no excuses.

2. **I invest for clear-cut, attainable goals.**   Not fuzzy, not silly; able to be measured step by step.

3. **I strive for extraordinary portfolio growth.**   I hitch my wagon to rising trends, and avoid the big falls.

4. **I maximize all of my tax-deferred investing opportunities.**   I don't feed the feds any more or any sooner than I have to.

5. **I put 100 percent of my money into stocks.**   I say "no" to "balance," "income," "bonds," and other bad words.

6. **I track the performance of the stock market, my holdings, and my alternative choices.**   I know what's going on, and if I don't like what's going on, I know where I should go next.

7. **I know when to buy and when to sell every asset in my portfolio.** I'm not emotional; I don't get stampeded; I don't fall in love or wallow in despair.

8. **I pursue growth in stocks throughout my entire life.**   That's where the game is played, and the gains are to be made.

9. **I never predict the direction of stock prices.**   Gypsies and Wall Street pundits are predictors; I'm a trend-tracker.

10. **I capitalize on market change and investment innovation.**   I pounce on new tools and new information that can help me be an even more effective maverick.

4

Empower Yourself: Turning Dreams into Goals

Have you ever resolved to lose weight, reduce stress in your life, or spend more time with your family?

How well did you keep (or are you keeping) those promises?

It's one thing to tell yourself you'd like to change your lifestyle. It's quite another to take those kinds of commitments seriously.

A maverick named Jennifer has found a way to accomplish that difficult job, in the realm of investing. She e-mailed me a three-point plan that she keeps prominently displayed atop her PC:

- *I will pay off my mortgage and own my home outright.*
- *I will invest for my son's education so that he never has to experience the burden of student loans.*
- *I will start and operate a nonprofit theater group in my community.*

Just from reading these statements, just from looking at the words she chooses, you can see how important these things are to Jennifer. Personally, I was struck by her determination to put her boy through college without saddling him (or herself) with a lot of debt. From her point of view, this is not a nice-to-have; this is an absolute must. Way to go, Jennifer.

What can you point to that's comparable? Have you identified the *compelling reasons* to change the way you invest? Is it the fear of living in a ramshackle shack in your later years? Or, more positively, is it the all-consuming love that you feel for your family? Or is it the image of that house, that car, or that boat that seems to keep popping up in your daydreams?

There's no right or wrong answer. The answer that's right for one person is likely to be way wrong for another. But in my experience, unless you can hold up a vision in front of yourself that's as powerful to you as Jennifer's is to her, you're unlikely to make the necessary changes in your life.

CREATING WEALTH

1. *I've heard a lot about Cisco and JDS Uniphase. Are these the best stocks to buy if you're a newbie?*
2. *We both would like to quit our day jobs when our youngest leaves for college in eight years. Which mutual funds do you suggest?*
3. *I bought Vanguard's S&P 500 and it's done nothing but go sideways. Is Vanguard's small cap growth index any better?*

When I got these e-mails, my reaction was, "Whoa, *Nellie!*" Yes, it's important to choose your investments wisely. But picking this week's hot stocks or last month's fancy funds isn't what creates wealth.

What *does* create wealth? Understanding what you're investing for. Setting genuine goals. And creating a game plan for achieving those goals.

When I probed the motivations of the investors who sent me those e-mails, it turned out that none of them had a clear vision of their goals. At best, each had a fuzzy notion that things weren't going the right way in their lives, and that "maybe the stock market can help." In other words, fuzzy goals led to fuzzy actions—which make real progress very unlikely.

In contrast, extraordinary wealth makers write down their goals. They then design personal pathways for realizing their big-picture dreams. Focused goals engender good plans, which in turn engender success, over the long run.

Financial freedom in retirement, world travel, world-class education for your child—you dream it, and there's a personalized blueprint for getting there. Better yet, once you make investing part of your lifestyle, you can't *help* but be successful. Maybe I haven't persuaded you of that yet. But stick with me. I will!

In this chapter, you'll begin by taking an honest look at your finances. Next, you will identify what kind of goal setter you are and what kind you need to be. At the same time, you will write down your investing goals, and discover when they will come true—using your own, individual numbers.

GETTING REAL

We pay bills for gas, electricity, water, cable, phone, and trash. We buy food and clothes with our ATM or credit card, never once touching the money. And despite a blossoming 401(k) that is starting to look pretty sweet on paper, it's really difficult to tell—especially far away from that quarterly statement—whether we're succeeding or slipping.

But *hey:* If you really want to be the zillionaire next door, you can't whine about how unreal the money seems, or about how far away those 401(k) dollars seem. *This is your life.* These are your affairs. You have to be totally committed to changing your habits and attitudes—even at the risk of some discomfort.

The first and most important rule is to *pay yourself first.* This is absolutely essential to successful investing and debt management. If you have access to a 401(k) plan, fund it with pretax dollars. If you have credit-card debt, stop using the cards, and pay off your balances with automatic withdrawals. And if you don't have the checking or savings account cash flow to buy a DVD player, for goodness sake, *wait!* The world won't come to an end if you use the VCR for another six months. Put two bucks a day into the DVD Fund coffee can in the kitchen, and see if you can keep from raiding it (it will take good discipline).

Maverick investors "get real." If you procrastinate when it's time to fill out your taxes, if you avoid frank discussions about your personal finances, the chances are that you need to rewrite your financial screenplay.

HONESTLY SEE YOUR WEALTH

If you're ever going to get out of debt and start investing more successfully, then you've got to get *organized.* You need to develop an honest and complete picture of your wealth (or lack thereof).

I know one maverick investor who made a collage of every financial statement she received. Bank accounts, investment accounts, 401(k) statements, credit card bills, insurance premiums—the whole nine yards. One side of the collage was debts; the other side was assets. She said she enjoyed every minute of it—once she got past the unpleasant ratio of debts to assets, that is.

If a cut-and-paste collage is not your style, fill out the sample worksheet that follows (Figure 4-1). By listing your assets, you'll be able to get a glimpse—albeit only two-dimensional—of your financial nest egg.

So what do you see? Be brutally honest with yourself. Are you satisfied with what's in plain sight? Would you like to be 20 times richer, and 100 times wealthier?

If you honestly see your wealth, you'll know what direction to take your goals. And here's the most interesting phenomenon of all, in this early

FIGURE 4-1   Asset Worksheet

Take Inventory of Your Current Portfolio
Tax-Deferred Liquid Inventory

What are your   <u>Types of Tax-Deferred Accounts</u>
Tax-Deferred Options?   IRA   Keogh
_____   Roth IRA   Pension
_____   IRA Rollover   Profit Sharing
_____   Sep IRA   Variable Annuity
_____   401 (k)   VUL (Variable Universal Life
_____   403 (b)

Type of account	Where invested	Value	Compounded rate of return achieved in last three years

Subtotal: _____ = **A**

stage of reorientation: You'll even begin to walk, talk, and act as though you're already experiencing the success you seek. Human beings have enormous capacities to *realize* what they can *visualize*. And that's why I keep coming back to this notion of the powerful idea: What can you visualize that will motivate you, for years to come?

FIGURE 4-1   Asset Worksheet from MI Seminars (*cont.*)

Taxable Liquid Inventory

Type of account	Where invested	Value	Compounded rate of return achieved in last three years

Subtotal: _____ = **B**

Calculating Your Individual Tax-Deferred Ratio

- Add **A** and **B** together. _____. This is the approximate value of your TOTAL portfolio = **C**

- Divide **A** by **C**. Your answer should be expressed as a decimal. This is your own, unique tax-deferred ratio. Write that decimal here: _____ = **D**

PLANNING STAGES—THE BENEFITS OF SETTING GOALS

Most people spend more time planning a two-week vacation than they do planning their financial future. Pretty silly, considering that it's the money that makes the trip happen, and not the other way around.

So why do people have so much trouble putting an investment strategy together? I think it's most often because they've never sharpened their goal-setting skills.

Now, *I know what you're thinking.* You're thinking that you've already heard all about the supposed benefits of writing down the details of your dreams. But listen to me, as I turn up the heat on you a little bit: it doesn't matter what you thought of goal-setting at some point in your past. You're not yet a multimillionaire, right? So I say that you can't afford to be rigid, blasé, or cynical.

Take that negative voice out of your head and lock it in the closet for a while—or *forever*, if you can. And open yourself up to a more flexible and more positive outlook.

Setting goals gives you direction and purpose. Even better, the very act of striving for achievement brings about greater levels of happiness. Done right, goal-setting:

1. Provides both short-term motivation and long-term vision
2. Increases your performance as an individual investor
3. Boosts your self-confidence

WHAT TYPE OF GOAL SETTER ARE YOU?

In my 25 years of investment counseling, I've come across four distinct kinds of goal setters. I call them the "no-goalers," "the goaltenders," "the adventure-seekers," and "the individualists." Let's look at them in that order.

No-Goalers

Are you too easy on yourself? Do you walk away from challenges because you're afraid to look silly? Have you made empty promises, year in and year out, without ever actually changing anything?

If so, you may be a No-Goaler. That's my term for the aimless wanderer—the person who claims to have "no interest in competing." You know what? I don't buy it. Maybe there's a Perfect Master out there who has risen above the rough-and-tumble of human existence. The rest of us—I believe—are still competitors at heart. If we think we aren't aggressive, or don't have ambitions, we're simply kidding ourselves.

Mostly, it's fear of failure. Think how many times you've edged up to the cliff edge of a major commitment, and then backed away. I know *I've* done it—and I've subsequently regretted it. Think how much more you, and I, and the rest of humanity could accomplish if we didn't have the chicken-out instinct.

If you're not prepared to stretch yourself to the limits, then you're not going to reach your potential for high net worth. Want to be a maverick? Want to get rich? Then get ready to start *stretching*.

Goaltenders

Do you hoard, rather than invest? Do you pinch pennies? Are you clipping coupons in the belief that a nickel saved is a nickel earned? Meanwhile, are you failing to *invest* those pennies and nickels in ways that over time can help make you wealthy?

If so, then you're what I'd call a Low-Goaler, or a Goaltender. The father of psychology, Sigmund Freud, might have told you that you were "retentive."

In the business world, they said that finance is playing the game, and accounting is simply keeping score. (At least, that's what the finance guys say.) Maverick investing is about playing the game—which of course involves some scorekeeping, but the key element is to *never lose sight of the goal.*

Stop trying to be perfect. Stop spending so much time worrying about the rules. Start challenging yourself. Again, let yourself *fail* once in a while. Failure will show you how to invest more wisely, and how to get closer to the things you want. Always set goals that are challenging.

Adventure-Seekers

Are you constantly searching for ways to hit the home run? Do you get a jolt when you hear a particularly spicy tip? Did you kick yourself because you weren't tech-stocked to the hilt in 1999? Are you still irked about having earned a meager 40 percent, while the Nasdaq rose 85 percent?

You might be an adventure-seeker. Sounds sexy, eh? In movie parlance, an adventure seeker might be an Indiana Jones type. And yes, rescuing the Lost Ark seems more appealing than living the life of a no-goaler or a goal-tender.

The fatal flaw: There's nothing sexy about taking risks that result in catastrophe. There's nothing erotic about being broke, and living poor.

When you set goals that are unrealistically high, one of two outcomes (or both) will occur. You may fall so far short of your expectations that you will eventually quit in disgust. Or, your discouragement leads you to do something incredibly stupid, leading to the eventual plunge of your spirits (and your portfolio).

Set goals that are ambitious, not ludicrous. For instance, 20 percent annualized growth on your investment mix is both ambitious and doable. (Some would even say, "sexy!") I've done it for years. So can you.

Individualists

As you've probably guessed, it's the mavericks who bear the title of "individualists." That's because our goals mean something personal, and individual, to us. They are *genuine*.

Again, your goals need to be personal, positive, precise, performance-oriented, and practical. Hit the nail on the head in these areas, and you can never go wrong!

GENUINE GOALS
Personal and Positive

Do you want to open a bed-and-breakfast along the coast? Are you interested in returning to school to get your Ph.D. in psychology? Have you ever wanted to run for public office on your own dime?

These are concrete, positive dreams that have personal meaning for some individuals. And the more personal and positive your dreams are, the greater the likelihood that you'll turn them into genuine goals.

We function better when we frame our goals in positive (not negative) words. For example, "I won't be able to retire if my portfolio continues to lose money" isn't quite right. It sets you up for gloom. Instead, why not get out a clean sheet of paper and write, "I will be able to retire comfortably if I achieve 20 percent growth over the next 17 years."

Everyone loves an upgrade. And you will love what positive goals do for your attitude towards investing.

Be Precise

Sometimes, goals can be so vague that it's difficult to know whether you're achieving them or not. For instance, you might decide to "contribute $2000 of my next bonus to my Roth IRA." But if you have no idea when that bonus is coming, or what the total amount will be, the goal is too difficult to pin down. You can't take it any farther.

Precise goals are measurable ones. They come with dates, times, and amounts attached. For instance, "$2000 in the Roth IRA by Christmas" translates into $166.66 per month, or roughly $38.50 a week, if you begin on January 1. There are no ifs, ands, or buts about $38.50 a week—you know what you have to do!

Be Performance Oriented

Let's say you're checking the quarterly results of your 401(k). You own two funds: one that earned 8 percent (Fund A) in three months, and the other that picked up 5 percent (Fund B) in the same period. Do you move money from Fund B to Fund A? Not if you're a maverick investor!

My growth goal is 20 percent per year, which translates into 10 percent over 6 months, or 5 percent per quarter. Am I on target? Absolutely! So I'm not going to obsess about rebalancing, rotating, or reacting. Heck—it's a beautiful day, and life is short. Why worry about money when you can go fishing instead?

Be Practical

Are you unrealistic about investing? Do you let the media, friends, or relatives tell you how much you should or shouldn't be making? Well, don't. Stop that stuff. Know what's possible, and pursue it.

Shoot high, but shoot at a target of your own devising, which makes sense for you. If you come in a little low, you can resolve to make it up over the long run. On the other hand, if you shoot for 20 percent compounded and earn 30 percent, you're gonna feel pretty darned good about yourself.

You can't *help* but be successful when you're practical, positive, performance-centered, precise, and personal. Why? Because the more genuine a goal is, the more likely you are to accomplish it.

FROM DREAMS TO GENUINE GOALS

Here's a useful exercise. In the "Dream Space" that follows, list 10 things that you want. Don't worry about putting them down in order. Don't analyze what you're writing as you go along. Just jot down 10 dreams.

_____

_____

_____

_____

_____

_____

_____

_____

_____

If you start running out of inspiration after about six or seven heart's desires, don't worry. (This happens to lots of people the first time they try this exercise.) Take a look at "Larry's List of Wants" (Figure 4-2). It may get you thinking about all the things you *would* have written down if I hadn't put you under all that pressure. . . .

Okay. Finished? Got your 10 dreams? Now make a second column to the right of your "I want" list. Then, with 1 being the most important and 10 being the least important, *prioritize* your dreams. Use every number between 1 and 10, but only once! (See Figure 4-3.)

FIGURE 4-2   Larry's List of Wants

1. I want to be able to shop in any store without ever having to look at the price tags.
2. I want to get out of debt without declaring bankruptcy.
3. I want to make sure my kid can go to college without she or me having to take out another loan.
4. I want to move into a bigger home.
5. I want to have enough money so I only have to work part-time when I'm older.
6. I want to see the world, from Australia to Zimbabwe.
7. I want to own a vacation home in Colorado.
8. I want more leisure time to play racquetball.
9. I want to give my wife a second wedding with all the bells and whistles we couldn't afford the first time around.
10. I want to have the kind of wealth that Richard Gere had in *Pretty Woman* ("an obscene amount of money").

Although you may not realize it, you're prioritizing dreams in a way that you probably haven't done before; that is, you're not assigning 1s and 2s to each item on a shopping list—you're forcing yourself to *choose*. By choosing one desire over another, you'll be able to devote the right amount of energy and time to making the most important dreams come true.

FIGURE 4-3   Larry's Dreams . . . Prioritized!

I want to be able to walk into any store without having to look at the price tags.   ____7____.

I want to get out of debt without declaring bankruptcy.   ____1____.

I want to make sure my kid can go to college, without she or me having to take out another loan.   ____5____.

I want to move into a bigger home.   ____2____.

I want to have enough money so I only have to work part-time when I'm older. ____3____.

I want to see the world, from Australia to Zimbabwe.   ____6____.

I want to own a vacation home in Colorado.   ____9____.

I want more leisure time to play racquetball.   ____8____.

I want to give my wife a second wedding with all the bells and whistles we couldn't afford the first time around.   ____4____.

I want to have the kind of wealth that Richard Gere had in *Pretty Woman* ("an obscene amount of money").   ____10____.

FIGURE 4-4   Top Three Dreams become Top Three Goals

1. **Dream:** I want to get out of debt without declaring bankruptcy.

    Goal: I will eliminate my insane dependency on high-interest rate credit cards by paying off $30,000 over the next five years.

2. **Dream:** I want to move into a bigger home.

    Goal: I will raise the $50,000 of additional down payment money to purchase a house with 5 bedrooms, 3 baths, and a backyard big enough for an enormous German shepherd.

3. **Dream:** I want to have enough money so I only have to work part-time when I'm older.

    Goal: I will have $1.2 mil in my 401(k) when I turn 55 in the year 2015, so I can begin taking periodic withdrawals and work a more humane 20 hours per week.

When you've finished, take a long look at the items that you've labeled 1, 2, and 3. How many hours or minutes in a week do you spend pursuing each dream? If this wish has the potential to be a goal, how would you make it genuine?

Now comes the fun part. Let's say you share Larry's passion for "moving into a bigger home." Well, now you need to make this dream more personal. You need to make it more *measurable*.

In Figure 4-4, you can see exactly how Larry turned his top three desires into genuine goals. He now has a time, date, location, and a variety of specs that fit his personal profile. You can do the same. You *must* do the same!

PERSONALIZE YOUR WEALTH

I hope that by this point, you've laid out a physical picture, an honest view, of your finances. You know how and why you need to set genuine goals. You've even begun writing them down.

Now it's time to personalize your situation—give it a signature file, if you will. Consider this e-mail from Aaron:

> My wife and I want to move to New Mexico and build our desert Oasis before we're too old. We both enjoy golfing. I want to teach kids reading skills as well—so I've found my reasons to invest. I've also done my homework. I know I'll need my $70,000 to grow to $1.25 million. How do I get there?

Aaron's effort at asking the strategic question, "How do I get there?" gives him a maverick edge. He's not hung up on the tactics of which fund.

He has identified his reasons to invest. He's taken an honest appraisal of his net worth. Plus, he's worked out a figure for his desert dream.

Where Aaron needs help is with his goal-setting. Although we know how much he has to invest ($70,000), we do not know how much he can add to the nest egg annually, or the time period he's looking at.

For illustration purposes, let's assume that Aaron is 40 years alone. If he contributed nothing to his account, but managed his account for 15 percent growth, he'd be able to move to New Mexico with **$1,145,657** at age 60. That's right: **$1.4 million** with no more annual contributions!

However, Aaron may want to get to New Mexico in less than 20 years. What will it take to get there in 15 years? Both he and his wife would have to set up an early retirement account (more in Chapter 20) in order to save outside of their retirement account. Remember that you can't access retirement accounts until age 59½. But if that's a good time frame for you, then start salting money away there!

MAKING IT REAL FOR YOU!

What maverick investors need to do is figure out the answers to three personal questions. If you've already made your "net worth" collage, the first two questions are a piece of cake!

1. **How much do you have on hand, now, to invest?**   You have a lump sum number—figure it out. What is the total dollar amount in your employer-sponsored plans (e.g., 401(k), 403(b), 457) and your individual retirement accounts (e.g., IRA, Roth IRA) combined. If you're married, add your spouse's dollars.

   What number did you come up with? That's your net worth, excluding taxable accounts and nonqualified tax-deferred programs. (We'll use those dollar amounts in subsequent chapters.)

2. **How much can you add on a regular basis?**   Many people simply don't believe that they'd be able to put aside $2000 a year. (Aren't things tight already?) In reality, these people only have to commit to a small and specific target of $5.50 a day. Honest: Do the math. (All right: I'll give you one day off). If the only thing standing between you and millions of dollars is the price of a meal at a fast food restaurant—which you probably shouldn't be eating every day, anyway— perhaps you can find the discipline to add the necessary amounts to your IRA every year.

   How much have you decided to put aside daily? Weekly? Annually? These are the contributions necessary to build wealth.

3. **When will you need the money?**   It's important to identify your
time horizon, since time is indeed finite. None of us will live forever.
Nor should any of us plan to accumulate riches until the age of 100
without taking from the nest egg (and as we'll see in later chapters,
the government requires withdrawals, in any case).

Remember the critical importance of *genuineness*. (If it's not you,
it's not genuine.) Be practical. Think in terms of a 10-, 15-, 20-, or 25-
year horizon. Make the timeline personal to you. For example, if
you're 30, you may be thinking in terms of retiring comfortably at 50
(i.e., in 20 years.)

IT ALL ADDS UP

By now, you may be able to guess what I mean by the statement, "It all adds
up."

First of all, I mean that over time, if you're a maverick investor, the
money does indeed pile up. It's amazing how even modest regular investments over a sustained period of time add up to a large nest egg, when managed well.

And second, I mean that the component parts of maverick investing all
add up. You start with what you're starting with: an honest and complete
statement of your current financial situation. What are your debts, and what
are your assets? Meanwhile, you develop a clear statement of your goals—
ranked in order of importance—and a time frame within which you want to
achieve those goals. And then you aim for maverick rates of return. I suggest 20 percent: high enough to be extraordinary, but not so high that you're
doomed to fail.

In fact, the opposite is true. *You're destined to succeed*—because it all
adds up:

Money + Time + 20% Compounded Growth = Financial Independence!

TURNING DREAMS INTO GOALS

• **It's the game plan, not the game ball, that determines your
wealth.**   Ordinary investors chase the latest fad, and as a result, they
struggle to attain ordinary results. Mavericks, on the other hand, are
goal-setters and milestone-celebrators. We set our eyes on the prize,
chart a course for getting there, and measure our successes along the
way.

- **Honesty is your best policy.**   Sure: You can brag about the 300 percent gain you made in two months—and conveniently leave out the fact that you made this gain on a tiny fraction of your net worth. But after the bragging stops, you're only be fooling yourself. And why do that? Mavericks don't shy away from the truth—beginning with the reality of their debts versus their assets. Being honest with yourself is the *only way* to figure out where you are, where you need to go, and how you can get there.
- **Good goals inspire action.**   Ordinary investors either rush through goal-setting, or skip this critical step altogether. As a result, their objectives—"I wanna be rich," or, "I wanna make 100 percent on my portfolio in 6 months"—are worthless. (Or if they're part of "fooling yourself," as just described, they're worse than useless.) Mavericks get maximum mileage out of genuine goals—attainable, upbeat, and personally meaningful goals.
- **How much, how often, how long?**   Three simple questions help you project the wealth you'll have for a genuine goal. *How much do you have in your 401(k)?* Example: $23,892. *How often can you contribute?* Example: every other week, 10 percent pretax, and 6 percent matching, which in our example comes to $7500 a year. *What's your time frame?* Example: 18 years. At 20 percent annualized growth, you'll have **$1.8 million!**

5

Ordinary Returns versus Extraordinary Growth

Have you ever wondered what it feels like to drive a high-performance car, or to live in a million-dollar estate?

Have you ever fantasized about how your life would change if you had virtually unlimited financial resources?

Have you ever thought about the things you would buy, the places you would visit, and the people with whom you would share your good fortune, if only you were rich?

Well, the difference between *envisioning* luxury and *living* in its lap is simply a matter of doing the right things, over the right period of time. Put another way, if you project your future wealth using your starting point, your regular additions, and the Maverick 20 percent compounded growth rate, you'll see *what* you can have, and *when* you could have it. You can determine what's at the end of the rainbow, as well as what's possible at significant milestones along the way.

Consider Tony, Katie, and Jarred (Figure 5-1). Each has unique goals and a different set of financial circumstances. Yet all three are able to project their wealth at 20 percent compounded growth. What's more, each can become a multimillionaire!

FIGURE 5-1   Tony, Katie, and Jared

1. Tony, 25, wants to live off retirement income and self-publish novels
    $5000 in IRA, $2000 per year . . .
    At 55, in 30 years, he'll have **$3.5 mil**
2. Katie Sue, 35, wants to live on investment earnings while financing public
    education initiatives in her neighborhood
    $20,000 in her 403(b), $3000 per year . . .
    At 60, in 25 years, she'll have **$3.3 mil**
3. Jarred, 45, wants to retire comfortably in Boca Raton, Florida, to live in a big
    house on a private golf course
    $40,000 in his 401(k), $10,000 annual contribution . . .
    At 65, in 20 years, he'll have **$3.4 mil**

Running the personal numbers and projecting what 20 percent compounded growth can do is *empowering.* In Tony's case, he knows that with $3.5 million in his IRA, he'll be able to self-publish books. With $3.3 million in her 403(b), Katie can look forward to becoming a public school advocate. And Jarred can rest easy that with $3.4 million in his 401(k), he'll be whacking plenty of dimpled orbs.

WHY THE TIME IS NOW: LESS CATCH-UP!

You've heard the old adage, "Lost time is lost money." Believe it. The earlier you catch the investing bug, the sooner you can purchase a beachfront villa in Maui.

Take another look at Tony, Katie, and Jarred. It's the youngest person, Tony—who invests less up front and less along the way—and who nevertheless reaches the $3 million mark at an earlier age than the others. Katie needs $3000 a year and Jarred requires $10,000 annually, just to catch up.

Typically, when I give a seminar to new mavericks, I ask the youngest person in the room to stand up. (When there are a couple of hundred people involved, this can be a fun exercise.) When they finally figure out who that person is—often a teenager, as it turns out—I point to him or her, and with a dramatic flourish, I proclaim to the rest of the group, "That young person over there is already *the richest person in this room!"*

Why? Because the greatest resource in the wealth-building equation is *time.*

Think about it. Time is the only fixed variable in the wealth-building equation (M + T + C = Wealth). In other words, it's the only variable that you can't manipulate. It is what it is. That's why you need to make the most of your time.

NEVER TOO LATE TO BE A MAVERICK INVESTOR

Are you concerned that you've let too many years pass you by? Do you feel compounding can't work for someone in your shoes?

Latecomers, take heart. The maverick path will make you plenty rich, regardless of your current situation. Why? Because, when you defy conventional rules, you're able to generate higher rates of returns than any financial planner's going to get for you.

Consider Daniel's story. He writes:

> I started with nothing at 49. Divorce, job layoff, despair—you name it and I've seen it. But I subscribed to your flagship service in 1989 and have since created an ostrich-sized egg worth $850,000 in just 11 years.
>
> I've been shooting for the maverick goal of 20 percent, and have been particularly fortunate to get closer to 30 percent in the decade. The funny thing is, now relatives and friends of acquaintances are coming out of the woodwork. Not to congratulate me, but to tell me what I'm doing wrong.
>
> "You have too much tech. You don't have enough tech. You should be doing this. Why aren't you doing that?" Would it surprise you to know that none of these "helpers" has a million bucks?
>
> Sure, I sacrificed. I've been maxing out my 401(k) and IRAs to the tune of $15,000 a year. But my will is strong and my vision is clear. I can see that million-dollar portfolio right around the corner. Wish me luck!

WHAT IS COMPOUNDING?

Nobody ever asks me, "Doug, what do you mean by 'money'?" And I can safely say that in 25 years of giving people help and advice, no one has ever come up to me and said, "Hey, Doug—define 'time' for me." I guess that means that people think they understand these two concepts.

When I talk about "compounded growth" at my seminars, however, I can almost always look across the crowd and spot plenty of dazed expressions. Many may be able to recite what they've read in a math primer—*compounding is the interest on top of both the principal and the interest earned.* But to most people, it's mostly a confusing mouthful. It doesn't seem particularly *real* to people.

Perhaps it's easier to understand what compounded growth *is* by what it *does*. In essence, it multiplies your money exponentially, giving you a return not just on your original investment, but also on the gains.

FIGURE 5-2   Understanding Compounded Growth

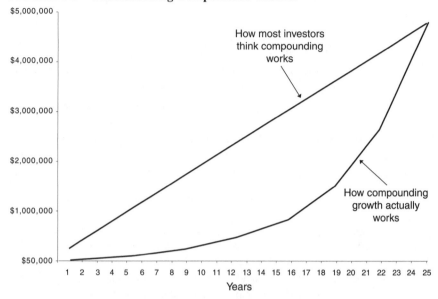

For example, $50,000 at 20 percent is $60,000 in year 1. In year 2, you have another 20 percent on the principal ($10,000) plus 20 percent on the gains ($2,000). Now you have $72,000. In 5 years, it's $124,412. In 15 years, it's $770,351. And in 25 years, that original investment of $50,000 with no additional contributions becomes **$4,769,811!**

When you look at the chart (Figure 5-2), you see that money does not compound in a straight line, moving from lower left to upper right. Instead, the line is only a little bit "uphill" at first, then it curves upward sharply, and then it gets closer and closer to vertical. This is a picture of exponential growth. Look at the left-hand side of the chart. Your compounded interest grows slowly at first ($2000 in second year), but by year 5 it swells to $124,412.

Now take a look at how the curve starts to point north by northeast in year 15. Your money reaches $770,351 on an original investment of $50,000. By year 25, the growth curve is shooting for the moon, turning your $50,000 into more than $4.7 million!

NOW ASK ME AGAIN
What is compounding? Before answering directly, allow me to inject my own subjective commentary on the subject: Compounding is probably what they should have taught you in math class, rather than trigonometry.

Can you imagine if we required every school to teach the basic realities behind compounded growth? I honestly think that if our society took this simple step, in 20 years our nation would be immensely stronger, and the lives of our senior citizens would be immensely richer—literally and figuratively.

Yes, you can lie with statistics. But this ain't statistics, it's simple math, and this math doesn't lie. Put $5.50 per day in an IRA compounding at 20 percent for 25 years, and *bingo.* You won't just feel like a million bucks, you'll be worth it.

YOUR TICKET IS 20 PERCENT

The historical rates of return for stocks, bonds, and cash are 12 percent, 8 percent, and 6 percent, respectively. Since financial planners typically recommend a mix of all three assets, and because they tell you to buy 'n' hold those investments, they expect you to be grateful for 8 percent. Even if your adviser is aggressive with a high allocation to stocks, he or she still won't seek more than 10 percent.

Hey, people are only human, right? Suppose I'm your nonmaverick financial advisor. Suppose I've got 50, or 100, or 500 people like you in my stable of clients. I've only got so many hours to give you, in the course of a year. In those circumstances, which of the following two strategies am I more likely to employ?

- Tell you to shoot for 15 percent, and have you get mad at me when we only achieve 12 percent?
- Tell you to shoot for 10 percent, and have you be happy when we crash through that barrier and achieve 12 percent?

Mavericks understand that 10 percent is *simply not good enough*—not for ourselves or our families. Therefore, we put 100 percent of our money in stocks or stock funds that consistently match or exceed the growth goal of 20 percent per year.

We don't diversify across asset classes. We don't settle for inferior investments. And we never hold onto any position during a bear market.

Isn't 20 percent an exceptionally high goal? Absolutely. Yet mavericks seek exceptionally strong returns, not ordinary returns.

I say 20 percent is your ticket because:

- **It is a genuine goal.**   It is upbeat, measurable, and growth-centered. Most important, *it is realistic* when you invest 100 percent in high-quality stock funds while managing the downside risk. Yes, I know that every single financial professional you choose to talk to on this subject is likely to snort and roll his or her eyes heavenward when you talk "20 percent." But what if I'm right, and they're wrong? Who do you *want* to be right?

- **It shoots for a million-dollar portfolio.**   Just run the numbers.
- **It challenges you to invest differently** from the herd.
- **It makes selection incredibly simple.**   Never underestimate the power of simplicity.

A PROCESS OF ELIMINATION

Have you ever been confused by tiny prospectus print, or hazy mutual fund objectives? Have you ever struggled to differentiate between "aggressive growth" and "high yield"? Do you sometimes get the impression that the names of funds in your 401(k) were designed to make you feel stupid?

The 20 percent growth target does something *really helpful* for you: It cuts through all the jargon and mumbo-jumbo instantly, and thereby simplifies your search for the right investments. Straight from the get-go, you can eliminate all fixed-income assets, bonds, bond funds, and balanced funds. If you see any of these words among your choices, just put a big, fat, red line through them. None of these will ever take you where you want to go.

Ever buy something on eBay, the Web-based auction house? (Maybe I shouldn't even point you toward this, since some people find it addictive.) But basically, eBay is a gigantic electronic flea market. People who want to sell you their treasures (or their junk) put the stuff up for auction. As a potential buyer, you go to the eBay search page, and type in what you're looking for. Say you're looking for scenic postcards of Paris. You type in "PARIS."

But you're only interested in the City of Light; you have zero interest in the small town of Paris, Texas. So on the next line down—the "exclude" line—you type in "TEXAS." The computer gives you a list of everything from Paris, France, and nothing from Paris, Texas.

In like manner, when it comes to picking your funds, you create your mental "exclude" line, and then you type in "bond" and all those other bad words.

FILL MY EYES ... WITH 5/10/20 VISION

One of the biggest concerns that I hear expressed by my radio callers is whether they've chosen the right stock fund for their 401(k). Although this is a valid concern, it's *not* the toughest item on the Maverick's agenda. Why not? Because when you have a strategic growth goal of 20 percent, the selection process becomes infinitely easier.

For example, 401(k) plans frequently offer between 8 and 10 funds and offer mutual fund choices (see Figure 5-3). Using 20 percent as your guide, as already noted, you can immediately put a red line through any bond or income-related fund. These investments don't have the ability to reach 20 percent in any year.

By now, you probably have three or four options left. Which of those funds is on track to reach 20 percent in a year? In other words, which of these choices gained 5 percent in the last 3 months, or 10 percent over the last 6 months—as well as 20 percent for the previous 12 months?

I call this "5/10/20 vision." And with only 8 to 10 funds in your 401(k), the chances are pretty good that only 1 or 2 will see this clearly.

Here are two possible complications. First, it's possible that your universe of funds includes *no* choices with 5/10/20 vision. If that's the case,

FIGURE 5-3   5/10/20 401(k)

Fidelity 401(k) for H&R Block
June 30, 2000

Henry, 38
Total Dollars: $100,000
Wants to retire at 55

Choices	Three Years	Five Years
Fidelity OTC	35%	28%
Fidelity Contra fund	19.96%	20.32%
Fidelity Growth and Income	16.42%	20.63%
Fidelity Magellan	21%	19%
Fidelity Advisor Opportunity Growth	Lemon	Lemon
Fidelity Asset Manager	14%	15%
Fidelity Asset Manager Growth	14%	16%
Fidelity Asset Manager Income	INCOME	
Fidelity Short Term Bond	BOND FUND	
Fidelity US Bond Index	BOND FUND	
Fidelity Retire MMKT	INCOME	

and if the stock market has been reasonably healthy in the previous 12 months, then you need to have a conversation with your 401(k) administrator—or at least with the person who negotiates with that person. What's going on here? Why can't we do any better than this? Isn't there any way to add additional investment options?

The second complication might be that the market has been dragging, overall, in the previous 12 months, and that *nobody* out there has been turning in great performances.

We'll talk about dealing with the "Big Bear" in later chapters. Meanwhile, focus on understanding the universe of options that are available to you today. You may have some good ones that you haven't been aware of before.

Remember, the point is to focus on 20 percent growth. That's what gets you to your goals. Yes, you've probably heard and you'll probably keep hearing those stories about the guy three cubicles down who's made a *big play in the market.* Forget about him. Most likely, he's like the guy who *wins big at the track*—except that he doesn't brag about all those days he *lost big* at the track. Stay focused on 20 percent growth. You'll win the game, and the challenge of picking the right investment will take care of itself—with a little love from you, of course.

THE SECRET OF MY SUCCESS
Those who have been on board with me for years already know the biggest secret to my success. I only buy stock funds with the ability to earn 20 percent compounded growth.

For example, in November of 1998, I recommended and purchased several funds that had shown remarkable near-term momentum. However, one of my selections didn't live up to its promise. It did not achieve 5 percent in the next 3 months, or 10 percent over 6 months. In fact, it lost 5.63 percent over 2 quarters!

Fortunately, as a maverick, I am not bound by the constraints of a buy-'n'-hold mindset. Instead, I determined that this position was not on target to reach 20 percent compounded growth, and I quickly dropped the underperformer.

But that's not all. When you sell, the new money affords new opportunity. My clients and I put the capital back to work in a mid-cap superstar that gained 100 percent over the next year.

The implications are clear. By selling a loser, I was able to purchase a winner. I was able to reevaluate the environment and run with a fund that was on track to reach 20 percent annual growth.

Nonmavericks struggle when faced with similar concerns. Some wait to break even. Others "rebalance" their portfolios, selling shares of their winners to put more money in their losers. Still others convince themselves that they need to wait five years before evaluating a fund's progress. These are classic traps that even the most experienced investors fall into.

Don't sell winners to pour money into losers. It doesn't make sense, yet this is one of the most common investing mistakes. Liquidating losing positions means admitting that you probably made a mistake, and few of us want to own up to that. But if you develop a sell discipline you will begin to develop the maverick ways that can propel you and your portfolio to that 20 percent nirvana.

Mavericks don't rebalance. We don't aim to break even. We aggressively pursue a high, yet achievable, rate of return.

Once you've seen what 20 percent can do for your wealth, you'll never want to look back! You'll want to do whatever it takes to achieve the maverick growth goal—beginning with learning the right questions to ask!

OVERVIEW OF ORDINARY VERSUS EXTRAORDINARY

- **Time and time again.** In the wealth-building equation (Time + Money + Rate of Return = Wealth), there's only one variable that's fixed: *time.* There's only so much that any of us have. That's why you have to make the most of it, pursuing extraordinary growth as soon as possible.
- **An extraordinary standard for extraordinary returns.** True, 20 percent is not for the timid. It's an extremely high rate of return. Yet that's exactly what Mavericks want. What's more, we're willing to invest differently from others to attain this goal.
- **And a tool for selection.** The good news is that 20 percent also makes mutual fund selection easy. If an investment doesn't show an ability to get 20 percent per year, it gets removed from consideration. Bye-bye, lemons. So long, underachievers. Let's go look for a *winner.*

PART 2

Maverick Insights into the Stock Market

6

The Players

W hat's the key to the pursuit of 20 percent growth, and the successful achievement of your dreams? As earlier chapters have made clear, there's more than one answer to this question. But one good answer is, *Understand the players in the Wall Street game, and make sure you know the right questions to ask each of them.*

Who are they? Brokers, planners, marketers, banks, accountants, insurers, media moguls, old-time gurus, new-time analysts, brokerage houses, fund families, online experts: These are the well-paid, highly influential participants in the investment game.

There are two mistakes that the investor can make, vis-à-vis these players. One is to take their word as the investing gospel, and do whatever they recommend (e.g., buy and hold). The other is to go to the other end of the spectrum, imagine that these intermediaries have nothing to offer, and invest without ever taking them or their advice into account.

Mavericks don't make either of these critical mistakes. We make it our business to understand how the "Street" works. We make certain that bigtime players are working *for* us, not against us.

Mavericks learn how to separate hype from valuable information. And mavericks arm themselves with knowledge, in order to distinguish the fair players from the frauds.

In this chapter, I identify 10 of the biggest players in the investment arena. I tell you who they are, what they do, and how they might be helpful—or dangerous. In the process, I describe the maverick techniques for turning the threats sometimes posed by these players into wealth-building opportunities.

PLAYER NUMBER 1: THE BROKER

At a minimum, a broker is an intermediary who buys and sells stocks on behalf of his or her clients, and earns a commission on that transaction.

Would you be surprised to learn that many brokers feel threatened by the online revolution? Well, don't be. In a recent issue of *Registered Representative* magazine, for example, one Salomon Smith Barney broker said that his biggest competitive challenge was differentiating himself from "all the noise of the discounters, Internet, and do-it-yourselfers."

If this statement reflects the fears of most commission advisers—and I think it does—then the message you should take away is that they don't want you comparing full-service firms like their own with discount brokerages. Nor do they want you accessing fund performance data on the Web. Why? Because if you started making those comparisons and going after those performance data, you'd quickly start asking embarrassing questions. Like, "So why are your recommended funds [funds on which commissions are paid at the time of purchase or sale] superior to these no-load funds that these other guys are offering? What, exactly, am I getting for that 5 percent you're taking out?"

The California Department of Labor states that the number of securities and commodities brokers will grow 51 percent between 1998 and 2008 . . . the fastest growth rate of any profession on the books!!!

Granted, there are thousands of honest, well-intentioned brokers out there. And there's nothing wrong with paying for personal attention as long as your account is growing. But mavericks make sure they get what they're paying for.

How can you avoid getting bamboozled by an inept broker? Start by checking out an individual's background at the Securities and Exchange Commission's Web site, *www.sec.gov.* Every legitimate seller of securities is licensed and registered. If someone tries to sell you something and doesn't show up on this Web site, assume that this person isn't a registered rep. Believe me: while the vast majority of brokers are legitimate, people run cons on the margin of every profession, fleecing people and making the legitimate players look bad.

Once you've determined that you're dealing with a legitimate broker, you need develop a list of what I call "nail-biters"—questions that you can ask that will tend to make brokers show their true colors. (Again, those colors aren't *necessarily* bad.) Here are a few of my favorites:

1. **How do you decide what stocks and funds to buy?**   If a broker claims to track every company in every industry, or if he or she claims to have a handle on each of the 9000 or so mutual funds that are out there—he or she is, uhm, in the *exaggeration* mode.

2. **How do you determine what investments to sell, and when?**   If a broker has no strategy for when to sell a stock or a mutual fund, he or she has little experience in protecting investor assets.

3. **How much money, in dollars, will you get if I buy Fund X versus Fund Y?**   Brokers only recommend things that they can make money on. (No surprise here: If you were a salesperson on the floor at a Volkswagen dealer, would you recommend a Ford?) You need to understand *whose*
   best interest the prospective broker is serving. It's not likely—but not impossible—that his or her best interests and yours track exactly.

4. **What incentives and perks other than money do you receive when I make this purchase?**   A broker is a salesperson first and foremost. If the broker is unwilling to be upfront about the types of incentives he or she receives, you may wish to think twice.

5. **What's the worst advice you've ever given to a client?**   A broker who claims that he or she rarely makes mistakes is either lying or hasn't worked very long. Conversely, a person who learns from mistakes—and is willing to own up to them—earns points for being trustworthy and competent.

Personally, I don't believe you should let brokers make financial decisions for you. Some have little to no professional experience, and many have never experienced bear markets. Most important, many have less personal wealth than you do! I sometimes tell my radio audiences that I'm amazed that a guy who drives a Rolls Royce would ever take financial advice from a guy who takes the bus to work. And yet, it happens all the time.

By now—Chapter 6—you already know the solution: *Be your own boss.* You have what it takes to become your own investment counselor. And by the way: If you're searching for special assistance for a portion of your money, you may be asking for more or better help than the average broker can provide. In many such cases, you'd be better served by stepping up to a fee-based planner.

PLAYER NUMBER 2: THE FINANCIAL PLANNER

What's the difference between a registered broker and certified financial planner (CFP)? The answer may surprise you: *education.* CFPs have to take rigorous college-level courses and pass a fairly arduous exam. CFPs also receive training that goes beyond the relatively narrow confines of investment, touching on fields that include debt management, insurance protection, and estate planning.

A first-rate education, however, doesn't always lead to first-rate thinking. In fact, the formal schooling that I would otherwise applaud often creates closed-minded financial planners. The better they learn their lessons, the more likely they are to follow the old-school rules—buy-'n'-hold stocks, reduce risk with bonds, and never, *ever* sell.

If you have a financial planner, try to recall the last time that he or she advised you to sell something. If you can remember getting that kind of advice, that's great. Now try to remember the reason *why* you were being told to sell. If the reason seems sensible—for example, you were overexposed to tech stocks, and you should rebalance to reduce risk—then congratulations. It sounds like you have a relationship with a skilled financial planner. They *are* out there.

But external circumstances are working against you, if you're trying to find (or hang on to) such a person. For example, the trend toward consolidation in the financial planning community is not likely to be helpful to individual investors.

Consider the case of an enterprise called National Financial Partners (NFP). They've gobbled up 75 financial services firms, in part by enticing them with private company shares of NFP. Once the conglomerate buys out a few hundred firms—and once the economic wheel turns again in a direction that favors initial public offerings (IPOs)—NFP may decide to go public, in which case all of these founding "partners" will get rich.

"But Doug," you may be saying, "I thought you *liked* the idea of getting rich!" Yes, I do; but I don't like the idea of investors like you and me thinking they're getting independent financial advice from a financial planner when we might be getting something very different. Take the case of the medical community today, which is squirming under the thumbs of the HMOs: *fewer tests! Fewer procedures! More volume!* Well, financial planning is going in this direction. Increasingly, the opinion of the financial planner reflects the opinion of his or her corporation. Now, the corporation's opinions may not be unsophisticated—with all those bodies, they *ought* to have some good ideas somewhere in the shop—but the chances that those ideas will fit your specific needs are fairly remote.

So that's a bad trend. Nevertheless, as you build more wealth in the future, you may want additional help. It's like a medical question: You may want a second opinion. To that I say, "Great!" Seeking additional perspectives is one of the best parts about being a maverick. At the same time, never give up your freedom and obligation to own your own performance. You may not always manage all of your assets, but you should always manage some of your assets. Take responsibility for yourself and your financial future.

If you're going to go with a planner, first take a focused tour of the Web. I like these resources:

- *www.napfa.org.*   The National Association of Personal Financial Advisors (NAPFA). When financial planners earn their income from the investments they recommend (i.e., commissions), it creates an obvious conflict of interest; specifically, they recommend the products they can make the most money on! (This is the Volkswagen salesperson dilemma cited earlier.) NAPFA decries the practice of commissioned-based counseling and only accepts fee-based consultants.

- *www.fpanet.org.*   The Financial Planning Association (FPA). This site is one of the planner's best resources and, by extension, yours! Find out more about the experience, education, and ethics behind the planning profession.

- *www.cfp-board.org.*   If you could conduct a background check on your financial planner, would you do it? You can! Click on "Consumers" and use the links to the National Association of Securities Dealers (NASD), the Securities Exchange Commission (SEC), and the North American Securities Administrators Association (NASAA).

But don't stop at a background check. Remember the "nail-biters" I listed earlier as a way to distinguish between the good and bad brokers of the world? You need to develop a similar set of questions to ask prospective planners, in your interviews with the candidates. (Yes, *of course* you're conducting interviews. Don't you do so when you hire a housekeeper? Your money deserves the same care).

In addition to the nail-biters previously cited, you may also want to add the following questions to your list:

- *How do you get paid? Commissions, salary, fees, combo?*
- *What do you get paid? If it's more than the average fee of 1 percent of assets, why?*

- *How many different companies and different products do you represent?*
- *How much money do you manage? How long have you been in business? References?*
- *How often will we meet? How often will we correspond?*

PLAYER NUMBER 3: THE MARKETER

Did you know that in January 1999, there were only three "Internet funds"—by which I mean funds that purported to invest in companies that did something more or less related to the Internet? And did you know that a scant one year later, there were *more than 30* such funds? Did they divide up the same pie into tiny pieces? No way. All of them enjoyed enormous cash inflows.

Give credit where credit is due: to the marketers. When the net-related stocks rose dramatically, the marketers—wet fingers in the wind—pounced on our emotions and created a slew of net-related mutual funds.

Consider Goldman Sachs's "Internet Tollkeeper." According to its marketing materials, this fund invests in companies that grow revenue by increasing "traffic" and "tolls." Well, great, that sounds good. Every business I know of is constantly looking for more customers, greater sales, and/or higher profit margins. So finding companies that do this can't be what distinguishes Tollkeeper.

In truth, the main thing that distinguishes Tollkeeper from the rest of the net-fund pack is the staggering cost of buying and owning it. You pay a 5 percent sales load for the privilege of getting in. (Welcome aboard!) You also pay 2.25 percent in annual management fees, 1 percent of which finances the fund family's marketing bill. And how was that performance? I'd say that Tollkeeper's 37.2 percent loss in the year 2000 illustrates how marketers are more than willing to lure investors into a commission-laced (I almost wrote "commission-riddled") product at the worst possible time.

Please, fellow mavericks, I implore you: Don't pay marketing fees, sales charges, and redemption penalties. If it's the Internet you're interested in, discover less costly ways to get involved. And it's like your friends at the U.S. Postal Service are always saying in those public-service ads: If a gimmick seems too good to be true, it probably *is* too good to be true.

Before you succumb to a marketer's breathless pitch, here are the curve-ball questions you MUST ask about the investment:

- **What does it cost to own this fund?** Look at transaction costs, such as a $20 or $30 trading fee. Also, see if there's a sales charge, usually designated by the "A" or "B" share tag.

- **What are the penalties or redemptions for selling?** Similar to general banking, many products have penalties for early withdrawal. It's called a redemption fee, and it can be brutal.
- **What is the performance record?** If your stock or stock fund has underperformed its peer group for one, three, and five years, that's a telltale sign. And if there's no performance record at all, you're better off waiting until there is one!
- **Does this product have an ability to earn 20 percent annual growth?** If your prospective pick does not provide any evidence that it can reach 20 percent during bull markets, look elsewhere.
- **At what price point will I sell this investment?** Never forget your sell-discipline. One more time: No matter what you purchase, you should have a clear understanding beforehand—*When am I going to sell?*

PLAYER NUMBER 4: THE INSIDER

Scenario number 1: It's suppertime. You're halfway through a glass of red wine. Slippers on, kids happy, and you're on glide path. The phone rings. It's someone from Citibank, reminding you that you have X dollars in Savings Account Y. They're just wondering if you'd be interested in moving your money to Investment Product Z—"a great opportunity."

Here's something I absolutely, positively guarantee that the script that this salesperson is reading from won't go on to say: "And Product Z is great for *us,* because it's the one with a hefty 5 percent sales commission!"

Scenario number 2: In early April, your CPA calls your office. He says that he's examined your portfolio and sees an opportunity for you to defer more taxes. He pushes you toward a new S&P index annuity product offered by an insurance company. Listen carefully (before you fire him): Does he go on to say that this is a product that caps your upside gains at 12 percent, no matter how well stocks in that portfolio perform?

If you think I sound a little annoyed here, you're right. What is the common thread in the two scenarios just presented? The common thread is the abuse of your personal information.

Think about it. Banks and accountants know *everything about us.* You'd think they would see that as a trust not to be abused. And yes, some do see it that way, and act accordingly. But others don't hesitate to invade your privacy, push your buttons, and trump you with the information you've voluntarily provided to them in the past. Hey—based on your profile, you're a *target.*

But you can fight back (and in fact, you'd better fight back). Specifically, you should take steps to separate your investing activities from your other financial affairs, including banking, insurance, and taxes.

Ask yourself these questions:

1. *Does my accountant work for me, or for a large brokerage company with its own goals?*
2. *Is my bank looking to make a profit at my expense?*
3. *How did my insurer know that I have $20,000 in my savings account?*
4. *Do any of these people—my accountant, insurer, banker—understand my needs as an investor, or are they trying to sell me a product?*

The experts will tell you that there are benefits to having a tax professional help you with tax-efficient investing. They will tell you about the advantages of moving all your money into your FDIC-insured bank down the street.

To this I say, *Tell it to a nonmaverick.* We mavericks don't let insiders—bankers, insurers, CPAs—become the dominant players in our investing world. We make investing part of our lifestyle, so that we can tell various insiders when and how we require their services. And we tell bankers and brokers *never* to call at dinnertime, and we explain to our former accountant why we took our business elsewhere.

PLAYER NUMBER 5: THE MEDIA
The demand for investment-related intelligence continues to outstrip the supply. Let's be honest with ourselves: The two motivators behind this demand are (1) greed, and (2) fear. As if the marketers weren't enough to play to our greed and fear, we also have the media, broadly defined. Colorful commentary, round-the-clock coverage, *Squawk Box, Moneyline,* thousands of financial Web sites—maybe there's an entertainment factor at play here, as well, but mostly I see these outlets as preying on our weaknesses.

It would be one thing if they were sophisticated in their understanding of the workings of the market, and therefore could give investors a leg up. But for the most part, they simply aren't. Consider *Smart Money*'s cover in March 2000. (*Smart Money* is a Dow-Jones magazine aimed at the hip young investor.) It read, "15 Great Tech Stocks," and went on to describe the ultimate technology portfolio.

Fair enough. But let's check in later in the year: By November 10, 2000, this portfolio had lost more than 40 percent of its value, while 6 of the 15 "must-own" stocks lost more than 50 percent! Of course, the NASDAQ debacle of 2000 played a prominent role in the portfolio's demise. But the lesson is still worth noting.

When we allow ourselves to be manipulated by our greed, we should expect to pay a consequence. And the media can cause more severe damage when they prey on our fears. For example, in September and October of 1998, *Fortune, Forbes,* and *Esquire* magazines led with bearish cover stories. On September 21, *Forbes* asked, "Is it Armageddon . . . or October 1987 revisited?" In October, *Fortune* asked, alarmingly, "The Crash of 1998: Can the U.S. Economy Hold Up?" Not to be outdone, *Esquire* went retro with its cover story, "Daddy, Where Were You in the Crash of 1998?"

Of course, there was no Crash of 1998, nor even the growlings of a bear in the nearby woods. In fact, the Nasdaq, Dow, and S&P closed out that year at record highs.

Were the media punished for making these bad calls? Hardly. The magazine publishers in question reaped bonanzas—in terms of ad dollars, subscriptions, and over-the-counter revenue—on both ends. First, they stampeded us with bearish features, and then they fired us up again with a wave of "resilient bull market" articles.

I'd be interested to know the median age of the editors and writers at *Smart Money* magazine. Ask yourself what you think that age *should* be, if you're going to take advice from them. What if the median age turns out to be under 30? Do you still want to steer your money in the directions they suggest?

Remember, your investing success (or lack thereof) is irrelevant to the media's bottom line. They sell ad space, air time, or e-mail addresses regardless of whether you become wealthy. Sure, writers and fortune-tellers like to boast when they're right. But they're not the ones with huge portfolio losses when the predictions go astray. The lesson? *Never rely on hot lists and headline-grabbers for leadership.*

So how do you use the media to your advantage? Use them for the facts and figures. Get the numbers you need from both online and offline sources, and use them in maverick ways. Online, I like:

- **Yahoo! Finance** for speedy and accurate stock/fund data
- **CBS Marketwatch** for easy-to-read performance percentages
- **Big Charts.com** for technical charting
- **SmartMoney.com** for "sector-map" tracking (remember, we're talking about charts, pictures, and numbers, rather than the opinions!)
- **Quote.com** for real-time streaming

I put CNBC on mute if I want to see the electronic ticker on TV. I read *The Wall Street Journal, Barron's,* and/or *Investor's Business Daily* to keep atop the general market environment. And that's the extent of my library.

You can also use the media for general education and inspiration. Television, Web sites, and radio shows all have the ability to spark your passion and boost your investor IQ. Just be wary of predictions and picks, and don't give in to greed or fear.

PLAYER NUMBER 6: THE SPECULATOR

Here's a cautionary tale. Superstar fund manager Ryan Jacob was a shooting star, a meteor, in the investing universe. He was the man credited with leading the first Internet-related fund, Kinetics Internet (WWWFX), to a 196 percent gain in 1998 and a 113 percent gain in the first six months of 1999. The 29-year-old Jacob believed so strongly in the so-called New Economy, and in his ability to pick winners, that he left his post at Kinetics to start the Jacob Internet Fund (JAMFX). Tens of thousands of followers poured $150 million into his venture as soon as it opened for business.

In its first calendar year in business—from January 1, 2000 to December 31, 2000—JAMFX lost 66 percent of its value.

As of June 30, 2001, its year-to-date performance was −41.2 percent.

Buy-'n'-holders who went in on Day One lost $6600 on every $10,000 they had invested. JAMFX wasn't just bad, it was *wretched*. It was the absolute worst-performing stock fund in a field of 6000 other possibilities. Think of that! It was worse than any other tech fund, any Internet fund, or any Russia fund.

When asked in mid-October about his performance, Ryan humbly offered the following explanation to Craig Tolliver of CBS *MarketWatch.* "Admittedly, one of our biggest mistakes early in the year was reacting to the sell-off in Internet-related companies as if it was a correction, when in fact it is clear now that it was a crash."

Two lessons from the Ryan Jacob story ring clear and loud. First, the New Economy speculators do not have special skills. They rode the dot.com frenzy up—and then they rode it back down. Second, fund managers do not get paid to sell. That means it's up to you, the maverick, to have an exit plan for leaving stocks and funds before a bubble bursts.

The so-called New Economy is responsible for another speculative craze, the initial public offering, or IPO. This is a beast something like the locust, which can only come out of the ground into the public view after a long period of dormancy. The idea behind an IPO is that at a certain point a company needs to go to the public markets in order to get the cash it needs to move forward. As it does so, of course, stock that was formerly private becomes public, and gets a value, and therefore becomes tradable.

The IPOs of 20 and 30 years ago most often involved "real" companies—that is, companies that had real products, real earnings, real management, and real track records. But the IPOs of the 1990s were different. Consider three of the wildest high-flyers—Linux, Priceline.com, and the Globe.com. Linux rocketed 2000 percent (from $15 to $320) on its first day of trading. Eight weeks later, the stock traded 60 percent lower, at $130; one year later, Linux fell below its offer price of $15.

Priceline? William Shatner's baby (Shatner was the company spokesperson) surged from $80 to $160 in April of 1999, only to subsequently lose 97 percent of its value in a free fall to $3.50 per share (see Figure 6-1).

And the Globe.com rose 606 percent on its first trip into the public marketplace, yet lost 98 percent of its value in less than two years—down from a split-adjusted high of $40 to a fraction of $1.

Dot Cons, Dot Bombs, The Great Tech Wreck, IP Oh No—whatever you want to call it, *just say no.* We mavericks work hard for our investment dollars. We can't afford to put real dollars into unreal companies. One of

FIGURE 6-1   Two-year Chart of Priceline.com

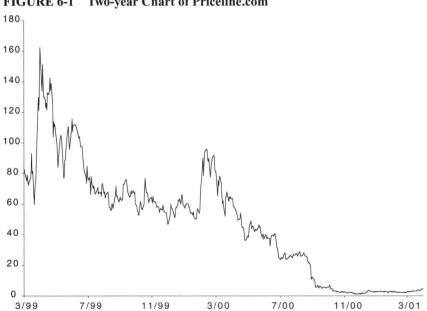

the keys to investing is finding substantial companies with real products, a reliable earnings stream, and strong growth prospects.

Now, that *doesn't* mean that we always stay away from new companies and new funds. What it means is that we stick to a sell discipline, at all times, so that we can't possibly lose 40 percent, 60 percent, or 80 percent. We would *not* purchase Priceline at $160, hold it for 10 years—buying at every dip, of course—and wind up with a bushel basket full of stock that's worth less than $5 a share.

Maverick investors generally say "no" to IPOs. We understand that initial offerings historically underperform major market indexes, usually by the six-month mark. We also recognize that three-quarters of IPOs fall below their offer price within two years—which, by the way, is a price that you generally can't even get unless you're on the inside.

The good news is you don't have to find the next Qualcomm or Cisco to become wealthy. All you need to do is get 100 percent of your assets into the stock ring at the right time (stock ring, not one individual stock), and have an exit plan for selling those assets. Time and compounding take care of the rest.

PLAYER NUMBER 7: THE ANALYST
Analysts are those people who do research of one kind or another, and then tell investors to buy, hold, or sell. Some work for investment banks or brokerages; others work for themselves.

Sounds sensible: Smart guys do some deep thinking, and then dispense their hard-won wisdom. But did you know that analysts rate 99 percent of *all* stocks as either "buys" or "holds"? Uh, oh: What does *that* mean? To paraphrase Garrison Keilor's famous line: Can *all* stocks (like all of the children in Keilor's hometown of Lake Wobegon) be above average?

In just the first four months of 2000, for instance, First Call/Thomson Financial found that fewer than 1 percent of the 28,000 stocks earned Sell recommendations. One more time, with feeling: fewer than 1 percent!

Why do analysts refuse to issue Sells? In some cases, because it is dangerous to their livelihood. An analyst can be shunned by the analyzed company for publishing negative news, and access is—or used to be—everything. A Sell-oriented analyst can be ostracized by his or her peers, or even fired from his or her own firm for bucking the system.

Consider clothing retailer Abercrombie & Fitch. In 2000, it dropped from $50 to $20, largely due to poor earnings. Yet it wasn't until the stock had already given back 60 percent of its value that analysts issued a downgrade—and even then, only from a Buy to a Hold.

Did anyone call for a Sell when the stock slipped to $15? Nope! Shares had now fallen 70 percent, requiring a 233 percent advance if the stock was ever to regain its formerly lofty perch. But researchers *still* refused to issue a Sell.

You'll find the exact same scenario for online bookseller Amazon.com. When the stock traded at the handsome price of $70 per share, the organization First Call (which keeps tabs on these things) found 24 Buys, 7 Holds, and no Sells on Amazon. When the stock dropped to $35 per share three months later—in other words, after Amazon had lost 50 percent of its value—there were *still* 24 Buys, 7 Holds, and no Sells. Down 50 percent, and zero changes in the analysts' perspectives.

So do analysts help get you out before a company hits the skids? Obviously not.

Equally dangerous are the superanalysts—the gurus who have achieved a near-godlike stature. You see them often on CNBC and CNN, or gracing the covers of investing magazines. Some investors hang on their every word. Unfortunately, listening to these analysts can leave you more confused than when you began. For instance, on August 25, 1999, Prudential Securities' venerable author and analyst Ralph Acampora told *Moneyline* that the Dow would close between 12,500 and 13,000 at the end of 1999. One month later, on September 28, Acampora announced that the Dow might close out the year as low as 8900.

Whoa! That's a pretty big spread for this guy—from 13,000 down to 8900. And to add some fuel to this strange fire, when the Dow hit 11,500 at the turn of the century, there were those on the Street who actually praised Acampora for "getting it right."

Is that as bad as it gets? No. Gruntal's Joseph Battipaglia predicted in the early months of 2000 that the Nasdaq would close the year at 5500. By mid-October, however, when it became painfully obvious that his target was unattainable, he downgraded his prediction to 4300. Of course, the tech index finished the year 2000 at 2471—45 percent lower than his original call, and 25 percent lower than his revised estimate.

Here's something else you should be aware of: To an ever-greater extent, analysts don't really know much more than you do. In recent years, the SEC has cracked down on the kinds of information that companies can make available to analysts, on the theory that the "little guys" in the market shouldn't be disadvantaged in this way. Today, most companies are running scared. Many have stopped talking to analysts in all but the most public settings—where, of course, they don't want to say very much anyway. In the summer of 2001, Congress held hearings to learn more about the analyst situation and how these recommendations affect individual investors.

Thankfully, you don't have to rely on junior researchers, senior technicians, or chief analysts to tell you when to buy or when to sell. Stock prices and stock indices form trends that are easy to track, and which *guarantee* that you'll be positioned to participate in every major bull market. Similarly, stop-losses of 12 percent, 15 percent, or 20 percent can keep you out of harm's way on the downside. They'll *certainly* do more for you than the analyst who never cries Sell!

PLAYER NUMBER 8: THE FED
Did you know that higher interest rates usually mean a cooler stock market? That's because interest-bearing investments—money funds, bonds, T-bills—start to look more attractive.

For example, the Federal Reserve and its current chairman, the legendary Alan Greenspan, hiked rates six consecutive times in 1994. Not surprisingly, this was the worst year for stocks in the 1990s. The S&P only rose 4 percent.

Conversely, the Fed slashed rates 17 consecutive times from July 1990 to September 1992. Despite a mini–bear market (1990), a scary war (the 1991 Gulf War, scary because of the threat to Saudi oil), and a recession (1992), the S&P ascended 17 percent. So although interest-rate hikes and cuts aren't directly related to the stock market (they actually affect the rate that banks charge their favored customers), they definitely can have an impact on the markets.

But the indirectness and unpredictability of this relationship means that *mavericks don't try to predict the direction of stocks on the basis of interest-rate changes*. It's just not a reliable enough cause-and-effect relationship. For instance, more volatile technology companies have been known to defy interest-rate moves. That's because many of them get their financing from the issuance of public stock, not interest-sensitive loans. And anyway, by the time Chairman Greenspan actually gets around to announcing something, the Street has usually anticipated and discounted the news.

So don't hang on the deliberations of the Federal Open Market Committee, or some other obscure branch of government. What you *should* do is let the market tell you how it feels. Major indexes and benchmarks will let you know if a particular industry approves or disapproves of the Fed's action. All you have to do is track the trends of those key indicators.

PLAYER NUMBER 9: THE BROKERAGE HOUSE
It's true when people say, "Nothing in life's for free." That goes double for the brokerage firms.

Fees, penalties, transaction charges, expenses. You may not see them on your monthly statement, but you're paying. (More than you might imagine!)

How can you get around this? One way is to ask the following three questions related to costs.

1. **What are the annual expense charges?**   Every investment other than an individual stock carries an annual management fee. Mutual funds, trusts, annuities—it doesn't matter. They all have "expense ratios," which means that there's a fee involved, somewhere.

    For example, the annual expense ratio for a typical mutual fund is 1.4 percent. So if your fund goes up 20 percent in a given year, and you began that year with $20,000, your statement at year's end will show $23,664, not $24,000.

    That may or may not sound like a big deal when your stock funds are rising in value. But here's the zinger: Fund companies get paid their management expenses *whether you make money or not.* In other words, if your $20,000 mutual fund loses 20 percent of its value in a given year, your statement at year's end will show $15,776, not $16,000.

    If you're paying more than the norm (i.e., more than 1.4 percent) for the management of your mutual fund—it may be time to rethink your strategy.

2. **What are the sales charges?**   Consider transaction costs. They range from $4.95 to $30 for online trades all the way up to $100 and $200 for broker-handled telephone calls. Load (commission) funds also nail you with up-front or back-door fees.

    For example, if you put $10,000 into Putnam Growth and Income (PGRWX), you'll pay 5.75 percent in an up-front commission, plus the 0.84 percent annual expense. If this fund rises 20 percent in your first year—which, by the way, it *won't,* because it's a repeat offender on my list of lemons, to be described in later chapters—you'll only see $11,215 in your account at year's end. That's right: $11,215 instead of $12,000!

3. **What are the penalties or redemption policies for selling?**   Similar to general banking, many products have penalties for early withdrawal. This penalty is euphemistically called a "redemption fee." And sometimes, redemption fees are brutal.

    Some mutual funds charge anywhere from 1 to 2 percent if you want to sell before a particular time frame expires. At one time, Fidelity was charging a 3 percent penalty if you wanted to sell Fidelity Small Cap Stock (FSLCX) within three years. Then the Securities and Exchange Commission (SEC) declared the penalty excessive.

One of those clear-cut arguments in favor of government inter-
vention! But the SEC can't be everywhere, nor should it be. It's up to
the maverick investor to stay away from brokerage houses that attempt
to lock your money up for longer than six months.

Choose Your Brokerage Relationship Well

Having said all that, the ability to invest long-term requires a relationship
with a brokerage house. Online, offline, full-service or discount, you will
need to put your money somewhere. And while cost is a major determinant,
it's not the only factor.

Here are the three items that I believe are critical:

1. **Customer service.**   Most of us tend to undervalue this aspect of life
   when we go shopping for our business relationships. We rarely check
   voice mail systems, response time, Web site quality, or rep knowledge
   before we enter into an arrangement.

   But that's exactly what mavericks must do. You need to be able to
   place orders 24/7/365 at a company Web site. And you can't waste
   time (and your good mood) on a twisted journey through voice or
   e-mail when you want to speak to a real individual.

   Make certain that your service reps answer phones and e-mails in
   a time frame that is consistent with your needs and expectations.
   Those people who choose a full-service firm should be able to expect
   a level of service that is equal to the cost of the relationship. Always
   calculate your annual cost at a full service house. Know what the
   company is charging, and add it up. Good service can come at a price.
   Measure it.

2. **Mutual fund offerings.**   When it comes to mutual funds, the most
   significant difference between full-service houses and the discount
   brokers is the menu. Full-service firms usually offer all load funds,
   with the emphasis on the house products. Merrill Lynch will sell Putnam funds to you, but the Merrill funds will find their way into broker recommendations. What you will *not* receive is a Vanguard fund
   recommendation. Why? Because Merrill Lynch can't make money on
   that transaction.

   Discount brokers now offer the mutual fund supermarket. The
   extensive list of both load and no-load offerings require you to make
   the selection. Most discounters and online houses offer search engines
   to help you select, but what I like is the choice. There are thousands
   of good money managers to choose from. Why limit your potential?

3. **Tools + research + advice = performance.**   I lumped these three
    service features into one category: performance. At the end of the day,
    isn't performance the feature that means the most? You can live with-
    out having a personal broker when your account is performing, can't
    you? When you break down the feature of performance into its com-
    ponents of tools, research, and advice, here's what you want to be
    looking for:

    Tools: Here is the first major difference between online and full-
       service firms. The online guys offer a lot of tools. The full-service
       firms have some, too, but would expect your registered rep to be
       using the tools for you. Mavericks do it themselves. That's a
       big difference between us and them ("them" being ordinary
       investors). We want tools and we use them.

    Research is mostly the territory of the full-service house. These are
       industry reports and analyst predictions about sectors and stocks.
       You would expect this research to be unbiased, since you are pay-
       ing for it in the form of higher fees. It rarely is, and—more often
       than not—broker-house economists and stock analysts tell people
       what they want to hear to maintain their invested positions. Once
       Big Wall Street has your money, it wants to hang on to it.

    Advice: I have been a client of a major discount brokerage company
       for 14 years, and I have never received an unsolicited phone call.
       They have returned my calls and communicated when required,
       but never have they called to sell me something. Don't call me,
       I'll call you: That's the way I like it.

    Some investors prefer the prestige of having their own broker.
    They feel good having someone whom they like and know do the
    research, use the tools for them, and make specific recommendations.
    Well, as far as I'm concerned, there is nothing wrong with paying for
    advice, as long as it is *valuable* advice.

PLAYER NUMBER 10: THE INFLUENCER

One last category: the people I refer to as the "Influencers." Sometimes,
influencers come in the form of authority figures, like our parents and other
family leaders. In such cases, their beliefs weigh on our life decisions,
including what career path we should pursue, who we should marry, and
yes, where we should invest our money.

Then there are those people one orbit out who exert another kind of
influence. Uncle Peetie, for example, gave you a no-interest loan five years

ago. Now he wants you to buy stock in Giant Gumball, Inc., a worldwide distributor of coin-operated gumball machines. What do you do?

When friends or family members help us, we often feel compelled to reciprocate. In fact, we often feel compelled to honor our loved ones simply because we like them, and we want them to like us.

How can you say "no" without feeling guilty, or causing turmoil in the family or some other tight-knit group? In essence, you must *offset the exchange,* either before it takes place or immediately thereafter.

In the case of Uncle Peetie, you can show appreciation at the time he gives you the loan by insisting that he take your payments with interest. Your insistence and follow-through fulfill the unwritten rules of reciprocation, and you won't feel pressured later to invest in giant gumball machines.

In other words, as a maverick investor, your challenge is to seek unique ways to satisfy the obligations you feel. If your dad thinks it is sacrilegious to sell the shares of Coca-Cola that he gave you as a gift, it's up to you to "teach the teacher." Show your father the benefits and opportunities that arise when you sell. You may even open up brand-new avenues of communication!

REVIEW OF INFLUENTIAL PLAYERS ON WALL STREET

1. **Player Problem.** Brokers who may not have your best interests at heart.

   Solutions. Become your own investment counselor, and/or develop a demanding list of direct questions like "What incentives and perks will you get if I make this purchase?"

2. **Player Problem.** Financial planners who may be providing stale, conventional advice.

   Solutions. Always manage a portion of your assets yourself, in order to understand how your adviser is helping you. Use several online resources to check the planner's credentials, and make the most out of questions like, "How many different companies and different investment products do you represent?"

3. **Player Problem.** Marketers who may be playing on your emotions.

   Solutions. Look beyond the pitch. Understand the risks and potential benefits a particular investment offers.

4. **Player Problem.** Media titans who may erroneously mislead and misinform.

   Solutions. Use the media for facts and figures, not picks and predictions. Choose your providers carefully.

5. Player Problem. Speculators who may seek to advance their own fortune at your expense.

   Solutions. Just say no to IPOs. Carefully evaluate so-called New Economy prospects. And always have a plan to sell.

6. Player Problem. Analysts who may be unwilling to issue Sells because they fear retribution.

   Solutions. Use simple market trends to participate in bull market moves. Employ stop-losses and other sell techniques to lock in gains or minimize downside risk. Keep in mind how little the analysts really know, in light of recent SEC rumblings.

7. Player Problem. Federal Reserve Board moves that may shake (or over-inflate) investor confidence.

   Solutions. Maintain a general knowledge of the Fed's (limited) impact on markets. Assume that the big boys have already the Fed's actions into account, well before those actions are taken. Rely most heavily on market trends, not interest-rate fluctuations.

8. Player Problem. Brokerage houses that may not provide you with the investments and customer service you demand.

   Solutions. Evaluate the performance of the investments, the costs of doing business, and your satisfaction with the arrangement. Exercise your right to fire underachievers and overchargers.

9. Player Problem. Influencers in your inner circle who may expect you to follow their lead and/or reciprocate.

   Solutions. Satisfy obligations to friends and family in unique ways that won't hurt financially or create feelings of bitterness. Persuade, teach, and influence the influencers!

7

The Playing Field

Have you been keeping large sums of money in checking or savings accounts at a bank because you think that's the only way to gain quick access to your dollars?

Or, to state it another way: Have you ever wanted to get into stocks or mutual funds, but held back because you thought it would be too difficult to get at your money when you needed it?

Do you think the only way to get an income stream from your investments is through a regular dividend?

Sometimes people invest too little of their capital because they don't understand some of the rules of the game, especially regarding their degree of access to stocks, bonds, and cash. The fact is that *all three of these asset classes are "liquid." (Liquidity,* in this case, means able to be turned into spendable cash readily.) You can get your money out any time, usually within 24 hours. You can even write checks from liquid account(s). What's more, if you need a reliable source of income, there are ways to plan for distributions without regular dividend payments.

Maverick investors know what stocks, bonds, and cash are all about. We make certain that we understand the playing field (see Figure 7.1).

FIGURE 7-1   30-Year Historical Returns of Three Asset Classes

	Stocks	Bonds	Money Market
1960–1999	12.20% 7.00%	6.00%	

CASH: THE ASSET WHO WOULD BE KING

In its various forms, cash is the least volatile investment on the planet. The returns hardly fluctuate. Assuming the world doesn't end, you can bank on getting your 4 to 6 percent. And you can go to bed knowing that you can reclaim your original investment (in other words, your "principal") at any time.

But what is "cash," exactly? Simple: It's that group of liquid vehicles that offers interest—including CDs, money market mutual funds, and T-bills. Each of these delivers a nominal rate of return (this is the 4 to 6 percent per year range just mentioned, on a typical 30-year time horizon). Cash is the safest of all harbors for your principal. Again: absent a calamity, you never have to worry about losing the amount you bring to the table.

Cash is where you begin when you're opening an account for the first time. You need a place to call home base—a perch and jumping-off place from which you can evaluate your stock or stock mutual fund choices. Cash also serves an important risk-reducing function; specifically, it's where you keep your capital when you're avoiding a significant downtrend, or stock market bear.

At the same time, however, *cash is trash* for lengthy periods. You don't want to spend a lifetime in an investment that only gives you 6 percent annual growth. One caller to my radio show couldn't figure out why I kept talking about accumulating millions of dollars over 25 years, when he—a devout saver and diligent buy-'n'-holder—only managed to reach $195,000.

Hypothetically speaking, here's what could have happened. Let's say that he had started with $20,000, and he had put away $2000 each year in his IRA for 25 years. Unfortunately, he had been contributing all of his dollars to a money market account yielding only 6 percent interest. With a basic, diversified, stock mutual fund that earned 12 percent, he would have earned $606,669.03. And at 20 percent, he would have earned $2,851,886.50.

$2.8 million versus $200,000? Cash may be a nice place to visit, but you certainly don't want to live there.

MAKING YOUR SAFE HAVEN PAY OFF

My dad is fond of saying that the second greatest thrill in the world is waiting in a cash account when the market is slip-sliding away.

Of course, 6 percent a year will not help you achieve your long-term aspirations. Your purpose for visiting the safe haven of cash is to preserve principal, protect gains, and wait for the opportunity to grow your portfolio at 20 percent.

Waiting in cash, however, is not merely an exercise in patience. This is a time for: (1) evaluation of your progress in the previous up cycle, (2) monitoring of current trend activity, and (3) preparation of your "buy" list.

Take note! The investments you previously held may not be the ones you'll want to purchase when it's time to reinvest. Why not? Because the same stocks and funds rarely repeat as leaders in a new uptrend.

Also keep in mind what cash is *not*. Cash is not the place to permanently allocate a sizeable chunk of your assets in the name of diversification. This is conventional foolishness that only serves to drag on your portfolio in good times, and give a modicum of relief in bad times that you haven't risked everything.

In bad times, cash is good. In good times, cash is a hobble—and mavericks let their stallions run without hobbles. That way, we're getting opti-

---

WHEN TO USE CASH (AND WHEN NOT TO!)

When to Use Cash

Getting started: opening your account
Home base: a place to start and end
Saving for a short-term goal
Waiting out a bear market
Waiting for a new opportunity

When Not to Use Cash

When the market is in an uptrend
When striving for growth
As an asset allocation play
When fully invested in stocks

mal performance when it's there to be gotten—and we're in our safe haven, working away, when it's not there to be gotten.

BONDS: MEANT TO BE BROKEN

What is a bond? It is a debt instrument. An IOU. You're the creditor (the lender), and the company or government you lend money to is the debtor. In essence, you're counting on an institution to pay you back your principal, plus an agreed-upon amount of interest, according to an agreed-upon schedule. Railroads, sewage treatment plants, and other Big, Capital-Intensive Things get built through bond financing.

Although this may sound similar to cash, there are several key differences. First, there's the risk that you may lose a huge chunk of your principal. The company, project, or institution that you lend money to could run into financial difficulties. More telling, bond prices fluctuate inversely with interest rates. In other words, they go down when the general trend of interest rates go up. (And vice versa.)

Bonds give limited upside potential. They average a mere 7 percent, historically—just a shade higher than cash. Yet, unlike cash, there's plenty of downside risk of losing money in the bomb—oops, "bond" market.

Bonds outperformed stocks in only one of the last eight decades—that is, in the miserable, one-of-a-kind 1970s. But take that analysis one step further: Bonds have *never* outperformed stocks in any 20-year period.

A NIGHTMARE ON BOND STREET

Charlie writes:

> You're always telling people to forget about bonds. Well, I'm 55 and retired already. I need a fixed income stream. That's why my broker allocated $200,000 to a High Yield. Isn't that the best way to invest my money, and still get the income I require?

Sorry, Charlie. Your broker's either misinformed, or he's slicker than you might imagine.

Unfortunately, the broker is hurting Chuck on a variety of levels. First, Charlie may be paying an up-front 5 percent sales commission load to the broker ($10,000 on the $200,000), when a no-load bond fund would have been easy as cherry pie to pick. (You've seen one bond fund, you've seen them all.) And Charlie may be paying the brokerage house 1.4 percent each year in an annual management fee. (There goes another $1400.)

What about income? Doesn't Charlie need to find a way to derive a steady stream of income in retirement? Well, yes. What Charlie's broker didn't tell him was that Charlie could invest in dividend-bearing stocks and stock funds. Alternatively, he could sell a portion of a position on an as-needed basis. Remember: Selling is a *good* thing, when it's part of a larger maverick plan! (Later on, I will show you examples of how to create spend-able income as a maverick.)

Let me make your life 10 times easier by taking a whole asset class off the table. *Just say "no" to bonds.* You don't need them. You don't want them. And as a maverick, you're never going to drag down your portfolio with this dreadfully inferior asset class.

Here's one final word of caution on bonds: You never know where the professionals are hiding them. For example, they hide under the umbrella of certain mutual fund classifications. Stay away from "hybrids," "bal-anced," and "asset manager" funds. Chances are, these tricky funds with the reassuring (but *vague!*) names are weighing down your investment with anywhere from 20 to 50 percent in bombs. Uh, bonds.

ARE BONDS EVER ACCEPTABLE?

What's an ironclad rule without an exception? Less interesting. Yes, there are a few exceptions to the rule on avoiding bonds.

The first is, "Give your stock fund manager some leeway." The fact is that most mutual fund managers allocate a tiny portion of assets to bonds, particularly in a falling rate environment. Under these circumstances, bonds fare rather well, and can give a savvy fund manager a little boost. If that's what's going on, you can give your fund manager a period of grace.

The second exception may grow out of your personal circumstances. Simply put, not everyone wants to pursue growth on their investments. If your age, risk tolerance, time horizon, or portfolio size has you looking at bonds, well, that may be okay. If your 65-year-old mother wants $6000 a year in income from her $400,000 nest egg—well, fine. Use government bonds directly, or bond funds. I impose my strict antibond rules for those of us mavericks who have to attain high growth objectives. If you already have $5 million in the bank, bond away.

Finally, if you are a conservative growth maverick with a rather low tol-erance for risk, growth and income and/or equity income funds that invest in bonds may work well enough for you. What you need to ask is, Does this mutual fund have the ability to get me to my specific growth target? If the answer is "Yes," then for you, it's a perfectly viable choice.

STOCKS: KEY TO THE MAGIC KINGDOM

When you buy a stock, what are you actually purchasing? You're buying partial ownership of a business. And as long as the company's in business, so are you.

The current share price of a stock represents what buyers and sellers believe a proportionate share of your company is worth. You want that valuation, or opinion of worth, to go up. Typically, that occurs when your company is growing.

It's all about growth—growth of the business, and growth of your portfolio. And you want each of your stock investments—individual securities, mutual funds, exchange-traded funds—to appreciate 20 percent or more each year.

Sound like a stretch? Consider the 1990s, where 84 stock mutual funds compounded at an annual rate of 20 percent or more. With just one of these mutual funds in your mix, you would have quadrupled—not doubled, not tripled, but *quadrupled*—your money in a mere eight years! No other asset class can touch this upside potential.

At the same time, there is sizable downside risk. Theoretically, you can lose your entire investment if a company goes belly up. Or, more likely, you could lose 40, 50, or even 60 percent of your money when there are more sellers than buyers for an extended period of time.

Yet there are a variety of proven techniques for managing risk and maximizing gain. For example, stock mutual funds—investments of pooled capital—let skilled managers do all of the stock-picking homework. You don't need to research an individual company's finances, products, and organizational structure. You simply need to see that your mutual fund is on target in a bull market with 5 percent per quarter, 10 percent over six months, and 20 percent per year.

"STOCKS FOR THE LONGEST RUN"

Conventional planners long have been training their clients to spread their capital across all of the asset classes. Sadly, that's a prescription for an ordinary 6 to 8 percent. Worse yet, this is exactly what planners want—to increase the likelihood that your returns will be in a nice, safe, *average* neighborhood. That way, everybody feels like they're keeping up with the Joneses, and no one gets left too far behind.

Unfortunately, 8 percent growth will not get you to your goals in a time frame that is consistent with your needs. And while the so-called historical average of stock investing is higher than 8 percent—in fact, it's 12 percent over 100 years, and 10.2 percent over 200 years—these are ordinary returns, as well. These are *buy-'n'-hold* returns.

Mavericks, on the other hand, can strive for 20 percent because they're as mindful of the Sell as they are of the Buy. And the good news is that there are many different types of stock vehicles in the twenty-first century—more than there ever have been in history—to get you to your personal promised land.

THREE ESSENTIAL STOCK VEHICLES

There are three chief ways to invest in equities: (1) individual securities, (2) mutual funds, and (3) exchange-traded funds (that is, funds that trade like stocks). As far as being a maverick goes, it makes no difference whether you're an individual shareholder, a mutual fund owner, an ETF explorer, or some combination of the three. What counts is getting 100 percent committed to this type of asset.

Having said that, let me tell you why I'm higher on mutual funds and ETFs than I am on individual stocks.

Investing in individual securities—again, stock in a single company—requires extensive research, which means you have to commit an enormous amount of time to this pursuit (see Figure 7-2). It becomes an avocation (or worse, a vocation!). Personally, I don't choose to spend all of my free moments with computer spreadsheets or in investor chat rooms. Life is short. I'd rather devote time to my family or the community.

PERSONAL REVIEW OF THE PLAYING FIELD

If you're ever caught between a broker and a hard place, here's how to remember what is right for you.

Cash. Home sweet home for evaluating investment choices and avoiding periods of excessive stock risk. It's a nice place to visit, but you don't want to live there.

Bonds. JUST SAY NO! They're portfolio deadweight. They're inferior to stocks on the upside, and inferior to cash as a safe harbor. This is the only asset class where the downside risk outweighs the upside reward.

Stocks. You've got ownership in a business. You can get your money out at any time. And it's the only asset class capable of getting 20 percent annual growth.

Individual securities. You pick several dozen companies, and make several dozen buy and sell decisions annually.

Mutual Funds. Pick a few professionally managed portfolios and make a few buy-and-sell decisions annually.

ETFs. Pick a few "baskets" and make a few buy-and-sell decisions annually. Do so, moreover, in a more cost-effective and trade-friendly manner than you can with traditional mutual funds.

FIGURE 7-2   MICROSOFT CORPORATION

Income Statements

(In millions, except earnings per share) (Unaudited)

	Three Months Ended Mar. 31		Nine Months Ended Mar. 31	
	2000	2001	2000	2001
Revenue	$5,656	$6,456	$17,152	$18,841
Operating expenses:				
Cost of revenue	752	952	2,220	2,710
Research and development	974	1,069	2,685	3,015
Sales and marketing	1,010	1,198	2,945	3,526
General and administrative	185	239	847	621
Total operating expenses	2,921	3,458	8,697	9,872
Operating income	2,735	2,998	8,455	8,969
Losses on equity investees and other	(4)	(46)	(33)	(126)
Investment income	882	706	2,202	2,584
Income before income taxes	3,613	3,658	10,624	11,427
Provision for income taxes	1,228	1,207	3,612	3,771
Income before accounting change	2,385	2,451	7,012	7,656
Cumulative effect of accounting change (net of income taxes of $185)	-	- -	(375)	
Net income	$2,385	$2,451	$7,012	$7,281
Basic earnings per share:				
Before accounting change	$0.46	$0.46	$1.35	$1.44
Cumulative effect of accounting change	-	- -	(0.07)	
	$0.46	$0.46	$1.35	$1.37
Diluted earnings per share:				
Before accounting change	$0.43	$0.44	$1.27	$1.37
Cumulative effect of accounting change	-	- -	(0.06)	
	$0.43	$0.44	$1.27	$1.31
Average shares outstanding:				
Basic	5,209	5,336	5,167	5,328
Diluted	5,543	5,563	5,536	5,575

See accompanying notes.

FIGURE 7-2   MICROSOFT CORPORATION (*Cont.*)
Microsoft Corporation

Balance Sheets
(In millions)

	June 30 2000	Mar. 31 2001 (1)
	Assets	**Current assets:**
Cash and equivalents	$4,846	$4,149
Short-term investments	18,952	25,869
Total cash and short-term investments	23,798	30,018
Accounts receivable	3,250	3,532
Deferred income taxes	1,708	1,841
Other	1,552	2,398
Total current assets	30,308	37,789
Property and equipment	1,903	2,159
Equity and other investments	17,726	17,463
Other assets	2,213	2,194
Total assets	$52,150	$59,605
Liabilities and stockholders' equity		
Current liabilities:		
Accounts payable	$1,083	$1,246
Accrued compensation	557	501
Income taxes	585	753
Unearned revenue	4,816	5,305
Other	2,714	1,935
Total current liabilities	9,755	9,740
Deferred income taxes	1,027	1,775
Commitments and contingencies		
Stockholders' equity:		
Common stock and paid-in capital— shares authorized 12,000; outstanding 5,283 and 5,336	23,195	27,647
Retained earnings, including accumulated other comprehensive income of $1,527 and $604	18,173	20,443
Total stockholders' equity	41,368	48,090
Total liabilities and stockholders' equity	$52,150	$59,605

(1) Unaudited

See accompanying notes.

Mutual funds and ETFs have 20, 30, 50, or even several hundred stocks in their one "portfolio." To keep up with each of these companies' financial standing adequately, you'd be tracking individual positions almost constantly. And by the way: Don't you also need to have new positions in the wings, ready to replace the old? Where are *those* ideas going to come from?

This is what fund managers get paid millions of dollars to do—spend their every waking minute on creating a winning stock portfolio.

Take it from me. You can make your life three gazillion times simpler. Learn to select a couple of funds rather than a couple dozen individual stocks. And one more key point: Most 401(k) plans—the place where everyone should concentrate their wealth-building activity—don't even offer individual stocks.

Frankly speaking, I couldn't be more excited about the doors that are open to mavericks everywhere with the ETF and mutual funds. Do I put my money where my mouth is? Yes. I allocate half of my personal portfolio to the ETFs with near-term momentum in a bullish uptrend.

Most important, more than the reduced expenses and immediate order execution, ETFs give mavericks the ability to reach the 20 percent growth goal. This benefit alone is worth its weight in gold.

8

The Maverick Bill of Rights

W hen it comes to potentially valuable info, do you often feel like you're one of the last investors to know?

How many times have you wished that you had never gotten involved with a particular broker or brokerage house?

Have you ever felt like you would be paying less money to the IRS, if only you understood the system better, and/or the cards weren't stacked against you?

It may seem like a pain to switch from one investment to another, or from one brokerage house to the next, but mavericks never sit on their backsides. If an adviser does not provide the customer service or value that you demand, show him/her the door. If an online or full-service firm sells you a lemon stock fund, find another company. You're *free*—but only if you act like it. And that's the subject of this chapter.

We need to exercise our freedoms, especially the freedom of investment choice. We need to take advantage of the opportunities that we have to move our money around—to shift our assets as the environment and/or our needs change.

Let's face it: As Americans, we're extremely fortunate investors. Our currency and monetary system are relatively stable. Our markets are (mostly) free of tampering, insider trading, and other shenanigans. Our government is quick to step in to cut off fraudulent schemes and scams. And meanwhile, we enjoy the freedom to choose from a wide array of legitimate investing opportunities. By way of contrast, in recent years large numbers of Albanian citizens—with few other places to take their money—have been fleeced in pyramid schemes. Over in Russia, currency devaluations destroyed the financial health of many citizens, and the evidence suggests that the strength of one's mob affiliations determines one's success as a Russian investor (and in many cases, one's physical safety).

So as Americans, we're fortunate—but we're not "lucky." Our good fortune is grounded in the U.S. Constitution, which provides the legal framework that specifically outlines our right to pursue and maintain our wealth. Most important in this regard is the Bill of Rights, which the far-sighted colonists huddled in the northeastern part of the country insisted upon before they ceded any of their authority to a new central government. The right to own property (which extends to a stake in a particular company) is protected by the Fifth Amendment. The right to secure one's personal effects, including stock holdings, against unreasonable seizure, is guaranteed by the Fourth Amendment. And the right to speak our minds—and by extension, get access to other people's good thinking—is protected by the First Amendment.

THE MAVERICK BILL OF RIGHTS
In Chapter 3, I presented the 10 beliefs or principles that aid mavericks in their pursuit of stock market success. Now I'm going to give you 10 powerful freedoms that, when exercised properly, give you the necessary edge in achieving your dreams. You will recognize some of the ideas behind these "rights" from previous chapters. But I want to restate these ideas in a way that underscores that *you* are in the driver's seat, and that you are *entitled to be there.* So here are the 10 freedoms in the Maverick Bill of Rights:

1. You have the right to grow rich.
2. You have the right to invest with *anyone* you choose.
3. You have the right to fire your broker for any reason.
4. You have the right to invest in *anything* you choose.
5. You have the right to *sell* any investment for any reason.

6. You have the right to know how well your assets are performing compared to similar investments.
7. You have the right to the fair disclosure of information.
8. You have the right to pay less to the IRS (lawfully).
9. You have the right to a second opinion.
10. You have the right to be a maverick.

Let's take a look at each of these freedoms as they relate to territory that is familiar to you—places like your 401(k), an online trading account, or even the house you live in. What you'll discover is a winning perspective on the best way to participate on the investing field.

MAVERICK RIGHT NUMBER 1: THE RIGHT TO GROW RICH

In *The Richest Man in Babylon,* the celebrated story by George S. Clason, a very rich man asks a scribe a question. "If you did keep for yourself one-tenth of all you earn," the rich man asks the writer, "how much would you have in 10 years?" The scribe answers, "As much as I earn in one year."

The scribe made a fundamental mistake: He didn't know about the power of compound interest. In previous chapters, you've learned that the power of compound interest earns you significantly more than mattress cash. By paying oneself first, the money that is wisely put to work in the stock market over 10 years may return as much as four times the original savings. In other words, after 10 years in the right places, $2000 may be worth $80,000, not $20,000.

Why is this lesson so powerful? Because it proves that anyone with the determination to build wealth . . . *can* grow wealthy (over time).

The maverick right to grow rich means that a person has the right to take meaningful actions to create individual wealth. It does *not* mean that the government, or one's family, or even one's employer is responsible for showering one with money. It means that you have the right to help yourself.

This is an important distinction—one that George Clason's Babylonian tale made eminently clear. If you count upon that inheritance, or pray for a "more equitable" distribution of wealth, you're likely to be disappointed. That rich uncle may need round-the-clock nursing care in his later years. (*You* may wind up supporting *him!*) And if the government can give it to you next week, they can take it away from you the week after. But if you maintain simple disciplines—like putting aside one-tenth of what you earn, and placing that money where it will grow for you—wealth will come knocking.

MAVERICK RIGHT NUMBER 2: THE RIGHT TO INVEST
WITH ANYONE YOU CHOOSE

Callers to my Maverick Investing radio show often ask whether they should stick with their full-service broker or switch to a discounter. Some wonder whether they should leave money in a former company's 401(k) or roll their money over to an IRA. And others inquire if it's smarter to choose a variety of brokerage houses, or keep the companies and paperwork to the bare minimum.

Although I have my own (strong!) preferences, it's *your* freedom of choice that we're talking about here. In fact, one of the beauties of being a maverick is understanding that you have the right to choose where, when, and how many providers you'll need.

For instance, I have one brokerage account with Schwab for all of my stock and stock-fund-related transactions. Schwab is not the least expensive player in the online world, but it's the discounter with the most mutual fund choices, and with the longest track record in the business. (I place a lot of emphasis on track records, and so should you). There are other good choices in the online world as well.

I choose Schwab because (1) I don't need a lot of highly individualized attention from a broker, and (2) I don't buy and sell individual stocks. But your case may be different from mine. You may want more personal attention. Or perhaps you'd feel more comfortable with two separate accounts for stock-related transactions—an online company for individual stocks, and a well-known family like Schwab for mutual funds.

The most important thing to remember is to *take advantage of your freedom.* Not only can you choose which and how many providers, you also have the right to say "when." For instance, when you leave an employer, you can roll those assets into an IRA account—be it Roth or traditional. You just need to contact the brokerage where you'd like to open up a new account, and fill out the paperwork.

Naturally, I have some recommendations for newbies. If you have less than $15,000 to begin, I recommend a single-fund family like Invesco. It has more than twenty choices across a wide variety of categories. What's more, it ranks high on everyone's lists for customer service and stock fund performance.

If you have more than $15,000, then you'll want to move up to a major discounter like Schwab. My money's at Schwab. Their Web site is intuitive and accessible. They've been around for a long, long time (track record). They have local branch offices when you want to talk to somebody face-to-face. And they have thousands of phone representatives, who actually pick up the phone and help you.

For those who want lower transaction costs, I'd look to Ameritrade. They have invested heavily in the Web infrastructure, and they have more than 4000 mutual funds to choose from. This speaks volumes about their commitment to the varying needs of their customers in the online world.

MAVERICK RIGHT NUMBER 3: THE RIGHT TO FIRE YOUR BROKER

Does your online broker experience technical difficulties every other time you deal with them? Are you paying for full-service advice, but getting counsel from a broker who seems to know less than you do? Did you discover to your dismay that the stock fund your adviser chose on your behalf was down 14 percent in a six-month period, when the average fund in that particular category was *up* 14 percent?

You do not have to stick with anyone, for any reason, ever. You are free to move your assets where you want, whenever you want—and don't let 'em tell you otherwise!

They may say they "feel your pain." In fact, they may try every trick in the book to hold on to you and your money. But the fact is, they *don't* feel your pain. They didn't lose any money on your transaction. They didn't cut back on their management fees. And they're not going to feel too terrible about the surrender charge you'll pay upon withdrawing your funds.

Don't get snookered. If it's time to hit the road, take your money and run. And if you're not entirely sure whether to fire your broker, ask yourself these three questions:

1. *Where's your money right this second?*   How clear are you on where you're keeping your assets? Do you have three accounts—one for buying stocks, one for your 401(k), and one for checking needs? Do you have six accounts? Ten? Why?

Mavericks take inventory. Get a grip on every financial account that you have—online, offline, full-service, discount service, and individual fund family. Once you know everything that you've got, you can better decide, "Should I stay or should I go?"

2. *What choices do you have in each account?*   With the exception of employer retirement plans, where you can't determine the number or quality of products, you want accounts that have as much choice as possible. Write down the actual number of choices you have in each account. If you have an IRA with Janus, write down 24. If you have a VUL with Ameritas, jot down 39. If you're on-line at Ameritrade, the number is something north of 4000.

3. *If you had an additional $10,000 to put in the stock market today, which (if any) investment company would you use?* This is the one question that helps you decide whether you're getting true value for your buck, or if you've been putting off the decision to fire your broker.

It's all about high-value relationships. Are you getting what you need, in terms of (1) choice, (2) service, and (3) performance? These criteria directly correlate with your investment success. In fact, using these criteria, you can measure your success!

MAVERICK RIGHT NUMBER 4: THE RIGHT TO INVEST IN ANYTHING YOU CHOOSE

In the previous chapter, you learned about the basic asset classes—stocks, bonds, and cash. You also encountered several choices within the stock category, including mutual funds, ETFs, and individual securities.

There are thousands of stocks and stock funds, more than 100 ETFs, and hundreds of variable annuities and insurance. And there's the oft-overlooked investment possibility: *nothing at all.* "Nothing at all" is a fine move (or nonmove), assuming that it's a reasoned decision based on short-term need, and not based on fear or other dark emotions.

You see, it's all about free will. If you *choose* not to decide, you're still making a choice.

MAVERICK RIGHT NUMBER 5: THE RIGHT TO SELL FOR ANY REASON

You can sell for any reason you like. But mavericks sell for *good* reasons, often related to eliminating poor performers. You have three tools for eliminating poor performers—three solid ways to fire underachievers that rob you of the opportunity to build wealth. They are:

1. Your 5/10/20 vision during bull markets
2. Trend tracking
3. Fabian Lemon List

5/10/20 Vision

You'll remember that 5/10/20 vision is your strategic technique for dumping any investment that's not on track to hit 5 percent per quarter, 10 percent per 6 months, and 20 percent per year during bull markets. If you're not getting these percentages when the market's up, then you need an upgrade.

Trend Tracking

Television analysts, software programs, economic forecasts, instinct, extinct—you name it. Everyone thinks they can devise a way, either by relying on economic data or on intuition, to figure out what various segments of the stock market will do.

But even the brightest quant-jocks, or the most intuitive stock empaths, eventually go down in flames. Why? Because when it comes to the future direction of prices, there are no absolutes. The only predictor of the stock market is the stock market itself.

What does this mean for maverick investors? It means that we have to track what various segments of the stock market are doing.

Hard? No—easy! There's a major index, or composite, for each of the important segments of the market. And when you know exactly what you own, you can always compare how well you're doing against a relevant composite.

At fabianlive.com, for instance, you'll see graphical representations of the Dow, the S&P 500, the Nasdaq, the Russell 2000, and the Wilshire 5000. You can use any one of these popular benchmarks to gauge how your small-cap, mid-cap, or large-cap stock or stock fund is performing. ("Cap" is short for "capitalization," which means how much money stands behind the company, which usually corresponds closely to the size of the company. A large-cap company tends to be bigger, according to standard business measures, than a small-cap company.)

For example, Janus 20 concentrates on large companies. It is fair to compare its three-month, six-month, and one-year numbers against the S&P 500. Similarly, Invesco Small Company Growth concentrates on up-and-comers—the little companies—and you can compare its percentages against the Russell 2000.

It's crucial to understand what each position in your portfolio represents, so that you can ask good questions and get good answers. For example, you wouldn't compare the performance of large-cap Fidelity Magellan with the Nasdaq index. (The S&P 500 would be more of an apples-to-apples comparison.) Similarly, you wouldn't choose to ask why your small-cap fund is losing out in a particular 3-month period to the Dow Industrials. You'd compare that fund to the Russell 2000.

The Fabian Lemon List

Kiplinger's magazine profiles 10 terrible investments in its annual "Mutual Fund Hall of Shame." Similarly, most online Web sources will tell you the week's worst performers. But when it comes to getting a quarterly summary of the hard-core facts on all of the fund industry's losers, the Fabian Lemon List is the place to go.

Why do lemon funds belong in the limelight? Because many families overcharge shareholders for products that underperform their peer groups, as well as the broader market.

SILLY REASONS WHY INVESTORS KEEP THEIR LEMONS

Have you ever held on to a bad investment because you were too embarrassed to explain its poor performance to your spouse? Are you determined to break even on a sour performer at all costs? Have you ever told yourself that you can't sell because of a penalty, or because of taxes that you might have to pay, or because your record keeping is on the casual side?

At one time or another, almost all of us have found reasons to avoid selling. Not surprisingly, we tend to come up with the highest volume of excuses when selling will result in a loss—either a loss of principal, a loss of face, or both.

Yet mavericks need to get beyond the "feeling bad" aspects of selling a loser, and recognize the positive implications of putting the proceeds of a sale to better use.

But first things first! Let's get rid of those excuses. Here I've outlined some of the common excuses that investors give for holding lemons, along with my counters for these excuses.

1. "But it used to be great."   Gentle reader: we're not talking about a family member, or a beloved pet. This is business. You shouldn't be any more emotionally attached to your investment than you are to your commute to work in the morning. Has the route stopped working, due to roadwork? Get a new route. Fund stopped working? Forget the good old days, and position yourself for a new buying opportunity.

2. "It'll come back eventually."   [*Sigh*] This is a *prediction*, and predicting is something mavericks do not do. It's also wishful thinking. You need to recognize the fact that this investment didn't get on the Lemon List by accident. It's been underperforming for years! There's something *wrong* here, and it ain't you (unless you just keep hanging out there forever). Put your money to better use elsewhere.

3. "I have to break even before I sell."   Wrong! Ask yourself this question: "If I had this cash today, even after a penalty for selling early or after a loss of principal, is this where I'd reinvest my hard-earned dollars right now?" If not, you're only trying to free yourself up from guilt, or spare yourself some embarrassment. Learn from the mistake, and move on.

When it comes to underperformance, how rotten is rotten? Three years of trailing a peer group average is a pretty safe bet. But because I'm so interested in track records, I go much further with the lemon list. I single out the U.S. stock funds that trail their peer averages for one, three, and five years, as well as those that lag behind the one-year average by at least 25 percent. And this is a peer-group comparison—I'm not even *talking* about how these bottom-dwellers stack up against popular benchmarks like the Dow, the Nasdaq, or the S&P 500!

In a typical quarter, my Lemon List contains anywhere from 4 to 10 percent of the stock fund population, representing billions of stock fund dollars. That means more money is languishing in underachievers than a normal distribution might imply.

Since the list changes each quarter, I can't serve up the most recent losers in this context—or even beat up on repeat offenders. For current lemon status, check out the search engine at Fabianlive.com.

MAVERICK RIGHT NUMBER 6: THE RIGHT TO KNOW HOW WELL YOU'RE PERFORMING

Reggie from Redondo Beach writes:

> I don't know how my funds can't be lemons. Only one came up on your search engine, but I have three positions that have lost money in the last three months and none of these are up 10 percent in the last six months. What should I do—should I sell everything?

Reggie has the right idea, as he tries to take into account both his 5/10/20 vision and the Lemon Search. Indeed, none of his funds are on track to meet his goal of 20 percent compounded growth.

But isn't it possible that some of his funds are outperforming their respective benchmarks? Isn't it conceivable that his small-cap growth fund is outrunning the Russell 2000 over the six-month period? Isn't it possible that his tech sector fund is up more than the Nasdaq for the previous three months?

That's why Reggie must employ the major market benchmarks as well. Depending on the type of investment he's looking at, he might check performance against the Dow, S&P, or Russell. For a more sophisticated check, he could compare his quarterly numbers against the mutual fund averages posted at Fabianlive.com. Here are some of the key benchmarks:

The Dow Industrials: This is an index of 30 "blue-chip" (in other words, stable, profitable companies with a long history of consistent revenue) stocks trading on the New York Stock Exchange

(NYSE). We use it to check the health of large-caps as well as gauge the mood of the nation.

The S&P 500:   This is the most widely accepted large-cap measure—a combined index of stock prices for the 500 largest companies in America. It gives us an indication of what investors feel about the largest, most established U.S. firms.

The S&P 400:   Ditto for 400 midsized companies.

The Nasdaq: This is the "New Economy" composite for issues on the Nasdaq exchange, a large percentage of which are "high tech." A reasonably good way to measure the health of the tech sector.

The Russell 2000:   Your small-company benchmark.

Willshire 5000:   An "everything-in-the-stock-market" index. It gives you the broadest view of stock market health.

MAVERICK RIGHT NUMBER 7: THE RIGHT TO FULL AND FAIR DISCLOSURE

You have the right to know the sales, earnings, and expenses of every publicly traded company. You have the right to know the top 10 holdings of your mutual fund. You have the right to know the cost, sales charge, or surrender fee charged by any company prior to the purchase of such asset. You have the right to know the cost of any transaction your broker may charge, before the purchase or sale is made. You have the right to know of any significant changes to the financial health of any company at the same time the media or insiders know.

You know what I'm going to say next: *Investors must exercise these rights of full and fair disclosure.* You must ask the questions and read the fine print. If you don't exercise these rights, people will take advantage of you. They will sell you things that are inappropriate, expensive, and costly to get out of.

MAVERICK RIGHT NUMBER 8: THE RIGHT TO PAY LESS TO THE IRS

I don't begrudge the federal government its tax bite. On the other hand, I take advantage of every opportunity the government gives me to minimize my tax obligation, which includes deferring taxes as long as possible (and perhaps finding myself in a lower tax bracket when the tax-due date finally arrives).

Let's look at a real case. Bette writes:

I am a single, 41-year-old woman, who earns $52,000 per year. Until now, I haven't invested in any retirement plans. Still, if I invest $200 per month in my company's annuity program, and I get 20 percent growth, I'll retire at 66 with $1,251,915. That sounds pretty good, but will it be enough 25 years from now? I can probably invest an additional $200 per month if I need more for retirement.

It's difficult to assess what is "enough" and what is not enough for an individual in retirement. People have different expectations, dreams, goals, and ideas about what they need and when they'll need it.

But in any case, this argues for amassing as much as possible for the retirement years. And a great way to get there is to *pay yourself first,* using the retirement incentives in the federal tax code. Pay yourself 10 cents for every dollar earned, in pretax dollars, and invest that money so that it is compounding for you.

If Betty invests 10 percent of her income—5 percent ($200) in her annuity and 5 percent ($200) in a Roth IRA—and if she achieves her maverick growth goal of 20 percent, she can retire at 66 with **$2.5 million.** My advice to her was, If you can find those extra dollars in your monthly budget, you should definitely salt them away. *Pay yourself first.*

Remember: you don't pay taxes for buying or selling within your qualified retirement plans: 401(k), 403(b), 457, IRA, Roth IRA, SEP. These are tax-deferred accounts—the places where Mavericks focus their wealth-building attention.

MAVERICK RIGHT NUMBER 9: THE RIGHT TO A SECOND OPINION
You're comfortable asking for a second opinion when it comes to a medical situation, right? So why not exercise this same conservative, common-sense approach to your portfolio? Get a second opinion on your position, your funds, your stock, your annuities, and your strategy.

Don't be afraid to question your broker (or yourself). And don't stop there. Seek the advice of successful people. Friends and relatives can give you second opinions. Your CPA or investment advisor can do it. Call me on my radio show. Get a new stimulus—a new perspective to help you evaluate what you're doing, or going to do, from a different angle.

MAVERICK RIGHT NUMBER 10: THE RIGHT TO BE A MAVERICK
As I noted at the beginning of this chapter, our Constitution guarantees our right to pursue happiness. What a blessing. You have the right to pursue your dreams.

I like to think that when mavericks read these 200-year-old words—the right to pursue happiness—they feel them as a very personal inspiration. I hope they feel a mixture of hope, excitement, and anticipation. And although we mavericks are not setting up our own country, I like to think we share some of the emotions our founding fathers felt when they succeeded in kicking the Brits out of their lives. We can do it *ourselves.* Sink or swim, we are our own masters. Seize the day, mavericks. Exercise your right to be different. Don't be afraid to make an informed and educated decision about your future. Don't blame somebody else for your lot in life. It's *your* life. Accept the challenge, and create your life's dreams by doing it the maverick way.

9

The Most Important
Money You Manage

Have you always thought that you should "invest conservatively" in your individual retirement account (IRA)?

Has anyone ever told you to "diversify" or "protect yourself from risk" in your 401(k) by purchasing a little bit of everything?

Or does your investment strategy hinge on hitting a grand slam? In other words, are you looking for that once-in-a-lifetime stock pick to hit out of the investment park with your taxable account dollars, while at the same time choosing to be careful with dollars you're setting aside for retirement?

It's natural for us to be biased against "taking chances" with our retirement money. After all, who wants to be broke and living in a shack when you hit your golden years?

But there's a difference between ordinary investor wisdom and extraordinary maverick thinking. Garden-variety investors treat their retirement dollars more or less as mattress-savings money, whereas mavericks go for serious growth with their tax-deferred dollars.

STRATEGIC TAX-DEFERRAL OR TACTICAL TAX MISTAKES
Pretax, post-tax, tax-efficiency, capital gains: These terms, and the concepts behind them, sometimes drive investors over the patience cliff. And

just to keep things interesting, these concepts are all interrelated and interact. No surprise, therefore, that lots of people simply opt for letting their tax situation dictate what to do. As a result, they often miss out on opportunities to build serious wealth with the tax code.

Mavericks, on the other hand, recognize the strategic importance of postponing taxes for as long as possible. We take practical steps to hold on to as much of our money as long as legally possible—letting compounding work for *us,* rather than for the government. At all times, we go for simplicity. We don't waste a minute of time decoding the mumbo-jumbo of the federal tax code; instead, we identify and implement simple deferral techniques.

Consider the types of questions that maverick listeners e-mail me regularly. Here's one from Cy in Long Beach:

> Should I contribute to my 457 retirement plan where I only have 17 choices, or is it better to open a taxable account with unlimited choice and seek 20 percent there?

Cy was on the right track, but had become overly focused on one question—choice—and was therefore losing sight of the bigger picture. (Don't worry; we'll get to "457s" shortly.) Unless all 17 of his retirement-plan options are on my Lemon List (see Chapter 8), he's almost certainly better off hanging out in that pretax neighborhood than moving into a taxable neighborhood. Yes, mavericks want as many investment choices as possible in their quest for 20 percent compounded growth. The reality is, though, that it is much simpler and much easier to achieve 20 percent in a tax-deferred retirement plan than a taxable account. (Later in this chapter, I'll show you how and why!)

Here's a question from Chris in Canoga Park:

> If I pull money out of my Roth IRA stock fund and move it to a money market account, will I pay tax? When I put that money back into the stock fund position, is it taxed there as well?

In this case, the question behind the question concerns *moving assets.* And the short answer to Chris's question is "no." In a tax-deferred account, when you shift money from a stock fund to a money position and vice versa, there are no tax consequences.

No matter whether you're thinking about these accounts as a way to meet middle-term goals (a means of funding a child's education) or longer-term objectives (retirement money), *deferring taxes is the way to go.* It is your passport to wealth—your ticket to growing rich. The more money you grow tax-deferred, the wealthier you're going to become.

WHY TAX DEFERRAL IS SO IMPORTANT

"Tax deferment" means just what it sounds like: Following the rules of the game as laid out by the Internal Revenue Service, you get out of paying some taxes now by agreeing to pay them later. There are many powerful arguments in favor of going this route. For example:

1. The numbers speak for themselves. Go to any Internet calculator and see the impact that annual taxation has on your progress. For instance, plug in "$20,000 over 25 years, tax-deferred," and contrast that with the same money over the same time period in a taxable account. Take any rate of return. For example: 12 percent compounded for 25 years earns you $340,001.28. If you realize that taxes can take 20 to 50 percent of the return away, you should assume at least a one-third discount off of your projection. Using our example, one-third of 12 is 8 percent. Eight percent compounded is $136,969.50—in other words, a difference of $201,758.00. With the compounded effect on having less money to work with after you pay taxes each year, you will earn at least *two-thirds less* over 25 years in a taxable account!

Surprised? Don't be. You will earn less—a lot less!—in a taxable account because you have less to reinvest each year. In a tax-deferred account, you can earn income on every dollar your investment earns, not just what is left over after taxes each year.

2. Guaranteed gains can't be beat. Sometimes, pretax investments provide other kinds of guaranteed gains. The most common example is employer matches of your contributions to your 401(k) or other retirement plan. If your employer is matching, say, 50 percent of your own contributions to a plan, that's a 50 percent gain on your investment before you've even started. There's simply no way to beat that! Grab those extra dollars, put them in your pretax account, and get them growing and compounding as soon as possible!

3. Pretax dollars are (relatively) painless. Yes, I understand that carving investment dollars out of your already tight budget may sound difficult, or even impossible. But let's say you agree to deduct 6 percent from your gross pay (that is, the biggest number on your pay stub, before the taxes and other deductions start being taken out). What's the hit to your net pay (that is, your take-home pay)? It's a measly 1 percent! If your take-home pay is $1000 per week, we're talking about a reduction of *10 dollars*. I promise you: you won't feel it. And meanwhile, you're salting away $60, because the tax you didn't pay is available for investing.

This is what we mavericks mean when we say, *Pay yourself first.* (I introduced this idea in the previous chapter.) Get the benefit from the compounding earnings on the amount you didn't pay to the IRS! If you max out your tax-deferred options, great—invest posttax dollars in good places. But whenever possible, pay the government many, many years from now. Don't worry—it will still be there, ready to take your money; and you'll be in a far better position to give.

4. Your tax burden *goes down*.   You actually have a smaller tax obligation when April 15 rolls around. When you put money into a 401(k) or traditional IRA, the deduction reduces your gross income, and thus reduces your tax burden. That's because the IRS looks at tax-deferred money as if it wasn't really earned. You can save effectively from each paycheck, and invest for your future at the same time.

5. Forget about buy 'n' hold.   As noted in previous chapters, people sometimes say that they have to buy 'n' hold because of all the dreary tax implications of selling. Well, listen carefully: This is a tax-deferred account. There are no tax considerations. Sell, capture profits, reinvest: no taxes, and therefore no excuses.

6. It's the most practical way to achieve 20 percent compounded growth.   I've saved one of the best arguments for last. If you were to sum up the benefits of tax deferral in a single strategic sentence, this would be it. When taxes don't enter into the decision-making process—when they don't even have the chance to erode your gains—and when a company matches a portion of your contributions, you have an excellent shot at 20 percent annually.

TWO PIES ARE BETTER THAN ONE

Have you ever had trouble separating your retirement accounts from your stock-trading accounts? Do you find it difficult to figure out your total assets? Do you ever wonder if you have too little or too much in the way of taxable money?

One exercise that I like to do at my seminars is to get people thinking in terms of two portfolios—a taxable pie and a tax-deferred pie. I ask people to split them up and write their various holdings on two separate sheets of paper. (See Fig. 4-1.)

Try this yourself. Ask:

1.   Is this a tax-deferred investment or taxable investment?
2.   What rate of return have I achieved on this investment in the past?
3.   What would happen if I were able to get 20 percent on every tax-deferred asset?

When you list each individual holding, you can quickly identify which are achieving the maverick rate of 20 percent. You can also determine the ratio of tax-deferred dollars to taxable dollars.

I'VE GOT A TAX-DEFERRED ... RATIO

More often than not, people find that they do not have as many tax-deferred assets as they should. For example, you have a 401(k), but you're not contributing very much to it. Or, you're investing conservatively within the plan. Or, you're unaware that you're allowed to have an IRA as well. (Certainly, if you're *aware* of that, you're acting on that knowledge, right?)

Although there's no perfect method for determining the right ratio of tax-deferred to taxable dollars, I like to key off of a person's age. Specifically, you should have the same percentage of tax-deferred assets as you've spent years on the planet. Are you 40 years old? Then 40 percent of your money should be compounding in a tax-deferred account. When you are 70 years of age, 70 percent should be in TDAs.

The point of this ratio is to focus you in on the options within the tax code. Multiple tax-deferred accounts can be used. I actually have four active TDAs (an IRA, a 401(k), a Variable Annuity, and Variable Universal Life). If you stop and think about tax deferral, compounding, and time, your future wealth should be accumulating faster and to a greater degree as you reach retirement.

It's all about knowing where your money is, making sure you have enough tax-deferred choices, and then maxing out those choices.

YOUR QUALIFIED ALTERNATIVES COME FIRST

*   **401(k), 403b, 457.**   If your employer has one and if you're eligible for it, *max it out.* In a 401(k) for instance, that's typically up to 15 percent, with a limit of $10,500 on personal contributions.
*   **SEP, Keogh, or Simple.**   Self-employed people can max out their plans, as well. Here are the limits: 13 percent of your income or $30,000 for a SEP; the lesser of 20 percent or $30,000 for a Keogh; and up to $6,000 with a Simple. I typically tell self-employed people that SEPs are easiest to set up and probably most effective for their needs, but in the same breath I tell them that they should consult a tax advisor.
*   **IRA, Roth IRA, Rollover IRA.**   Many people don't realize this, but you can have an individual retirement account (IRA) in addition to an employer plan. In such cases, the contributions are probably *not* deductible from your taxes. (Your accountant will tell you.) Nevertheless, the money in the account grows tax-deferred. Big bonus!

In a Roth IRA, the contributions are not tax-deductible, but the money grows tax-free, and you can withdraw it tax-free. In a traditional IRA, the contributions are tax-deductible, but only when you do not have an employer-sponsored plan.

The verdict? Unless you're rolling over a substantial dollar sum, where you'd have to come up with a lot of tax dollars, the Roth is probably your best bet. Note, though, that there are income restrictions on the Roth. For single-wage earners it's $95,000; for married couples it's $150,000.

NONQUALIFIED PLANS FOR ADDITIONAL TAX-DEFERRAL NEEDS

What if you want to save for a child's education? What if you have a large chunk of cash that you want to shelter from taxation? What if you have life insurance needs, or want to protect your estate for your heirs?

There are a variety of nonqualified tax-deferral plans, like the Education IRA and the fast-rising 529 College Plans. There are also a number of insurance products—fixed annuities, variable annuities, variable universal life policies—all of which provide advanced deferral strategies. I will describe these new and flashy (but solid!) investment vehicles in Chapter 20.

MAVERICKS TAKE IT TO THE MAX

A defining characteristic of a maverick—one that sets you apart from the typical investor—is *your commitment to maxing your tax-deferred dollars*. Ordinary investors (or at least the starry-eyed among them) look for 3000 percent gains on a single tech stock in their trading accounts. Mavericks max out their tax-deferred opportunities for 20 percent compounded growth.

To summarize, there are three ways to max out your tax-deferred money. First, you can contribute the maximum amount that your employer allows—usually 15 percent, up to $10,500—in your 401(k). Second, you can max out the number of accounts at your disposal. For example, you and your spouse might have a 401(k), a 403(b), two Roth IRAs, and an Education IRA. If you are behind in your savings for retirement, we look to the Variable Annuity or the Universal Variable life products to play catch-up. Finally, you can max an IRA by parking it at a discount broker, where you increase your number of investment choices tenfold.

Now that you understand what I mean by "the most important money you manage," you're ready to learn about the maverick allocation of that money. Maybe you won't be surprised to hear that *it's all about stocks*.

PART 3

Maverick Investing Techniques

10

How to Invest 100 Percent in Stocks Throughout Your Life

W hat are the three most important things in real estate? *Location, location,* and *location.* The idea behind this old maxim is that *where* you put your resources, in terms of commercial or residential real estate, is the most important factor in determining the long-term success of that investment. Yes, you have to operate your property well, but if it's in the wrong place, no amount of skilled management is likely to dig you out of your "locational" hole.

The same is true for investments like those we've been talking about in this book. Where you allocate (or position) your money will ultimately determine whether that money turns in an ordinary or an extraordinary performance.

Ordinary investors follow the herd. They do what an investment house tells them to do—which most often means buying some mix of all three of the asset classes described in Chapter 7. It might be 50 percent in stocks, 30 percent in bonds, and 20 percent in cash. Or it might be 60/30/10, 55/25/20, or 45/40/15. Whatever the combo, it is designed for results of about 8 percent annualized growth—that is, *mediocre* growth, by maverick standards.

Mavericks know that the only allocation that makes sense in a bull market is 100/0/0—100 percent equity investing. Stocks are the only asset class that counts—the only one with the ability to get 20 percent compounded growth year after year.

This doesn't mean you won't have a cash position while you're evaluating alternatives, or you won't move your money to cash before a severe downtrend occurs. What it does mean is that extraordinary investors *commit to stocks for life.*

WHAT'S THAT RATE AGAIN?

There have been times in history when owning a representative slice of the entire stock market, such as the S&P 500, has afforded wealth-builders 20 percent compounded growth. Conversely, there has never been any time when a bond or cash position has rewarded investors this handsomely.

Consider this message from Marshall:

> Doug, I understand why stocks are so terrific. But every day, the Dow seems to jump up and down by hundreds of points. I want to invest 100 percent in stocks. But if it scares me, shouldn't I control risk with 70 percent or 60 percent, maybe 50 percent?

Think I tried to talk Marshall out of that kind of allocation? Well, actually, I *didn't.* For those who choose to be ordinary—for those who believe that 8 percent per year is enough for their family's future, and/or simply can't live with the kinds of short-term fluctuations that Marshall cited—asset allocation is an adequate strategy. I'm very candid on my radio show on this point: Not everyone is cut out to be a maverick.

The maverick approach takes commitment, a long-term perspective, and the discipline to ride out the short-term bumps and grinds of the market. Mavericks recognize that bonds and other fixed-income instruments are unlikely to sustain a given standard of living. (And they're *highly* unlikely to enhance a lifestyle!) Mavericks are dedicated to making more for our retirement—so that our money outlives us, and not the other way around.

GETTING IN WHEN STOCKS ARE ALREADY HOT, HOT, HOT!!!

Here's another concern that a radio listener, Mark, shared with me recently:

> Doug, I've got a lot of money sitting in cash. I keep waiting for a big, huge sell-off before I invest. But it's just not happening. How do you get in the market when it just seems to go up, and up, and up?

It's certainly understandable if—like Mark—you're nervous about buying into a stock market that may be near its peak (and there are always commentators out there ready to tell you that this market is near its peak).

So how do you figure out exactly where you are in the cycle of highs and lows?

The answer is, you don't. That's a thinly disguised form of prediction, and *mavericks don't predict.* What you do is first look to the market's trend. If the big-time indexes are above their long-term trend lines, we recognize that we should be invested. The market is up 77 percent of the time. What you *should* do, when you are entering the market in the middle of a cycle, however, is divide your money into three more or less equal parts. Invest the first third now. If stocks fall apart, you will have protected the majority of your assets in money accounts.

But if things go in the other direction and stocks rise by 5 percent, you can comfortably put another third in. Now you are 66 percent invested. Once again, wait for the broader market to rise by another 5 percent. When that happens, you can invest the final third. (This is "incremental purchasing," a subject to which I'll return in a later chapter.)

The goal is to get 100 percent invested in stocks. If you've followed the maverick strategy just outlined, you've now achieved that goal. Feels good, right? But don't get too comfortable, because you still have some maverick responsibilities ahead. In Chapter 14 (Locking in Gains and Stopping Losses) and Chapter 16 (Trending and the Art of Selling), I'll show you exactly how to manage the risks of a 100 percent equity position.

A LANDMARK STUDY MAKES THE POINTS

In 1986, Gary P. Brinson, L. Randolph Hood, and Gilbert Beebower published a study in the *Financial Analysts Journal* that studied four factors in determining portfolio success. They looked at expenses/costs, portfolio manager activity (that is, buying and selling), investment policy (asset allocation), and the actual investments themselves (e.g., Stock Fund B, Stock Fund Y, Bond Fund C, Bond Fund I, etc.).

As a result of this study (as well as several subsequent studies), researchers concluded that they could explain more than 90 percent of performance by investment policy (asset allocation) alone. In other words, according to these researchers, by far the biggest determinant of success was not the manager's activity, or the particular fund choice, but *the location of the assets themselves.*

These are *my* kind of researchers. And although there have since been a variety of challenges to this 90 percent estimate, few experts dispute the conclusion that asset classes matter. For us nonacademics, the message is clear: Get the asset category right. This is the *strategic* decision, on which everything else hinges. For mavericks, it's stocks—100 percent stocks.

When you get that strategic decision right, you can then move on to figuring out which stock funds are right for you. This is the *tactical* decision—the way that you'll implement your strategy.

All of the research points in the same direction: The higher the percentage of stocks in your portfolio, the higher your total returns. If I haven't persuaded you of this, go ask the opinion of anybody whose financial savvy you respect (or someone whose advice you're already paying for). Ask him or her, "If stocks generate the best returns, and if I have a way of minimizing the downside risks of owning stocks, why shouldn't I be invested 100 percent in stocks when the markets are in good shape?"

Listen hard to the answer. I bet the person you talk to will either (1) agree, or (2) argue with your premises ("you can't minimize the downside risks of owning stocks!"). I bet he or she *won't* say, "Oh, you'll do better in bonds over the long run."

BALANCING? JUST THE TIRES, PLEASE!
Joe from Idaho asks:

> Doug, I've got Robertson High Yield and Stevenson Aggressive Growth in my 401(k). I've tried to maintain 50 percent in each. Yet every time I turn my back, my growth fund position is at 70 percent and my High Yield is at 30 percent. I've been rebalancing, back to 50/50—just like everyone says to do. And once again, it's at 70 percent and 30 percent. Should I keep rebalancing?

What's going on here? Idaho Joe's wrestling with a problem caused by some bad advice that good times have made worse. Some guy named Everybody has been telling Joe that the secret to a healthy portfolio is maintaining "balance" across asset categories. In this case, Everybody seems to have told Joe to put half of his assets in stocks and the other half in bonds, and make sure that ratio was maintained over time.

So Joe started down that "balanced" road, and lo and behold, things got out of balance. Why? Because the stock component of his portfolio grew faster than the bond component. His 50 percent stock position turned into 70 percent of the total value of his portfolio, while his bond position has shrunk to a 30 percent share. (Once again, in different words: It's not that he's lost any money in bonds, but their value has grown so much more slowly than that of the stocks that they've become the weak cousins in the portfolio.)

What do you think of Everybody's advice? Do you agree with Everybody that Joe should sell shares in his winner, the stock fund, so that he can more buy shares of his bond-fund loser?

The answer is, "Of course not!"

Wall Street recommends "balance," and then regular "rebalancing" to get back to balance. But mavericks ignore the advice of "Everybody." We don't sell a stock fund that's sizzling in order to buy a bond fund that's fizzling. It just doesn't make sound economic sense. We don't root for bond markets to have their brief moment in the sun—that is, during bear markets, when stock prices are depressed—in order to feel a little better about having bought these low-yield turkeys in the first place.

We don't buy them in the first place. Let your auto mechanic worry about "balance," and keep him away from your 401(k).

THE MYTH OF ASSET ALLOCATION (OR, WHAT PEOPLE REALLY DO)

One more thing about asset allocation: *While it may work in theory, in practice it is often a myth.* Even people who want to stay with their original asset mix—say 60 percent stocks, 30 percent bonds, and 10 percent cash—simply don't do it. Either they're not as conscientious as Joe is about following bad advice, or they get seduced by the Bull. In other words, once people start to see the success of stock positions relative to other positions, they stop rebalancing, and charge off toward 100 percent equity investing.

"But Doug," I can just about hear you protesting, "Isn't that exactly what you want me to do?" Well, yes. But I want you to get there according to a *plan*. I want you to get there following a blueprint that minimizes your risks, and maximizes your returns.

Mavericks get to 100 percent equity investing *early* in the cycle. They get there with a plan, and a purpose. They understand how and why they're fully invested, and they know exactly when and how to sell.

In contrast, ordinary investors tend to hit 100 percent equity investing during the peak of market cycles, with no idea when they should sell. Then all hell breaks loose, and these latecomers can't find the exit.

REASONS WHY YOU MUST NOT USE ALL THREE ASSET CLASSES

By way of review, let's take a look at the reasons you must shoot for 100 percent equity investing:

1. Anything less won't get the job done.   If you decide to put a lot of bonds and cash into your equation, the best you can hope for is 8 percent per year. Project 8 percent compounded growth on your total portfolio to see just how much longer it will take to reach your goals (if, indeed, you can *ever* get there in one lifetime!).

2. Cash is a seriously weak link.   Weighing down your portfolio with cash is like strapping a block of concrete to your ankles. Wear cinderblocks as footwear only when there's no other good alternative.

3. Bonds require "bad times" to be effective.   Are you basically a negative kind of person? Do you sit around hoping for a recession, slow growth, or economic troubles? Then bonds are for you. (Remind me not to go out for a beer with you.) Bond managers (and, of course, bond sales-people) are the only people I know who actually root for a stock market col-lapse. Ironically, as it turns out, you can do almost as well with cash instruments as you can with bonds, and you can (1) completely avoid the downside risk of a bear in bonds, and (2) avoid the necessity of wishing misfortune on your friends and family members who own stocks.

4. People make the wrong adjustments at the wrong time.   Sooner or later, an unbelievably high percentage of investors arrive at 100 percent equity investing. My point is that either you'll get there according to a plan, or you'll find yourself irresistibly drawn to it—like a moth to a flame—creeping up from 50 percent to 70 percent, then 90 percent, and finally all the way in. The question is, do you want to get there early and leave on time, or do you want to get there late, and leave too late?

INDIVIDUAL SECURITIES OR MUTUAL FUNDS?

There are three ways to invest in equities—(1) individual securities, (2) mutual funds, and (3) exchange traded funds (ETFs). We'll talk about ETFs in Chapter 18 (Riding the Waves of the Future).

Right now, however, let's focus on the never-ending debate among investing professionals: individual stocks versus mutual funds.

As far as being a maverick goes, it makes no difference whether you're an individual shareholder, a mutual fund owner, or both. What counts is getting 100 percent committed to the asset class.

Having said that, let me tell you why I choose to invest exclusively in mutual funds.

- They're easy to track.
- I can select from the best managers in the world.
- I don't need very many of them to diversify.
- I'm able to get 100 percent invested in equities.
- I achieve my goal of 20 percent compounded growth.
- They are low-cost to use.

Individual securities, on the other hand, require extensive research and an enormous amount of time. You need something like 15 or 20 stocks to diversify adequately (meaning, to minimize the damage resulting from company- or industry-specific meltdowns). You need to track all of those positions, and always have new candidates ready to replace the old. Most 401(k) plans—the place where everyone should concentrate their wealth-building activity—don't even offer individual stocks. And the volatility of individual securities can make it extremely difficult for you to sleep well at night.

WHAT'S YOUR OVERALL GAME PLAN?

There are a number of issues that an individual stockholder needs to keep fresh in his or her mind:

1. How will you get 20 percent on your total portfolio?   It's not uncommon for individual equity advocates to call up my radio show and brag about the 100 percent gain they just realized in, say, SkyHighTech.com. But when I push them to reveal *exactly how much of their total portfolio* was in SkyHighTech, something interesting tends to happen. "Well, that's hard to say, Doug," comes the evasive answer, this time in a quieter tone of voice. "You know, I have a bunch of other stock positions at the moment."

If 100 percent of this high-flier's portfolio was in SkyHighTech, then he actually doubled his money. Good for him. I hope he sleeps well at night. And by the way: These guys almost *never* call me up to tell me about how they just *lost* 90 percent of their money on SkyHighTech.

If only half of this guy's portfolio was in SkyHighTech, well, he's achieved a 50 percent return. Again: good for him! But if only one-seventeenth of his money was in SkyHighTech, then he's gained between 7 and 8 percent (taxable)—not too hot, especially if (1) there's some sleep loss involved, (2) his other picks aren't doing as well, or (3) he's got substantial bond and cash positions dragging down the rest of his "average."

2. Bull markets will cover up a ton of sins.   Sometimes, when things are streaking, you almost feel like you can do no wrong. Everything you buy goes up. But gamblers usually pay a heavy price for not knowing what they bought and why. Make sure you know what you own, and why.

3. All capital is at risk.   As hard as it is to believe, it is very possible to *lose all of your money* with one stock. I've had some very nice, very naive callers to the radio show ask me what they could do about a company that no longer trades on a particular exchange. I hate answering that question, because the answer is, *Nothing.* They've lost their entire investment in that stock.

Mutual funds, even the lemons, almost never just evaporate into thin air. But they *can* fall prey to a bear market. And having the awareness is one reason why we're mavericks.

YOU INSIST? THEN ASK THESE QUESTIONS FIRST!

So I haven't talked you out of those individual stock positions? OK, then; here are the questions that I'd ask myself before venturing my capital on an individual corporation.

- At what price point will I sell this stock? When it drops 15 percent from a high? 20 percent? 25 percent?

- By selling this investment, what do I stand to gain? Protection of principal? Opportunity for growth elsewhere?

- Am I the type of person who would rather hold a bad stock than experience that bad feeling that results from selling at a loss? (Yes, everybody who plays in this game has experienced that bad feeling.) If so, what will I do differently than I have in the past, in order to keep my emotions out of the selling decision?

- Has this stock or sector demonstrated the ability over time to compound at 20 percent annually?

- Will this company contribute to sufficient diversification within my individual stock portfolio of, say 10, 15, or 20 stocks? Will its purchase result in my being weighted too heavily in one particular segment of the economy or my portfolio?

- Do I feel obligated to invest in this company because I work for it? Am I bowing to peer pressure—a friend, a relative, a neighbor?

- If I buy this stock, what percentage of my total portfolio's value will be wrapped up in this one company?

- Is this a bad quarter, or a bad investment? How quickly is this company able to pull out of a slump? What evidence is there that the bad times won't get worse?

- Will I have the ability and fortitude to keep tabs on the company's finances? Will I stay in touch with the company's management, market share, and book value?

- If I keep this stock, am I exposed to an unnecessary risk of a dramatic price drop due to poor earnings or bad management?

- What do I know about the company's current earnings? Is the company overvalued, by traditional price-to-earnings measures? What about its finances? Its historical profitability? Its relative strength within its industry?

- What do I know about the company itself? Do I visit its store, or use its products and services? Can I explain what the company does in 50 words or less?

- What indicators tell me that now is the right time to make a buy? Is it P/E ratios that are lower than the broader market? Price-to-book ratios that are lower than the company's industry?

As you can see, buying individual stocks requires a bit more effort than opening an online account and choosing a ticker symbol. For me, the questions come down to the technical aspects of managing risk, emotions, and opportunity. But an individual stock enthusiast must also take into account the fundamentals of a corporation—its profitability, its earnings, its price relative to earnings. Peter Lynch and Warren Buffett call it "doing your homework." So if you play this game, make certain you do it with gusto and dedication.

If you don't know anything more than what your fiance's coworker has to say about GetRichQuick.com, then you might as well gamble in a casino. In fact, your odds at the casino may actually be better, especially if you play a good hand of blackjack.

MAKING YOUR 100 PERCENT ALLOCATION TO EQUITIES WORK FOR YOU

In this chapter, I showed you the importance of 100 percent equity investing. I attempted to explode the myth of asset allocation, and described ways to work toward a total stock portfolio.

But up cycles and bull markets don't last forever. That's why mavericks prepare for change. In the next chapter, I'll tell you everything you need to know about preparing for change. Specifically, I'll show you exactly how the stock market works during a raging bull, and what mavericks do to keep from investing their emotions along with their assets.

11

Market Psychology: Recognizing the Effects of Up Cycles

Have you ever jumped on a bandwagon or an investing fad? Have you ever purchased a stock that you desperately hoped would double in value, only to watch it fall apart after you bought in?

Have you ever prayed for a stock to come back, so you could sell it and break even?

As with most crazes, our emotions make us act in ways we'd rather forget. But it's even worse with stocks. Why? Because when the stock market is hot, people abandon their carefully worked-out strategies in favor of chasing lottery dreams.

Mavericks stay outside the emotional currents of investing. Wherever stocks are today—chic, or in the doghouse—mavericks know that the environment will eventually shift in the other direction. Just as sure as the sun comes up in the east, a long, bull cycle will mature, and give way to a short, violent bear period. Similarly, when just about everybody has called it quits and run up the white flag, an up cycle will emerge from the ashes.

Market psychology is all about change, and mavericks embrace change. We manage the risks of down cycles, and we take advantage of the opportunities in up periods.

BOOM, BUST, AND BOOM: LESSONS FROM
CALIFORNIA REAL ESTATE

Maybe you haven't yet experienced the highs and lows of the stock market. Let me introduce you to the subject with a case history from a separate but similar field: real estate. Specifically, let's look at property in the Golden State.

Throughout much of the 1980s, California property smoked the salmon out of the expert's forecasts. Prices appreciated 150 percent, meaning that a house that began the decade priced at $100,000 ended the decade worth $250,000. If a person had put $10,000 down to buy that $100,000 house (in other words, a 10 percent equity stake) and hadn't sold that house, then he or she enjoyed unrealized gains of $150,000, or a 1500 percent return. "Unrealized" simply means that the increased value still resided in the house, rather than in some other investment.

The economy was rolling. The Cold War was ending. The Hype Masters jumped into the fray, trumpeting those 1500 percent returns. By 1989, everybody wanted in on the new California Gold Rush: real estate.

Then interest rates—caused by too many people and businesses chasing too few dollars in the national economy—cooled the housing market. Mortgages got too expensive, pricing out whole categories of buyers. Zillions of new units came onto the market at once, as developers tried to cash in on the boom. Supply overwhelmed demand. Suddenly, builders of condominiums couldn't unload their units. Office space went unrented. Nationwide, the real estate market went into the tank. And it wasn't long before latecomers who had bought at the market high—in our example, $250,000—were in the hole for big money: say $50,000 to $70,000.

It took the next half-decade for home prices to get hot again, leaving people emotionally devastated and financially strapped. Some filed for bankruptcy; others walked away from their loans. Most simply made their payments, hunkered down in their homes, and waited for better times.

What lessons can we learn from these kinds of real estate declines? Three things:

1. Most markets—real estate, stocks, bonds, even chickens—move in cycles, driven by complicated factors of supply and demand. They have downs, as well as ups.
2. Market insiders and media experts only paint rosy pictures about the near-term future. Why? Because that's what puts gasoline in their BMWs!

3. Change happens. The only way to deal with change is to expect it, prepare for it, and find ways to take advantage of it.

THE PSYCHOLOGY OF CHANGE
Many of the biggest changes come in the smallest packages. Cindy from Iowa writes:

> Doug, I started listening to your radio shows on the Internet and I'm trying to be a maverick for my newborn girl. She's only three weeks old—very cute little nose!
>
> I want to invest aggressively for her future. I don't want to wait until she's dating before I begin to save for her education.
>
> Anyway, I was wondering if you had any "New Economy" stocks that you thought might be good to hold until she's 18.

I love the fact that Cindy is already thinking about her daughter's education. So few people start planning as early as the first few weeks of a newborn's life—probably because it's so hard for young parents to imagine how quickly the next 18 years will go by.

But Cindy, with all of her foresight and good intentions, has been snookered. The snookering has taken two forms. First, she's become convinced that long-term investing is synonymous with holding a stock for 18 years. Second, she has let the media define what is worth owning—a tech-oriented "New Economy" stock versus an "old-fashioned" industrial.

Mavericks think otherwise. We understand that no investment—no index, sector, industry, stock, or fund—will be right forever. Nothing stays on top forever. "Old" isn't necessarily bad, just as it's not necessarily good. Things *change:*

- The hot market-cap category will shift, from large to small to medium and back again.
- Styles will come in and go out of style: for example, growth to value and back to growth again.
- Sectors will wax and wane: old to new to "new old" to "new new."

THREE REASONS WHY A SO-CALLED "NEW ECONOMY" WILL HURT
Tech "versus" the rest of the economy, record lows on cash levels, rising household debt, a bulging trade deficit, and sky-high levels of margin buying (that is, buying stock with borrowed money)—these are just a few of the danger signals in the roaring 2000s.

What happens when there's no more cash left to buy more of this high-priced stuff? What happens when the tech sector finally isn't able to float the rest of the economy higher and higher? (The Nasdaq woes of 2000–2001 give some clues on *this* score.) When prices sag, and when institutions begin to call on their margin account holders in a big way—including all those high-tech zillionaires who have margined their stock to fuel a glitzy lifestyle—could stocks tumble across the board?

Mavericks do not predict when an up cycle will lose its luster. But we absolutely, resolutely resist the idea that a "New Economy" has created a risk-free stock environment.

There are three reasons why New Economy hype will hurt the ordinary investor:

1. New implies old . . . even ancient.   People trip over themselves to climb aboard the "what's new" canoe. Nobody wants to be on the aged steamboat. But that's exactly where the ordinary investor winds up. Believe me: As a novice or part-time investor, you are *highly unlikely* to be invited into the New Canoe. The Big Boys already have all the limited seats reserved.

And you know what? That's *just fine.* Mavericks are broad-gauge, adaptable, flexible, and opportunistic. We recognize that out-of-vogue sectors become hot, while the latest and greatest eventually slip to the bottom of the pile. We don't waste a lot of time scouting out (and fighting for a place in) that New Canoe.

2. New is static . . . not dynamic.   If you buy-'n'-hold "new," you're either saying that (1) the technology revolution is over, and we've arrived at the End of History, or (2) this company you're buying will be the industry leader forever.

In reality, the economy is always new and always changing, and companies are *always* going into the tank. That's why mavericks protect themselves from extreme downside slides with stop-loss percentages.

3. New grows tired . . . fast.   At the beginning of the 1990s, Japan's Nikkei stock exchange was supposed to embody all that was good about the "new global economy." Then Japan's astounding economic expansion ended, and conditions deteriorated. Rather than beating the world, the Nikkei languished in obscurity for the next decade.

Believe it or not, our economic expansion will come to an end as well. (As I write this in the spring of 2001, the talk is that Europe has to step up to the plate to prop up the faltering U.S. economy.) But for mavericks, this only means even greater opportunity. In fact, when you lock in your gains at the end of a cycle, you're able to prepare for the start of the next up-trend.

PSYCLE CRAZINESS

Raging bulls produce a lot of hot air. Predictions for the Dow and the Nasdaq climb. Media hype increases exponentially. And as a result, greedy and/or impressionable individuals start to raise their personal projections for annual growth—from 20 to 30 percent, from 30 to 40 percent, or even higher!

In this overheated environment, old Wild-Eyed Doug starts looking too conservative for some people's taste. Consider an e-mail from Anonymous, who chastised me for setting my sights too low, and berated me for even *mentioning* downside risk:

> What on earth is so "maverick" about putting dollars in a mutual fund that probably won't get you more than 15–20 percent? Many of my stock picks have gone up 30 percent IN ONE DAY. Try getting that from a mutual fund. What's wrong with going after bigger gains? What's the worst thing that could happen? Lose half of it? I say if you're really maverick, you let it ride.

Maybe this guy is just as good as he thinks he is. Maybe he'll have the skill and luck to get his money in and out of the right stocks at just the right times, and live to enjoy the profits of his high-stakes approach.

Or maybe not. Maybe he's more like a lucky drunk staggering from one table to the next in a casino. He may be on a roll now, but check back in after an hour or two: *He is bound to take a fall.*

I didn't take offense at Anonymous's scoldings. In fact, after hearing from all the experts that the maverick's 20 percent is too high a target, it's refreshing to be criticized for being too cautious. Maverick investors don't shoot from the hip (we *certainly* don't stagger from table to table). We don't rely on a bull market to make up for our greed or lack of discipline. Instead, we're progressive individualists who blaze unique trails to personal wealth.

Obviously, there's nothing a maverick enjoys more than growing his or her total portfolio by 30 or 40 percent in a banner 12-month period. But that's a bonus—the upper-upside to a solid, long-term strategy. It's completely different from the person who makes unrealistic projections, and then takes unnecessary risks to reach those lofty goals. And believe me: When you risk enough, often enough, you'll get *hurt.* That's why they call it "risk."

STAYING OFF THE COOLNESS LADDER

Maverick investing is as much a mindset as it is a technique.

Mavs are cool because we let our unconventional investing lifestyle speak for itself (it's something in the way we *walk,* I think). We know that stock mutual funds alone achieve the most impressive results. We know that the answer is in ourselves.

In sharp contrast, emotional investors—those with relatively low financial self-esteem—think that the answer is Out There, somewhere. As a result, they find themselves climbing what I call the "Coolness Ladder." They quickly move off the Coolness Ladder's lowest rungs—from CDs and savings accounts, for example—to bonds (*an OK move, as a transition*). Then they move on to mutual funds. (*Good move, if done right. Stop there.*) But they keep scrambling up that ladder, looking for the answer Out There. Why not sector funds, such as telecom, health, and so on? *They* sound cool.

As the bulls run ever more wild, the emotional investor keeps scrambling upward, looking for ever "sexier," ever sleeker investments. If they start with individual "blue chips" like AT&T, IBM, and Intel, it's only a matter of time before they shift toward the infrastructure stocks—the Ciscos and JD Uniphases—followed by Net stocks, chat-room selections, and IPOs. Before a person realizes how far up the ladder he or she has ascended, that person is speculating on future prices in a margin account.

Mavericks are *way too smart* to be seduced by the Coolness Ladder. We prefer the road less traveled; we get an emotional lift from creating our own path to financial success. Most important, we're extra vigilant when the herd is up to its eyeballs in margin. A maverick history lesson: Run-ups and record levels of margin preceded two of the worst bear catastrophes in market history—in 1929–1932, and again in 1973–1974.

Maverick investing means ignoring the incessant chatter that pushes people toward the Coolness Ladder. It means calmly stepping away from stocks when indicators signal a downturn. It means hanging up when the guy on the phone uses the "M" word (for margin). In most cases, it means leaving the IPOs and other high-risk ventures for the crapshooters.

"Really, Doug?"

Yes, really. I'll explain.

IPO INSANITY

In every market cycle, things happen at the bottom, and things happen at the top (to this extent, we mavericks are allowed to engage in predictions.) At the top, buyers are out of control, and sellers control the tempo. Gimmicky investment products pop up everywhere, as exchange workers, brokers, advisers, investment banks, and fund companies all look to cash in. Perhaps most telling, it seems that almost every company from Portland, Maine, to Portland, Oregon, tries to go float an initial public offering (IPO).

For those of you who are new to this realm, this simply involves taking a private company public—that is, going through the necessary steps to make shares in the company available to the public, and agreeing to play by public company rules. It's a way for a company to get access to new capital. And it's a way for owners of the private company to get liquid and/or rich, as well as a way for investment bankers (who run the process) to do very well themselves.

If you want a totally biased, fun, and informative perspective on IPOs, read *License to Steal* by journalist Timothy Harper and an anonymous Wall Street–based coauthor. (Make sure you get the right *License to Steal,* since there are a couple of books with the same title.) This is an insider's look into borderline and outright illicit financial activities. Among many other things, the author talks candidly about how his company underwrote just about any IPO that came down the Street. For example, the authors tell us about one colorful scheme as follows:

> Once they took a vacation to Wyoming or someplace, moose hunting or something, and came back with an IPO that called for the owner to create a chain of dude ranches throughout the West. I don't think any new dude ranches were ever opened, but in the meantime, the IPO raised several million dollars.

So that's the kind of foolishness (to pick a kind word) that goes on when investors are overheated, and deal-makers are less than principled. Who gets hurt? The little guy who buys the dude ranch story. In general, I'd say "just say no" to new businesses that lack a real track record of offering a solid product or service.

At the market bottom, it's a very different story. There's no money to be had, in any case, so private companies put their IPO dreams on hold. Brokers look for sales positions outside of financial services. Newspapers focus on the financial carnage, and generally overlook what is, in many cases, a great buying opportunity.

Again, the little guy—by whom I mean the individual investor—gets hit the hardest. Buy-'n'-holders lose their resolve, sheepishly pull out of equities, and warn their children never to get tangled up in stocks.

But that's not all. Years later, many of these same confused souls call me on my radio show, lamenting the money they lost during a panic, and bemoaning the opportunity they lost during the ensuing market turnaround.

DOTTING THE COMS

In light of what I just said, should a maverick investor *ever* consider an IPO? Only if you treat the newcomer with the same unwavering scrutiny as you would another individual stock. In that spirit, let's look at the IPO madness that grabbed so many headlines in the late 1990s.

Clearly, most IPOs soared heavenward on the overall updraft (think "hot air") of the Internet phenomenon. No surprise, then, that dot.coms and dot.com spin-offs accounted for most of the 144 percent rise for IPOs in 1999. Yet even as the millennial clock was ticking into the year 2000, the media missed or minimized the real story: The biggest names in the IPO world were actually hurting, and struggling. CBSMarketwatch.com was down 65 percent from its peak. William Shatner's Priceline.com had slumped more than 50 percent. And the globe.com was already 80 percent below its high-water mark.

By March 2000, *Fortune* was reporting that many Net companies were using nontraditional methods of accounting (when you read stuff like that, look out). Soon, popular Net IPOs like Microstrategy, eToys, and iVillage were down 80 percent from their all-time peaks. Three out of four IPOs dipped below their offer price within the first two years of trading.

Nevertheless, I continue to get scores of IPO-related e-mails weekly. For example:

> Doug, I was thinking of becoming more of a maverick. What do you advise on MP3.com?
>> What's your impression of Martha Stewart?
>> WebMethods gained more than 500 percent. Is this a good buy?

Simply put, the vast majority of these new companies haven't been around long enough to prove their merit, their stamina, or even their fiscal reliability. And you simply have to understand what you're buying into. If you don't, then *don't*. Only buy things you understand. If your child knows more about MP3 music than you do, stay the heck away from MP3.com, *whatever* it is. Or if you know something about Martha Stewart's taste, and if you'd sooner let your six-year-old take indelible markers to your walls than let Martha decorate your home—then stay away from dotting the coms.

SEEING THE CYCLES

Have you ever felt like you're in an investing traffic jam, where the only lane that's NOT moving is yours?

The key to getting in front of the traffic is to understand market cycles. No, you can't predict their length, direction, or magnitude, but you can profit handsomely by recognizing their impact and general progression.

For example, you can spot general market trends—up cycles and down cycles—by using one or more of the big-time benchmarks. As noted earlier, the Russell 2000 gives you the trend of small-caps, while the S&P 500 serves as a barometer of the large-cap arena. And the Wilshire 5000 provides the picture of the entire show.

Individual segments of the economy also have cycles, although they tend to be far too volatile to permit meaningful trending. (In other words, they bounce around so fast that following trend lines is not very productive.) Another quick history lesson demonstrates this phenomenon: The energy sector delivered impressive returns from 1981 to 1985; health proved exceptionally robust from 1991 to 1995; and telecom closed all the circuits between 1996 and 2000.

Not surprisingly, conventional advisers argue that you should buy and hold all segments of the economy. (Diversify! Buy 'n' hold!) That way—as the argument goes—at least a portion of your money will *always* be in the right place, even if the rest of your assets underperform.

By now, you know where this argument is going: Spreading your assets around reduces your ability to achieve maverick returns. In fact, the only thing you guarantee by diversifying clear across the market is ordinary results throughout your life—in other words, 12 percent if you invest exclusively in equities, or 8 percent if you asset allocate with bonds and cash.

Mavericks have bigger aspirations. That's why they use momentum tactics for picking the fastest segments—whether they're large-caps, small-caps, value, growth, old economy, new economy, health, telecom, or tech. (We'll get into the nitty gritty of "momentum" in Chapter 15: Selecting the Maverick Way.)

PSYCHOLOGY OF GREED

Get a load of these incredible statistics from 1999:

- More than 170 funds rose 100 percent.
- The Nasdaq 100 scored a 102 percent increase in valuation.
- IPOs ascended an average of 144 percent.
- The Internet Fund rang up 220 percent.
- Qualcomm appreciated 2100 percent.

When you see numbers like these, what do you feel? Surprise? Jealousy? Fund envy?

Stats like these bring out the "greedies" in people. James from Bloomington, for example, called my show to explain how he rolled $40,000 into a single tech stock at $30. He liked the company so much, he even purchased another $20,000 on margin.

In the Nasdaq's early 2000 shakedown, the stock fell to $7.50. The "greedies" left James with shares worth $15,000 and a personal loss of $45,000. I must say, I *hate* hearing stories like this. I hate the fact that James succumbed to greed, and that he was encouraged to do so by the sharks who are always out there in the water, swimming around with those little pin-striped fins sticking up.

Everyone wants a larger asset base. Everybody is vulnerable to fund envy and "top 10" addiction. That's why you simply have to develop your goal-oriented, growth-focused, maverick approach to investing. In fact, this is about the only thing I've found that's suitable for managing powerful emotions (especially the greed that emerges during a dramatic up cycle).

MY FAVORITE MISTAKE

Emotions are the most powerful forces in the universe. Allow me to make the case that emotions like greed and fear are the greatest threats to your financial well-being, because they make you invest like an idiot.

To be perfectly honest, I've met Greed. And while he's entertaining, sharp-witted, and exceptionally confident, he's *not* the sort of guy you want to offer the guest bedroom to. Trust me. I've been there. As I mentioned in this book's introduction, I lost over $35,000 investing in stock index options because my first trade was a success, and I got the greedies.

Ironically, the very same emotional forces were working against investors the year I became serious about the stock market. In 1979, as fears of inflation and fears of "missing out" gripped the public, I watched the price of gold go from $275 to $850 an ounce. People waited in monstrous lines outside the Jonathan Coin Shop in Los Angeles, desperate to purchase American Eagles and South African Krugerrands at the $850 price point. Sounds nutty in retrospect, right? And I'm sure I don't have to tell you what happened to the price of gold shortly thereafter.

Am I condemning options and commodity trading? Absolutely not. I never try and talk expert hang-gliders out of hang-gliding, either. But for the average guy on the street—certainly including me, and probably including you—options trading and hang-gliding are good things to avoid. Greed and thrill-seeking are poor motivators. They can damage your wealth and health.

MARKET PSYCH IN PERSPECTIVE

In this chapter, you learned about the seductive power of up cycles—everything from IPOs to the Coolness Ladder. I showed you how cycles operate in real estate, the broad market, and within individual sectors. I also gave you insight into the biggest up-cycle challenge of them all—*greed.*

In the next chapter, we'll become intimately familiar with the trappings of a downtrend. Some say it can never happen again. I say a bear is Wall Street's dirtiest little secret—but only until it escapes from its cage.

12

Wall Street's Dirty Little Secret

Have you ever plunked down a hefty chunk of change on a single stock, only to watch your investment get cut in half?

Have you ever chased declining prices because a broker said to buy the dips?

Were you one of the millions of people who banked on the S&P 500, then watched in frustration as others got in on the Nasdaq early?

In the stock market, as in nature, tides turn. Winds shift; currents flow quickly in new directions. Hot becomes cold; sizzle becomes fizzle. It can happen to an individual stock, a major segment of the market, or the whole enchilada.

Since we mavericks aim to have 100 percent of our money in equities (at the right times), we have to take precautions. That means we plan for change; we prepare for the time when stocks will be hit by a hurricane.

Ignore the hype that promotes the "indestructible economy." Instead, be realistic and hard-nosed. Plan for the worst. Ask yourself:

- What would I do if the economic environment shifted?
- What would I do if the market pulled back 25, 30, or 50 percent?
- How will I feel if I lose $10,000, $100,000, or $500,000?

BEARS HAPPEN

Why all these negative questions? Because Wall Street has a dirty little secret: *Bears happen.*

Did you know that in every decade there's been at least one occasion when all of the major indexes fell more than 20 percent for a period of three months or longer? The last official bear, as measured by the S&P 500, reared its head in 1990. By historical standards, it was a relatively tame reversal.

And it was only a blip on the screen. Except for that ugly moment in 1990, the '90s were nothing short of spectacular. What are the key take-aways from that amazing 10 year run? I see two, and they pull in different directions. First, mavericks have to be in the game when the game is hot. Second, even in the best of times, the stock market can get whacked upside the head, and the smart investor takes steps to protect himself or herself.

Could we see a more serious drop than 2001? Sure. Will it be in 2005? Very possibly. Could it happen in 2008, when baby boomers start to retire in large numbers and require income? The longer into the cycle we go without a serious correction, the more likely it is that we'll live through one. (And how about that word—"correction"? Wall Street has trained us to use highly positive words to describe routs and disasters. You gotta love these guys!)

In truth, of course, there's no way of telling when the next painful down-cycle will occur—only that it will. And when it does, *it will begin with a correction of 10 percent.* That's the one thing that we can say, truthfully and consistently, about every slip, slide, crash, bump, and bear on record.

So if you had been buying the dips and selloffs in late 2000 like there's no tomorrow, you lost your shirt as stocks dropped more than 40 percent after already being down 35 percent. This was a time where a correction became a major bear market. And it set many investors back more than seven years on their road to wealth. (I calculate that timeline based on the Nasdaq returning to a historical return of 15 percent over the next seven years.)

MY PERSONAL EXPERIENCE

In 1973–1974, a merciless bear mauled shareholders across the United States. Blue-chip industrial stocks declined by as much as 50 percent. Small-cap stocks took a 65 percent beating.

This was no nasty little Nasdaq mood swing, nor even a quarter-long "crisis" like the one we lived through in 1998. Instead, this was a grinding, relentless, seemingly endless assault that continued for a full 19 months, and wreaked enormous economic, social, and psychological havoc.

That Big Bear came to our house. At the time, I was a recent high school graduate, a sun-worshipper, and a surfer. Left to my own devices, I would have spent most of my time at the Huntington Beach Pier, focusing more on the summer south swells than the plummeting stock market. But the financial carnage intruded upon my Endless Summer.

Many of my friends' parents lost their jobs, and then their houses. Many lost more than half of their net worth. Most investors (I later learned) were too heartsick and disillusioned to leave their much-diminished fortunes in stocks. Even those that *did* buy and hold on to their positions didn't break even until 1981, some seven years later, on average.

As I noted in the introduction, this was a challenging time for my family, as well. As an investment adviser, my dad struggled to survive during the mega bear market of 1973–1974. He witnessed the devastation of investors' portfolios and experienced the change in attitudes toward stocks. For a while, things were tight and tough in the Fabian household.

So I learned to listen for the growling of the bear. But did the experience make me market-phobic? Hardly. Today, I'm always completely at ease with my portfolio—even though I have 100 percent of my money in equity funds 80 percent of the time.

But at the same time, I never let the CNBC media talking heads persuade me that they know which company will double in value over the next six weeks. (They don't.) Nor do I allow an overzealous academic—or worse, an agent of Wall Street with a book contract—to sell me on a "Dow 36,000." And if I'm not chomping down on Dow 36,000, I'm not taking the bait of Dow 100,000, either.

The truth is, *stocks can and do go down.* Sometimes, they can even get knocked to the canvas. And if you're badly positioned, you can get knocked to the canvas along with them.

THE 1970S ARE HISTORY—AREN'T THEY?
Some New Economy advocates say that bears are simply bad memories— scary ghosts left over from the ancient past. That's simply not true. Down cycles will always be a part of your investing future. If you don't have a game plan for a mudslide in stock prices, you could easily get wiped out, just like all those unhappy investors in the 2000–2001 technology debacle. For example, Mark from Rockville, Maryland, wrote:

> At one time, I had $200,000 saved up for retirement. Then my portfolio declined 10 percent in what appeared was a natural pullback in stocks. No

big deal, right? Three days passed before my broker called me up. It was October 19, 1987, and everyone was selling like crazy. Of course I got out. I had to save what was left. As it turns out, all I had left was $120,000. And I haven't returned to the stock market since!

I hate stories like that. Mark didn't just lose the money he worked hard to accrue. More important, he lost his appetite for investing in stocks, apparently forever. This combination—lost money, lost confidence, and lost opportunity—is the triple-whammy that mavericks must avoid at all costs.

Remember, the market is not logical, it's *psychological.* That means our emotions play a bigger role on Wall Street than does common sense. It also means that, while the 1970s are history and the 1987 crash is long gone, Fear and Greed—and their offspring, the Big Bear—never go away.

FEAR ITSELF
Greed is like a muscle car with a hot engine and a rotten suspension: It's tempting, and it's totally unforgiving. The tail starts to spin out. Fear is the brake pedal you slam on. Rather than improving the situation, stomping on the brakes turns the scary spinout into a full-fledged disaster.

In the investing world, greed and fear take many forms. Think about your own investing history. Have you ever refused to sell a bad investment because you wanted to wait until you could break even? That's both greed and fear (the fear of losing).

Psychology is a strange thing. Studies have shown that the pain associated with giving up $1000 is far greater than the pleasure of winning $1000.

Panic is even more insidious. That's when the fear of losing everything overwhelms us. The urge to run for cover becomes impossible to resist. That's stomping on the brakes, even when some part of your brain is saying, "Gently! Gently!"

Fortunately, you don't have to succumb to devastating anxiety attacks. Maverick investors can lock in profits and avoid periods of emotional and financial turmoil. It's easy. We simply maintain our commitment to selling stock positions when the bear sign first appears.

THREE CONDITIONS FOR A MAJOR BEAR MARKET
One of the worst things an investor can do is fall sleep at the switch during a major bear market.

In the investment universe, this is equivalent to falling asleep at the wheel and crashing into a telephone pole—not something you want to experience! Maverick investors make plans to avoid the grisly effects of a drawn-out, ego-deflating, fiscally destructive down cycle—the major bear market—and then they *act* on those plans.

How do I define a major bear market for the twenty-first century? I say we're in a bear market when the following three conditions pertain:

1. A marketwide drop of 20 percent or more (*magnitude*)
2. A six-month or longer period of "below 20 percent" activity (*duration*)
3. The overwhelming majority of investors loses hope in building stock market wealth (*psychological shift*)

The good news is that these three conditions rarely come together all at once. As we've seen throughout the 1990s, a number of indexes dropped 18, 25, even 30 percent from their respective peaks. Still, a "buy-the-dips" mindset prevailed. In fact, we never witnessed a bearish duration of six months or more during the 1990s, nor did investors ever quite throw in the psychological towel until the year 2000.

Based on the psychology of down cycles in the twentieth century, it is reasonable to anticipate that a major bear market will still begin, as it almost always has, with a 10 percent correction. That's exactly what happened to the Nasdaq in April of 2000. From its high of 5048, the index dropped 30 percent in 30 days, and everyone expected it to bounce right back. The index did recover short-term, but each rally was met with another bear market sell-off, shoving the Nasdaq to new lows. This turned out to be many investors' first bear market. As we move into the twenty-first century, remember one thing: The longer the down time, the greater the anxiety and trepidation. At some point, the investment community will capitulate. Worse yet, the media will publish headlines that echo investor fears—captions like "Stocks are Dead," and "Never Coming Back." This occurs with every bear market.

Fortunately, mavericks will be sitting pretty by that point. Having already employed one or more of our selling strategies (stop-loss, trending, 5/10/20 vision), we will have moved the bulk of our assets to money market accounts. Best of all, just as the flock is headed south, we'll be riding the next up-cycle north.

BEAR FACTS
Don't want to get hit crossing the Street? Then be like a maverick: Look both ways

Consider these down-cycle realities:

1. Stock prices go down five times as fast as they go up. Buy-'n'-hopers say they'll hold through every storm—hail, sleet, and cyclone. And in the long term, that strategy may "work." But while your money declines 50 percent in value in a matter of months—say, from $50,000 down to $25,000—it may take years for the Street to give you your buy-'n'-hold money back. (If that's "working," I'm looking for a higher standard to which to hold my money!)

2. The media get ugly on you. Just as everything in the media tends to be highly gushy and Pollyanna-ish during the market's up-cycles, the media become total Eeyores—ultranegatives—at market bottoms. It's virtually impossible to escape. The *last* things investors saw after the 1987 crash were headlines announcing, "Hey, this is a *great* buying opportunity!"

3. An average market decline is 33 percent over 16 months. Can you take the heat? Can you stand watching your portfolio sink from $100,000 to $66,000 over the course of a little more than a year—and with no sign of recovery in sight? If you said "no," then good for you—you have some maverick impulses! Lose a third of your portfolio's value? You shouldn't *have* to. If you're 100 percent committed to equities, and you implement a down-cycle avoidance strategy, you'll never ride a bear's back to the bottom of a canyon.

Sure, all that buy-'n'-hold hype is persuasive. And it's actually worked fairly well for the last two decades. You could have done nothing more than purchase the S&P 500, hold it, and you'd have achieved almost 18 percent.

My question to passive investors who say they will buy 'n' hold through any set of circumstances is, Do you want to bet that the extraordinary 1980s and 1990s are about to be repeated? Can you afford to buy 'n' hope for 18 percent over the next two decades?

BUY 'N' HOLD COULD COST YOU 25 TO LIFE!
Buy 'n' hold is not a benign, low-risk practice. In fact, I'll argue (as long as you'll keep listening to me!) that buy 'n' hold is dangerous, and that those who recommend it are either ignorant or irresponsible.

Let me give you an example. Let's say that in October of 2002, you have $50,000 in your 401(k). You're 30 years old. You're planning to retire with a million-plus dollars by the age of 55.

Now let's add a twist of lemon. Let's assume that October 2002 makes bear tracks similar to those that marked the 70 percent inflation-adjusted loss on the Dow from 1969 to 1982. People beginning a journey in late 1968 needed to buy 'n' hold until *the year 1993* before they broke even! So if the same thing happens to you—the 2002 buy-'n'-holder—you would need to keep the faith until 2027 (the year you turn 55) just to get your original purchasing power back. Nobody should invest for 25 years and find himself or herself in the same place where he or she had begun. Of course, my example extrapolates from the 1970s, and that dismal decade wasn't exactly typical. But neither were the roaring 1980s and 1990s.

So please don't kid yourself. Buying and holding through a down cycle can be catastrophic. In fact, if you do not know when to sell, you could be setting yourself up for the mistake of a lifetime.

BEAR MATH

Have you ever gained 50 percent, then lost 33 percent, and finally found yourself back at the starting gate? According to an e-mail I received recently, that's what happened to Tim:

> Doug, I got an IPO at an amazing price. I got in at 26 and it went up 100 percent—in less than three months! Then it got killed alongside other Net stocks for accounting irregularities. I checked the losses with my online tracker, and it was supposedly down 50 percent. But I was actually down 100 percent because it returned to my Buy price of 26. How am I supposed to track my portfolio online if the numbers are inaccurate?

Unfortunately, Tim is not versed in what I call "bear market math." When you've doubled your money, which means that you've achieved 100 percent on your investment, a 50 percent loss takes you back to where you had started. (In other words, Tim's online tracker was correct.) If Tim had lost 100 *percent,* that would have meant that his stock had gone to zero. In other words, he would have lost *all* of his money, not half. (See Figure 12-1).

Consider another scenario. You purchase 100 shares of SuperFly.com at $50, for a total of $5000. It climbs 60 percent to a price of $75, making

FIGURE 12-1	**Breakeven Chart**		
If you've had a loss of . . .	then you need a gain of . . .	If you've had a gain of . . .	it only takes loss of . . .
50%	100% to break even.	25%	20% to break even.
If you've had a loss of . . .	then you need a gain of . . .	If you've had a gain of . . .	it only takes loss of . . .
70%	233% to break even.	82%	45% to break even.

it worth $8000. You practically *twitch* with excitement. You believe you have The Gift. (I know: I've been there; done that!)

Then SuperFly gets swatted for a 40 percent loss. Well, at least you're still up 20 percent, right? Wrong! All you've got now is $4800. (Check the math for yourself.) My point is simple: Gains are only as big as they sound. Losses are even more painful than they sound.

So be a maverick. *Avoid losses.*

THE UPSIDE OF DOWN CYCLES

I've discussed the calamities associated with riding a bear all the way down to the valley floor—the double whammy of losing a sizeable portion of capital, and locking what's left up long enough to make itself whole again.

But there's a wonderful, redemptive bright side to down cycles. Those who don't participate in them can still participate in the huge advances that always follow down cycles. In fact, they can participate *more,* and more confidently, because they protected their capital the whole time that the bear was growling.

But to do this, you must be prepared to *sell,* at the right time. In the chapters ahead, you'll learn and practice three habits that will form the basis for your sell discipline. These include, for example, preset stop-losses—in other words, lines in the dirt that clearly identify how much you're willing to give back before selling. They include the use of benchmark trendlines for determining when to stand aside. Finally, your sell strategy will involve rotating out of weak positions into positions of strength.

So let's turn our attention to the first of these three habits—the stop-loss strategy.

13

Stop-Loss Strategy: Locking in Profits, Setting Up New Buys

Have you ever wished you could get into the stock market with *all* of your money—and not have to spend time worrying about how much you have at stake? Do you ever long for some kind of simple safety net that could get you out of stocks before they plummet? Do you want to reduce risk, and still supercharge your returns with aggressive growth picks?

Well, you *can* accomplish all these things—with less risk, and less worry. The way to do so is to adopt a *stop-loss strategy*.

What's a stop-loss? Simply put, it's a preset limit, expressed in percentage terms, of what you're willing to give back on your unrealized gains or on your original investment.

Naturally, we all want to sell at the highest point. But we mavericks know that it's impossible to predict when the absolute market peak has been reached. We also know that until you sell, you haven't actually locked in a profit. Unrealized gains are just that: unrealized. They can get away from you.

A preset stop-loss not only cuts your losses; it also allows you to realize your profits, as close to the market high as possible. The approach draws a line, affording you the opportunity to get out of the game after giving up only a (small) predetermined amount, and locking in your gains. For example: Let's say your aggressive growth fund runs for an impressive 60 percent gain over a given 18-month span. Let's also say that you've said that you don't want to give up more than 12 percent. If and when your fund loses 12 percent of its value, you move to the sidelines.

Couldn't you just let it ride? Well, sure you could—but at unnecessarily high levels of risk. For example, Robertson Stephens Emerging Growth fund was up in 182 percent in 1999, then another 40 percent in the first quarter of 2001. Then during the bear market from March 31, 2000, until April 1, 2001, the fund lost 67 percent. If you stayed for this whole ride, you gave back all of your gains.

Remember, you're investing every one of your hard-earned investment dollars into stocks. You need to guard against the downside associated with a major bear market.

KEEPING THE WEALTH YOU CREATE

What are the two most important aspects of managing your own portfolio? First, making your money grow at an aggressive rate that's right for you (I choose 20 percent). Second, and just as important, *protecting the money you create.*

If your plan is to be passive—to ride out every storm, to never execute a sell order—then you don't really *have* a plan. Without a plan, you are an Average Joe, and you shouldn't expect much more than the historical average return on stocks, or about 10 to 12 percent annually. But beware. Even that expectation may be unreasonable, if you don't take the necessary steps to protect yourself from an extended downtrend or extremely poor investment choices.

We've talked about the reluctance many people feel toward selling. Despite the clear-cut advantages of selling in certain market circumstances, many people elect to ride out the storms. What's *your* excuse? Taxes? A reluctance to admit that you made a mistake, somewhere back there in the past? A dread of telling Uncle Stanley that his great investment tip was, in fact, a turkey? (You name it; I've heard it.) Excuses don't cut it. When you don't actively safeguard your assets, eventually you're going to get burned.

Here are three compelling reasons *not* to ride out stock market storms:

1. The stock market doesn't always rebound quickly. It may take a very, very long time for you to get back to where you started. For example, from 1965 to 1980, the Dow Jones Industrials went nowhere. Actually, *less* than nowhere. The Dow ended 1965 at a reading of 970, and 15 years later it finished at 964. The market won't be particularly interested that your kid needs that tuition paid this fall, or that you were planning on retiring in two years. Hey—welcome to the dark side of buy'n'hold.

2. You've got the whole thing at stake. If Doug's going to mouth off about striving for 100 percent stock allocation, then Doug has to state clearly how to manage risks inherent in that strategy. You can't build wealth without putting all your assets to work. You can't *protect* wealth without taking prudent precautions.

3. You keep the wealth you create. I want you out of the market well before the bear comes knocking on the door. But I certainly want you out before you lose most of your gains, or—God forbid!—your original stake. Protect your principal; lock in your profits. *Enjoy* your newfound options. Reevaluate the field, expand your horizons, and get into something that's sweeter.

ADVANTAGES OF A MAVERICK SAFETY NET

The stop-loss approach is a safety net for the fully invested maverick. It's not a perfect methodology. At times, you'll sell and you'll wish you hadn't. Other times, when the gain turns out to be small, you may feel like the stop-loss action was hardly worth the effort.

The advantages far outweigh the negatives, however—particularly when it comes to new opportunity. Any time you sell a position, you're a "free agent" again. You're in a position to evaluate all of your choices and to select the better opportunity.

Here are the biggest advantages of using stop-losses as part of your investing lifestyle:

1. A simple, unemotional discipline. Greed and fear can break your financial bones, but a stop-loss will never hurt you. That's because it is purely technical. There's no emotional stake on your part whatsoever. You let your profits run as the position soars to new heights; you say goodbye and cut the cord at the exact moment your investment hits its predetermined sell point.

It can be a mental discipline, where your online tracking system alerts you to pay attention. Then you can determine your final exit strategy. The easiest thing to do in investing is to lose money. Mental stop-losses alert you, and finalize when you're going to sell. And with individual stocks, you can even put in place standing stop-losses in the "sell" field of your online trading account. When that stock hits the predetermined floor, it's *gone.*

2. A legitimate risk-reducer. If the market is heading a certain distance south, you can't afford to chase "falling knives." Eventually, the assumption that the selling pressure will end proves foolish. This is especially true in a bear market. Remember that every bear begins with a minor correction of 10 percent. Then once the bear starts charging, the 20, 30, and 40 percent losses build up fast. If we are going to play the game, we must hold on to the majority of our chips to play another day. In fact, when first taking a stock position, your initial goal is risk reduction (a.k.a. capital preservation). The longer you're in, however, the more flexible you can be to move the stop-loss up with the price of the equity. That way, you lock up profit as well as preserve principal.

3. A focus on strategy.   You know when to sell before you even buy. No emotions, no uncertainty.

Remember, smart generals seek battles only after they have tipped the balance in their own favor (or when they simply have no other choice). When you "sell before you buy"—in other words, when you know going in when you'll be going out—you have already assured your investment success, or at least your survival.

4. Out of poor performers, and into great performers.   Owning an investment that is imploding never bothers me—for long. That's because I don't own it for long. Because my stop-losses are in place, I know that as soon as the evidence of underachievement becomes clear, I will *act*. I will sell the mule, and go buy a thoroughbred.

Would you invest with a fund manager who freely admits that 60 percent of his trades are losing propositions? Probably not. But what if I told you that this individual's five-year track record puts his funds in the top 3 percent of all stock funds? *Then* would you take another look?

Without naming names, this highly successful fund manager understands the importance of selling. He doesn't sit on sagging investments out of a misplaced sense of pride, watching his gains (and then his original investment) getting eaten away. Instead, he uses the equivalent of a stop-loss. He *bails*. He thinks of selling not only as a way to cut losses, but also as the way to create the ability to buy something better—something that's likely to generate substantial profits for the investors he represents.

That's how I want you to think.

SETTING THE STOP-LOSS
Here's a note that arrived in my e-mail box recently:

> Doug, it seems the markets jump by 2 percent to 3 percent on a daily basis. With that kind of volatility, I'm afraid I'll get stopped out of my stocks and my sector funds too quickly. How can I choose an appropriate stop-loss for my investments?

Of course, I like the general direction of Doug's thinking. He buys into the idea of stop-losses, but worries about losing out when market volatility triggers his stop-losses prematurely. But let me back up a stop, and look at two of the assumptions that lie behind Doug's questions, both of which strike me as incorrect. The first is that stop-losses are the same for everybody (they aren't.) And the second is that they're the same for every type of investment (again, they aren't).

In fact, these are very personal decisions—decisions that *you* have to make. How much can you afford to lose? If you already have considerable gains on an investment, what percentage of those gains will you give up? If you're just going in, how much of your principal are you prepared to lose? For instance, if you put $10,000 into a stock fund today, could you live with it going down to $9000 (a 10 percent drop), $8500 (15 percent), or $8000 (20 percent)?

We're really talking about your tolerance level, here: if you're losing sleep at a 20 percent loss, then you've gone beyond your tolerance level. Remember: Mavericks don't lose sleep over money (life is too short).

Once you gauge your tolerance level, you'll want to consider the nature of the investment itself. For conservative to moderate growth funds, you might be looking at a stop-loss range of between 8 and 12 percent. For sectors like financial services or tech-laden aggressive growth funds, you'd need greater leeway, perhaps in the 10 to 15 percent range. And for individual equities, I recommend a range of between 15 and 20 percent.

STOP-LOSS TRADING IN ACTION

A member of the maverick community told me this happy story in April 2000:

> Doug, I had half of my entire 401(k) allocated to an aggressive growth fund. With heavy tech exposure, I felt a 15 percent stop-loss would do the trick—keep me protected, and for the most part keep me fully invested.
> I was up 45 percent from November '99 through March 2000. Then came the tech wreck. I calmly sold when my fund pierced the 15 percent veil, and I locked up a 27 percent profit.
> At first, I worried that I sold at the wrong time. But then I thought about it some more. I already locked up a year's worth of profits and the tech volatility was too scary for my blood. So I shifted those assets to a more moderate growth choice.

Why does a guy like me like a story like that? Easy: It is full of rewarding maverick lessons. This investor learned that even with a relatively high 15 percent stop-loss, the time came to *sell that stuff*. He found that selling didn't feel great—in his case, mostly because he worried that maybe he had gotten out too early—but subsequent events showed the wisdom of his choices. He discovered that following a strategy deliberately (I like his use of the word "calmly"—very maverick) locked in profits, and set him up for the next round of successes. And perhaps most important, he learned that he'd sleep better at night by pursuing a course of moderate growth.

THE SIDE EFFECTS OF STOP-LOSSES

Most medicines have side effects. In some cases, the side effects go away after just a few doses, as your body gets used to this new ingredient in the mix. In other cases, the side effects persist—for a long time, or forever— but the patient persists in using the medicine because it's clear that the advantages of taking it far outweigh the disadvantages.

Stop-losses have several side effects. Before you use a stop-loss, you should understand these side effects, and think about how they might affect someone like you.

1. Selling can make you feel the "blues."   There's something inherently exciting about taking your seat at the blackjack table. *You're in the game!* Getting strapped into your seat on a roller coaster is an even more extreme version of this. You feel *alive.*

And conversely, leaving the table or getting off the roller coaster can create a real sense of letdown. If that experience made me feel really alive— maybe for the first time in weeks or months—what am I going to feel like now? What is there to look forward to, when you're not in the game?

All I can say in response is, (1) these blues are temporary, and (2) these blues are far less painful than the blues you get from blowing your whole stake by staying in too long. You have to learn to *celebrate those gains.* I spent some time one night at a casino (not a usual hangout for me, I should say). I was with a friend, who soon found himself up $300 at the blackjack table. Then he hit a rough patch, and went down $75. He looked at me, I looked at him, and he walked away from the table up $225. As he was cashing in his chips, I was thinking to myself, "Hey—this guy's a natural-born maverick." But then he turned to me with a troubled look on his face and said, "Maybe I should have hung in there. I bet I could have gotten back up to $300." Needless to say, I hustled him out the door, and into the Las Vegas night.

Executing a stop-loss is a lot like cashing in those chips. It's not that you've lost the urge to keep playing. You may even believe that you have the skill or luck to turn things around, recoup your "losses" (did my friend *lose* $75, or *gain* $225?) and keep rolling forward.

My advice is, *Don't.* At least in a casino, you're just playing against a set of known odds. In the market, you're playing against a whole universe of factors, none of which can be affected by you, individually, in the slightest little bit. When the market starts going south, take your winnings to the bank, and learn to feel good about that.

2. You will get stopped out early.   Well, of course you will. There will be plenty of times when you'll hit your stop-loss, you'll sell, and the market will do an immediate about-face. Zoom—up 10 percent in a week! And when this happens, you may be tempted to curse yourself—or maybe me—for being so *cautious.*

If you want to curse me now and then, that's OK. But my advice to you, again, would be, *Get over it!* It's true: You may get stopped out early as much as 30 percent of the time you act. But mavericks are fully invested; therefore, they must reduce risk. A stop-loss is your insurance against the one time out of four that a spade comes up and the position goes into the toilet.

3. The more complex a portfolio, the more complex stop-losses can get.   When you're buying funds at different times, and of different types, it becomes more challenging (especially for new mavericks) to keep track of all this stuff. You might have 12 percent for this sector fund, 10 percent for that diversified stock fund, 15 percent for a blue-chip industrial, and 20 percent for a highly volatile tech play.

My advice to newbies is to keep it as simple as possible. For example: Invest in conservative to moderate growth funds only, and use one stop-loss percentage that is appropriate for this type of diversified mutual fund.

THE THREE STAGES OF STOP-LOSS PROTECTION
If I told you that eight months from today, one of your stock funds would gain 32 percent, would that be cause for celebration? I think you'd say "yes." And if I asked you whether this is a good reason to consider stop-loss protection? Again, your answer should be "yes."

What do I mean by this? Let's say that you buy Fund G at 25 in February, and put a 12 percent stop-loss in place. Fund G moves to 37.5 over the next 8 months—a 50 percent unrealized gain. Then it hits a broad market selloff in mid-October, and drops to 33. That's a 12 percent sag, which triggers your stop-loss, and you sell. (Again, you might be inclined to feel defeated, where in truth, you walked away with a healthy 32 percent gain!)

The stop-loss process has 3 stages.

Stage 1.   Here you focus on the protection of principal. Your primary aim is to avoid a catastrophic loss. For instance, you happen to have bought at a market top, your stock fund drifts more than 12 percent from the price you bought in at, and you get out.

Stage 2.   In contrast to the previous example, your fund heads for higher ground shortly after the buy-in date. So you move your stop loss up with the price movement of your investment. In other words, if your stop loss is 12 percent, you would only sell when the investment drops 12 percent from the highest point reached *after* the date of purchase. This is called a "trailing" stop loss. That sounds a little jargon-y, but if you think about it, the term makes sense: Your stop-loss percentage is trailing along behind your rising investment. Your goal in Stage 2 is to reach a break-even point. Specifically, you want your stock fund to rise far enough that your 12 percent stop-loss cushion guarantees the entire amount of the principal invested.

Stage 3.   Now your trailing stop-loss is working toward pure profit. Your goal here is to protect the asset base, including gains. So if your fund steadily rises 35 percent over the course of a year, then sells off 12 percent, you're going to lock in at least 20 percent.

Although 20 percent may not sound like an enormous victory after seeing your portfolio rise 35 percent, it beats the heck out of the alternative, which in many cases is watching all of your gains evaporate. What's more, as I've said many times already, as long as there is strength in some aspect of the market, mavericks can put their money back to work in a brand new opportunity.

OUT OF THE DARK, INTO THE LIGHT
Colin had this to say about stop-loss protection and shares of the Nasdaq 100:

> I really like the philosophy of setting stop-loss percentages for my investments. Right now, however, I'm in a bit of a bind.
> When I bought my QQQ shares at 70, they quickly rose to 120—a staggering 70 percent jump. It then fell to 102 in the recent selloff and I sold. I had reached my 15 percent stop-loss.
> My question is, how do I know when and where to get back in?

Colin, listen carefully: You're already a winner. Because you got stopped out of your QQQ position, you have brand-new money to invest. You're not tied to the Triple Qs, or anything like them. In fact, you're likely to find stronger short-term strength in a sector of the market other than technology. (This is called *rotating up,* a buy methodology discussed in Chapter 15: Selecting the Maverick Way.)

In most cases, you are going to rotate up to a stock or stock fund showing stronger near-term strength than the position you left behind. However, if you choose to deal with the same exact investment, consider a preset percentage that you'd be willing to buy back in at.

This works like the stop-loss in reverse. For example, you'd wait for your prospective investment to rise 15 percent from the low point it reached from the date of your sell. So if the QQQs fell to 96 from 102, then climbed 15 percent to 110, Colin would buy the QQQs once again.

STOP-LOSSES WITH INCREMENTAL PURCHASING

Beads of sweat, rapid beating of the heart, lightheadedness, shaky fingers: These are the warning signs of stock-market queasiness.

I learn a lot from my radio-show callers. One thing I'm constantly reminded of is that while everybody's story is unique, there are a number of underlying themes that are pretty constant. One theme that is constant is anxiety. A lot of people—especially newbies and those who've been hurt by the market in the past—are extremely gun-shy. Buying makes them queasy. Unfortunately, so does *not* buying. What to do?

To those of you who have yet to stick your big toe in the water, and also to those who've experienced a bear attack, I offer a solution called *incremental purchasing*. Here's how it works: You start at some sort of home base, such as a money-market fund. You divide your available investment stake into three equal parts, and then invest the first third in stocks.

Welcome back to the game! But now what? If the market tanks, you lose ground, but at least you will have protected the majority of your assets in those money accounts.

Let's say, though, that your new investments go up by 5 percent. It's time to put another third of your original stake in. After you've done that, you're now 66 percent invested. Once again, following my incremental purchase approach, you wait for your second investment to rise 5 percent. When that occurs, you'll invest the final increment to achieve a 100 percent stock allocation.

Many people like the simplicity of incremental purchasing, but wonder how to employ stop-loss protection at the same time. Mario from Montauk Point writes:

> Doug, my first increment is up 7.49 percent, the second is up 1.21 percent, and the third is down 5.05 percent. I wanted to implement a stop loss at 10 percent, but I'm not sure how to do it. Do I regard these as a single investment, or as separate investments?

Ideally, you'd begin using your stop loss at the time of your first incre-ment. In this case, Mario would have had a 10 percent stop loss protecting the initial increment. Once his stock had moved high enough up to invest a second one-third of the pie, he'd regard the price received for the second one-third as the purchase date for his 10 percent stop loss. With everything in the stock market, the stop loss is set 10 percent off the high reached by the third and final increment.

IT'S NOT DOLLAR-COST AVERAGING!

Some people confuse periodic investing—a totally unmaverick way of par-ticipating in the stock market—with incremental purchasing. Periodic investing is simply putting a set amount of money on a regular basis, say $200 a month, into an investment account.

That's not what I'm talking about. What I'm talking about is a method of risk-reduction that requires the market to continue trending higher *before* additional increments are placed into action. Don't buy a ticket on a sinking ship!

Is periodic investing a method for reducing stock market risk? Wall Street wants you to think so. They've even developed a special name to tart it up a little bit, calling the gimmick "dollar-cost averaging."

The idea is that if you make steady purchases such as $200 a month, you'll get some shares at a high price, some at a low price, and some at a fair, or average price. This way, as the theory goes, you'll do better than if you randomly pick and choose your spots to get in. If you think my sum-mary may be unfair, look in the front of almost any quarterly statement from your mutual fund. It's almost always there, prominently displayed: "the wisdom of dollar-cost averaging," or some variation of that phrase.

If bears never came to the picnic table, if dandelions never took root in rose gardens, maybe dollar-cost averaging would be just as wonderful as its proponents claim. But think about it: If you persist in pumping dollars into a stock investment that has gone sour—either one that keeps declining, or one that just bumps along on the bottom of the ocean floor for months or years—you're doing nothing more brilliant than throwing good money after bad.

In the real world, some stocks and some stock funds *never* come back from the destruction caused from a bear. Or by the time they do, they've made you waste a decade of opportunity.

Consider the one-time largest company in the world, IBM. Between its peak in 1987 and its trough in 1994, the once bulletproof Big Blue lost a whopping *60 percent* of its value. It then began compounding at an annual rate of 42 percent for the next five years—by any measure, an astounding comeback. But for those believers who stuck it out through in the late 1980s and early 1990s, it took more than a decade just to get back to even.

There will always be at least *some* good examples of dollar-cost averaging over time, with solid stock funds or indexes. But mavericks fight the urge to go on autopilot for three reasons. First, we have a goal of extraordinary growth. You can't get 20 percent doing dollar-cost averaging. Second, what if you hit the bear, react badly, and finally give up on stocks because you can't take losing money year after year? And finally, what if you choose a bad fund or stock to dollar-cost average into? Mavericks seek wealth a different way.

TRACKING STOP-LOSSES ON THE WEB

Many investors experience difficulty implementing a stop-loss approach with pencils, paper, and Post-its. The good news is that there is excellent technology available to help you get the stop-loss job done. So find that technology, and use it. Do all the dirty work online.

You can track your portfolio at scores of investment sites, including (for example) Yahoo! Finance. There, they let you put in a lower limit—a preset price at which you want to sell your stock or stock fund. And here's the cool part: you can set it up so that your online provider *alerts you when a stop-loss has been hit.* This is exactly the kind of stuff that the Net and the Web were invented for. Take advantage of it.

I also recommend the use of charts. Most people (including me) can grasp a *picture* of numbers better than they can grasp the numbers behind the picture. At BigCharts.com, for example, you can plug in a trailing stop-loss so it appears on your screen right atop the investment you're tracking. (Think of it as a little conscience, floating up there.) Another thing to remember is that it's simple to change the parameters for a trailing stop-loss, and then see the resulting change on a chart.

Get the point, here? There's simply no better way to succeed in the twenty-first century than to track your portfolio online. In the next chapter, I'll profile the ups, downs, ins, and outs of portfolio tracking—both online and off.

14

Monitoring the Market, Tracking Your Portfolio, and Examining Your Options

D o you ever wonder if your portfolio picks are performing as well as they should be?

Are your investment statements more confusing than your long-distance phone bills?

Have you grown accustomed to puzzling over dollar totals in your accounts, wondering where they come from, and never really knowing whether you're doing well or not?

Mavericks don't settle for confusion. Mavericks *measure* their success, on a regular basis. We monitor the big-time benchmarks—the Dow, the S&P, the Nasdaq—once a week. We do a quick checkup on our portfolio positions monthly. And we carefully examine investment opportunities each quarter.

Strangely enough, Wall Street doesn't *want* you to evaluate your success. They'd prefer that you buy their products without a fuss. But why would that be? Isn't an informed customer always the best one, when someone is selling a great product or service?

I think so. When you're able to measure the success of the products and services that investment firms offer—when you can identify how your holdings, as managed by them, stack up against other products and the market at large—you get the clear picture you need in order to know where to invest.

In this chapter, you will learn everything you need to know about monitoring, tracking, and securing your success. I'll show you what resources you need at your side, the steps you need to take, and when to take those steps. I show you how to make measuring your performance part of your (maverick) investment lifestyle.

GO WEST, YOUNG MAVERICK
If you decided to drive cross-country—let's say, from New York to California—I bet you'd do more than just chuck a few pairs of socks into the back of your PT Cruiser. I bet you'd lay out some kind of time horizon—say, seven days. You'd identify various milestones, tour stops, and preferred routes beforehand. You'd get an up-to-date roadmap and charge up your cell phone. And once underway, if you found yourself getting off schedule, you'd probably make the necessary adjustments.

In this scenario, I'm assuming that you have a goal that you're trying to achieve—getting from here to there—within a set period of time. Of course, *lots* of cross-country trips get made without any kind of goal in mind, and every good life includes a healthy dose of spontaneity. But if you have an audition for a major movie role in Hollywood—if you've got dreams that you can taste, smell, and touch—you're not about to take an impromptu detour south for say, a three-day Mardi Gras party in New Orleans.

Investing is about achieving dreams. To win, you have to plan your financial trip, and you have to evaluate your progress along the way. There's simply no other way to get there.

What kind of planning am I talking about? Is this necessarily a huge commitment—a marathon of introspection and self-scrutiny? No, not necessarily. Maybe the best way to answer the question, and to introduce the larger topic of planning, is to give an actual example provided to me by the husband in a husband-and-wife team—both 35 years old—who put it together in this fashion:

Ultimate purpose(s):   The wealth to put my two children through college, own a home overlooking Lake Tahoe, spend leisure time with my wife on the ski slopes, and learn more about carpentry.

Goal: $4.7 million

Time horizon: 20 years

Net worth in 401(k)s, IRAs, other accounts: $75,000

Future contributions by self and spouse: $10,000 annually

Milestones at 20 percent growth:

5 years: $261,000

10 years: $724,000

15 years: $1.9 million

20 years: $4.7 million

Is this a plan? Yes—and an excellent one, at that. Now let's look at the reasons why a great plan is an indispensable tool.

FIVE REASONS TO EVALUATE YOUR PROGRESS

Some wise individual once said, "if you don't know where you're going, any road will do."

He's exactly right. I think there's a corollary idea, too: It feels good to know that you're on the right road. Think back to the last time that you were been lost, out on some dark highway somewhere, and out of the darkness popped a road sign telling you that you were exactly where you wanted to be. Well, that's what progress-tracking is about, except you don't have to go through the getting-lost part.

And switching to a gardening metaphor: Keeping an eye on your garden's progress is very satisfying and productive. You get to enjoy watching those sprouts push up through the ground. You get to take the weeds out before they can cause much trouble.

Here are five good reasons why you absolutely, positively *must* evaluate your investment activity on a regular basis:

1. Awareness means fewer mistakes.   Mavericks look to the big-time benchmarks (Dow, S&P 500, Nasdaq, Russell 2000) weekly to see which segments of the market are trending higher and which are trending lower. As a result, we're less likely to be caught off guard by a major downslide.

2. Awareness means new opportunities.   Let's say that you're monitoring the Russell 2000 and discover that, after months of turmoil, small-caps are heating up. By staying on top of the cyclical activity of this index, you can move money into a small-cap growth stock or stock fund with greater confidence.

3. Evaluation reveals what's working and what's not.   For example, resources such as Yahoo! Finance give you the ability to track your portfolio online. No number crunching. No paper shuffling. You can track exactly how well your investments are faring, relative to peer-group averages, the big-time benchmarks, and your quarterly growth target of 5 percent. (Remember: I'm using 5 percent quarterly, and 20 percent annually, as representative maverick goals. You may choose to shoot higher or lower.)

4. It confirms that you're on target for 20 percent.   The maverick growth goal is not lazy, hazy, or halfhearted. When you carry out your quarterly review, you'll look to see if your total portfolio achieved 5 percent. You'll see which of your holdings accounted for the most gains, and which are dragging performance down.

5. Evaluation drives the buy, sell, and hold decisions.   Mavericks eliminate emotions and predictions from trading. How? We use trend charts and performance percentages—objective, unemotional, tangible evidence—to decide when and what to buy, sell, or hold.

AVOIDING OVERKILL

Being a maverick means being aware of how well your money performs. But some people take tracking their portfolio to unnecessary extremes.

Salvador from El Monte writes:

> Doug, I look at my portfolio every day and I know exactly what I have in my account at all times. I'm not just on top of my investments, I live them!

Constant checking of one's dollar worth gets people into trouble. Why? Well, aside from the fact that there's a whole lot more to life than money, an excessive focus on day-day-day results is too often tied to greed (I'm not sure whether the greed causes the obsession, or vice versa, but it doesn't really matter). Greed is bad because it often overrides common sense. Worse yet, greed investors tend to jump out of stocks at the worst possible moments—that is, at the very bottom of the market floor.

Don't let dollar signs seduce you. Mavericks focus on a compounding rate of return—examining percentage gains and losses on a monthly basis. You do this the same way you'd examine a bill or a bank statement.

Granted, the ease with which the media and the Internet provide us with instantaneous quotes and figures tempts us to visit more frequently (I have an author friend who checks his books' rankings on Amazon.com every day, even though day-to-day changes in those rankings mean little). The key is to avoid getting obsessive. If you understand the relationship between your investments and the big-time benchmarks, and you simply monitor the trends of the market once a week, you'll always know where you stand.

WHY EVALUATE? IT HELPS YOU WITH PLANS B AND C

"The majority of [people] meet with failure because of their lack of persistence in creating new plans to take the place of those which fail."

That's a line written by Napoleon Hill, author of the best-selling wealth-building book of all time, *Think and Grow Rich.* The quotation points toward one of Hill's fundamental tenets: If Plan A ain't working, create and implement Plan B.

Mavericks recognize the importance of having this kind of flexibility. We're ready to sell when a good investment goes bad. And we're prepared to buy when a surprising alternative shows promise.

The evaluation process not only helps us understand the performance of what we've already got, it also makes the discovery of better investments possible. That's why we:

1. Monitor the market weekly
2. Track our portfolios monthly
3. Examine our choices quarterly

RESOURCES, RESOURCES, RESOURCES!

Pagers, cell phones, daily papers, weekly periodicals, the *Journal, Barrons, USA Today,* Yahoo! Finance, CBS Marketwatch, CNNfn, your 401(k) Web site, your online account, Fabian.com—etc., etc., etc. These are just a few of the tools available to keep you in touch with the market, with your personal positions, and with the wide universe of investment options.

How often should you evaluate? A few minutes a week, a half-hour each month, and one or two hours quarterly. You're not looking to overthink and overdo. The idea is to make investing fact-based and systematic. I'd feel terrible if I turned anyone into one of those computer nerds who never gets away from the screen long enough to smell the roses. Monitoring your portfolio doesn't mean that you must make a career out of your money plans—but effective and efficient monitoring can save your life's goals. (Among other things, it can keep the greedies at bay.) The fact is, you're going to be watching the market anyway, so you might as well monitor it in ways that will keep your plan on pace.

ARE YOU AGGRESSIVE, MODERATE, OR CONSERVATIVE GROWTH?

Maverick investors are *growth* investors. They seek rates of return that can only be achieved by aggressively pursuing growth, rather than cautiously preserving capital. In essence, growth investing is the continuous pursuit of an ever-increasing standard of living.

Before you evaluate your portfolio, you'll want to determine what kind of maverick you are. This is not merely "risk tolerance"—which is commonly defined as how much risk can you handle and still sleep well at night. There's more to it than that.

Specifically, you need to take a look at the way you live. For example, if you're a surgeon whose career demands being on-call at a hospital, you do not have the opportunity to trade or implement stop-losses as actively as others. For this reason, you might need to consider moderate or conservative growth.

Similarly, experience plays a part in the type of maverick investor you are. Many early-stage mavericks need to build their confidence up when they're investing 100 percent in equities. Typically, that means a newbie should turn to conservative growth options first.

Are you AG, MG, or CG? It'll depend on:

1. **Your risk tolerance.**   Figure out the stop-losses that will provide you with the necessary levels of comfort.

2. **Your experience level.**   Start conservative, and consider moving toward moderate and aggressive levels.

3. **Yourself.**   Family, career, desire. If there are practical limitations on your time, you might consider more moderate or conservative growth.

BEFORE YOU EVALUATE ANYTHING . . .

Before you evaluate anything, you need to know the characteristics of your investments. Here are five features of your stock or stock mutual funds that are critical to effectively measuring your progress.

1. Is it AG, CG, or MG?   Figure out what you already own. If you do not have any investments at the moment—in other words, if your wealth today is 100 percent in cash—then you can skip this preliminary step. But if you have a hodgepodge of products that you've collected over time, make up a list of what you own, and what type of investments they are. You can determine your current funds' growth orientations by reading their stated objectives. In the case of individual securities, read each company's annual report. What are they saying about their orientation?

2. What are the "drawdown" stats?   "Drawdown" is the amount a stock or stock fund is likely to give back from its high to the end of a cycle. For instance, an aggressive growth fund might rise like gangbusters—at a clip of 40 percent—over an exciting nine-month stretch. But the same fund might have a 20 percent drawdown—give back 20 percent—in the next six scary weeks. How do your investments perform when the market is down?

3. What's the market-cap?   While you usually don't have to worry about confusing distinctions between small-, medium-, and large-caps, you *do* want to know whether your investments deal with small, medium, or large companies. Again, it's important to know what you have so that you can (a) adequately diversify, and (b) understand which of the big-time benchmarks most closely represent your investments. Also, the larger the companies, the more stable the investments' values.

4. Diversification.   This word is perhaps the most abused word in the investment lexicon. For purposes of understanding your stock fund, you simply want to know if it is heavily concentrated in a particular sector, like technology or health care. If it's heavily concentrated, then it's not diverse—for better or worse.

5. Relationship to big-time benchmarks.   When statisticians get cranked up, they tend to start tossing around twenty-dollar words like deviation, variation, and correlation. Rest easy: Although we're interested in statistics, twenty-dollar words aren't important for our purposes. You simply want to understand and be able to read trend lines (which capture statistics over time). For example, does your small-cap move in the same general direction as its big-time benchmark, the Russell 2000? Similarly, does your large-cap travel in the same general direction as the S&P 500—up when the index is up, and down when the index is down? Note my emphasis on *direction*. We're not looking for the same price movement—just movement in the same direction.

Once you know the characteristics of your fund, you'll know which big-time benchmark to check on weekly. You'll know what type of investment should replace an underachiever. You'll also understand how to evaluate your choices quarterly. For instance, if you—a moderate maverick at the Invesco fund family—have new money to put to work, you would investigate all of moderate growth choices at Invesco.

MONITORING THE MARKET WEEKLY

Most weeks, months, even years, the bull is in charge. But every now and again, there's a down cycle for a particular segment of the economy—and sometimes, across the entire stock market.

Mavericks monitor the markets weekly so that we're not caught off guard, or slammed by a protracted bear market. We avoid unpleasant surprises.

How? That's what this chapter has been about. We gather quick snapshots of the big-time benchmarks; we check the price movement of the Dow, Russell, S&P, Nasdaq. We want to know:

- Is this segment of the market still trending higher?
- Is an up-cycle ending and a down-cycle beginning?
- How far are the indexes above or below the trendline?
- What percent did this index rise or fall this week?
- If I'm investing in (for example) aggressive growth, what percent did my stock or stock fund rise or fall this week?

The purpose of weekly monitoring, once again, is to eliminate the possibility of a surprise and to increase our general level of awareness. Wall Street won't like it; advisers advise against it. But mavericks prepare for the possibility of getting stopped out of a position. We also follow the trends to decide whether we'll buy, sell, or hold a particular segment of the market. Just because we check the market weekly doesn't mean that we make changes weekly. In fact, it would take a highly unusual series of circumstances to get me to make changes on a weekly basis. Again, life is short.

TRACKING YOUR HOLDINGS MONTHLY

Have you ever looked at your electric bill and felt that something was out of whack? Did you investigate further? Did you compare the cost to what you had paid in the previous billing cycle? Or maybe with the previous year, in order to take seasonal fluctuations into account?

Tracking your portfolio monthly is a 15-minute exercise designed to let you make sure everything is right with your positions. You're building awareness about (1) the relationship between your fund and its chief benchmark, (2) the percent change in performance, (3) short-term momentum, and (4) progress toward the 20 percent compounding goal.

Here's the process:

Step 1: How are my funds (stocks) doing in relation to their respective benchmarks?   For instance, the Nasdaq moved 4 percent higher in May. Did my tech sector fund move in the same direction?

Step 2: How are my funds (stocks) performing on a percentage basis?   For example, the Dow Industrials moved 1.1 percent higher in November. How did my large-cap value fund do?

Step 3: What evidence do I have concerning near-term momentum?   Mavericks determine short-term strength in terms of 4-, 8-, and 12-week momentum. The question we ask and answer is, "How well is my fund doing over these (or similar time frames)?"

You can get this information in *Investors Business Daily* (IBD), or on a number of Web sites, including fabianlive.com and CBS Marketwatch.

You do this because you simply want to get a feel for recent strength, gauging whether your fund is picking up speed or tapering off. If this is your first month with a position, it is highly unlikely that the information gathered in 30 days would justify making a move. But if it's your third month of underperformance, you might rotate up. (I'll cover the outs and ins of rotation in the next chapter, Selecting the Maverick Way.)

Step 4: What type of progress are you making in relation to your goal of 20 percent annual growth?   For instance, your small-cap growth fund dropped 3 percent in the month of October, while the Russell 2000 grew 1.9 percent. Here, your fund is out of sync with its benchmark, down 3 percent rather than up 2 percent, and it has fallen short of the 1.67 percent monthly target for achieving 20 percent per year.

Again, if this is your first month of ownership, it's too soon to pull the trigger. Nevertheless, you now know that you need to keep an eye on the price movement of your small-cap investment. By the close of a quarter, you may have the ammunition to shoot an underperforming position.

TRACKING YOUR AVAILABLE CHOICES QUARTERLY

If there's one thing that frightens beginning mavericks, it's the perception that they'll have to do homework. But what if that homework required only one hour every three months? What if you knew beyond a shadow of any uncertainty, that single hour would create a lifetime of opportunity and successful financial gain? Would you find the minutes? Of course you would. And you *will*.

Tracking your available choices on a quarterly basis is the backbone behind the milestone. From a strategic perspective, you're determining whether (1) your total portfolio performance is on target for 20 percent growth, (2) you have lemons in your mix, and (3) individual positions are staying the course of 20 percent.

From a more tactical standpoint, you're checking to see (1) how individual positions compare to their peer-group averages, and (2) how alternative choices at your brokerage house performed. Specifically, you will look at those choices that match your growth orientation (AG, MG, or CG).

QUARTERLY STRATEGIC REVIEWS

It only happens four times a year. The quarter closes. The media publish the numbers and in the process create lists of winners and losers. And you get a three-month statement of activity. What do you do about it?

Strategic Move 1:   You want to get the two most recent statements in your hands to make a quick worksheet calculation.

Value of Portfolio at End of Quarter B   _____

Value of Contributions C   _____

Value of Withdrawals D   _____

Value of C – D   _____

Adjusted Value of Portfolio at End of Quarter B   _____

Value of Portfolio at End of Quarter A   _____

Value of B – A/A   _____

Did you get 5 percent growth on your total portfolio? This is the most fundamental question you need to answer. Because in the end, it's all about the scoreboard—it's all about total investment performance.

If your entire portfolio picked up 5 percent in the quarter, then congratulations: You're on track to reach your goals. If not, something has gone sour. That's why you're next move is to check for lemons on the Fabian Lemon List.

Strategic Move 2:   This simple check takes less than a minute on Fabian.com. Simply type in your ticker symbol or fund name to check your mutual fund portfolio. You can also search for lemons by category, like large-cap growth or small-cap value. And you can print out the entire list. In most cases, you will upgrade that lemon immediately. Sell it and seek another choice. Period.

Strategic Move 3:   Checking in on your portfolio also means checking in on the market. You will look at the performance of the big-time benchmarks and the general mutual funds categories. Sometimes the market is flat or slightly lower in a quarter. This may mean you're not on track for this 90-day period, but no action is required. As long as our holdings are performing relatively well to the market and their peer group, we wait it out. Mavericks don't change for the sake of change. We change when change is necessary. Allow the benchmarks to be your tea leaves.

You have your money somewhere: Aim, Dreyfus, Fidelity, Janus, or wherever. And if you pick up any major financial publication, you'll also have the most comprehensive stock fund info on the planet. The trick is to put this info to work in a down-and-dirty quarterly review.

You're going to want to be focused in these quarterly reviews. And by "focused," I mean that you want to concentrate exclusively on the choices that you have within your current brokerage relationship(s). Don't look at those top-10 lists with envious eyes. Don't ruin your eyes poring through those lists of 10,000 different mutual funds. That won't help anything. Stay at home, and stick to your knitting.

For example, if you're at Dreyfus, check out their stock fund choices. Did your specific selection get 5 percent in the quarter, 10 percent in the six-month period, 20 percent in the year, and 20 percent compounded growth across three years? If so, you have a keeper. If not, you have some decisions to make.

Strategic Move 4: At this point, you'll compare your funds to their Lipper peer averages. They may not be lemons, but they may be hopelessly mediocre.

This is the time to ask the question, "Am I getting the performance results that I have a right to expect from this fund company?" If not, take your business elsewhere. If you've found a single tragic holding, however, you'll probably want to keep your account there, and simply upgrade within the fund family.

MAKE THOSE CHANGES

I said it in the beginning of the chapter and I'll say it again now: Maverick investing is about achieving dreams. By planning your financial trip and evaluating your progress as you go, you're able to identify the best investments to own at the best possible time.

In the next chapter, I'll show you exactly how to upgrade from a poor performer to a healthy achiever; I'll teach you the techniques for rotating up to short-term strength. And I'll tell you the secrets necessary for picking winners—straight out of the chute!

PART 4

Maverick Advancement in the World of Investing

15

Selecting Your Investments the Maverick Way

A re you overwhelmed by the thousands of fund choices that show up in newspapers and magazines? Are you picking a little bit of everything, and winding up with too much dead weight? Do you feel like you are constantly selecting the wrong investment, no matter how informed you try to become?

Believe it or not, choosing the winners of tomorrow, on a reasonably consistent basis, is not all that difficult. The trick is to adopt a fruitful investment framework, and apply that framework systematically. Many of us fail in our investments because we succumb to peer pressure and other kinds of persuasion. Officemates, uncles, analysts, accountants: We listen to people who seem to be knowledgeable—even when all the evidence suggests that they're not!

Is it ever wise to act on that hot tip slipped to you at the water cooler? Absolutely—but you're never going to know *which* hot tip is the legitimate item. (Here's an experiment: Track some of those hot tips over the next few months. How many of them turn out to be as hot as they were billed to be?) That's why I say that when it comes to making maverick decisions for your portfolio, you need to hold yourself accountable. You, and you alone, are responsible for your success. You're the overseer, the manager, and the ultimate selector of everything in your pocket. You need to make the picks, and you need to do so in a way that maximizes your chances for success.

WHAT ARE YOU REALLY WILLING TO RISK?

I ran an informal poll at my Web site in the spring of 2000 and asked 850 club members whether they were aggressive, moderate, or conservative mavericks. Maybe you won't be surprised to learn that 95 percent of the respondents reported that they were either aggressive or moderate. Fewer than 5 percent called themselves conservative.

Well, it's human nature for individuals to think of themselves as courageous and adventurous. But when it comes to losing money, most of us are far less bold in real life than in our imaginations.

Think about it. How do you feel when $20,000 becomes $12,000? I'm not talking about giving back gains. I mean how would you feel if your initial investment of $20,000 dropped to $12,000. Can you stomach that kind of downdraft? Are you able to accept a 40 percent loss of your principle in the same spirit as a 40 percent gain—in other words, that it's all part of the high-stakes game you're in?

Consider the first year of the twenty-first century. Tech-focused thrill-seekers watched their portfolios climb 20 percent, 25 percent, even 30 percent from January to mid-March of 2000. Then the Nasdaq nose-dived 40 percent over the next two months, and $20,000 became $12,000!

Can you hang this tough? Should you *have* to?

Understanding your real risk tolerance requires a different kind of focus. It requires that you look at an index or an investment from its high to its low–in other words, from its peak to its trough. Find out how many dollars your account would lose, in the slide from top to bottom, and then ask yourself, "Can I sleep at night with this sort of downside action?"

REVISITING YOUR RISK MAKEUP

Consider this e-mail from Jackie in Louisville:

> Doug,
>
> I'm looking to move into a bigger house in the next three to four months and I need a place to make about $5000 quickly. I'm 35 years old and I have a very high tolerance for risk. Because I am quite aggressive, I'm willing to put $25,000 into a fast-growing stock or fund that is reliable. What stock or fund will get me 20 percent in three months without too much chance of going down?

Oh, my. Like the rest of us, Jackie would like to live in heaven before his time is up on earth. We'd all love an invincible investment–one that fights like a battleship, but won't sink like one. In the beginning of my answer to Jackie, I gently focused him on the question of *risk.* All well and good to call yourself "aggressive," with a "high tolerance for risk." But tolerance for loss can't be measured on the upside; you must determine your risk makeup on the downside.

Consider the Tolerance Chart on the page that follows. If you find that you're *never* ruffled—not by volatile price swings in up or down markets— then you are, indeed, an aggressive growth maverick (AGM). In my experience, *fewer than one in five mavericks* belongs in the aggressive growth category.

If you seem to do well in the face of volatility, as long as the general trend of the market is up, you're a moderate growth maverick (MGM). This category embraces the vast majority of us—able to stomach a choppy market on the upside, yet unable to cope with a crash or a drawn-out bear. A historical footnote: Moderates who invest too aggressively—that is, MGMs who are seduced into acting like AGMs—are the most susceptible to selling in a panic, or selling at a market low.

If you crave peace and calm—if you struggle with upswings, downswings, and sideswings—you're a conservative growth maverick (CGM). Sporting this label doesn't mean that you can't thrive as an investor. It simply means that you're likely to give up a little upside in exchange for avoiding the white waters and rollercoaster rides over your investing career.

Downside Risk (Not Tolerant) ———▶ Downside Risk (Very Tolerant)

Brief Table:

AGC—Tolerance drawdown of 10 to 20 percent

MGM—Tolerance drawdown of 8 to 10 percent

CGM—Tolerance drawdown of 5 to 8 percent

I want to emphasize that regardless of your profile, you should be able to pursue maverick returns (which for me, personally, means 20 percent per year). Those who are more aggressive may have a better shot at generating fantastic returns during exceptional bull runs, but they also risk sub-par performance in other years. Conservative mavericks, by contrast, achieve reliable results that could range from 14 to 17 percent over longer time horizons.

If you're still not sure about your maverick profile, take a look at factors like market experience, personal interest, and career choice. If you're a newbie to investing, if you hate monitoring the market regularly, or if you do not have the chance to track stocks frequently, stick to a conservative growth path. On the other hand, if you've been around the block a few times, remain cucumber-cool in sticky situations, and have easy access to the Internet, stride right through that door labeled "AGM."

UNDERSTANDING FUND CATEGORIES

I've presented this spectrum—conservative to aggressive—because one of your first jobs in selecting investments is to bring your picks into alignment with your own investing profile, as just defined. You're unlikely to develop a new personality to match your funds or individual stocks; therefore, you have to make picks that match your investing personality.

So how do you figure out whether a particular fund is aggressive growth (AG), moderate growth (MG), conservative growth (CG), or—God forbid!—no growth (NG)? Where does the Janus Fund (for example) fit into the mix? How about Invesco Telecom or Vanguard Windsor?

The mutual fund industry created multiple categories that the experts use to distinguish differing fund styles. These are terms like "emerging market," "large-cap core," and so on. You can read the prospectus on your investment to determine its classification. Or you can look up the designation in quarterly reviews by *The Wall Street Journal,* the *Los Angeles Times, Barron's,* and many other financial publications. You can even call your fund family and ask.

Once you know the Lipper classification of the fund, use the following table to determine whether it is AG, MG, or CG:

Aggressive	Moderate	Conservative	Slow Growth
	S&P 500 Index		
Small-cap growth	Large-cap growth	Large-cap value	Balanced
Small-cap growth	Large-cap core	Multi-cap value	Fixed Income
Small-cap core	Multi-cap growth	Mid-cap value	Bonds (11 categories)
Science and tech	Multi-cap core	Small-cap value	
Gold	Mid-cap growth	Equity income fund	
Emerging markets	Mid-cap core		
International Sectors	Global		

In the chart, you can see that all science & tech, small-cap growth, and emerging market funds fall into the Aggressive Growth domain. Conversely, multi-cap value and equity income funds reside in Conservative Growth.

So what about the example previously cited—Invesco Telecom, the Janus Fund, and Vanguard Windsor? Invesco Telecom concentrates in a specific sector, Science & Tech, making it an aggressive growth vehicle. Meanwhile, the Janus Fund is a moderate investment because it focuses on large-cap growth, and Vanguard Windsor goes for large-cap value, giving it a distinctly conservative flavor.

Sometimes my newbie mavericks tell me that this exercise makes them a little uncomfortable. They locate themselves on the risk-tolerance spectrum, and then they examine what they already own and find a mismatch. I reassure them that this is a good and healthy process. It sets you up to make the choices necessary to achieve longer-term success *in your personal comfort zone.* In most cases, it sets you up to make good changes.

For instance, an AGM (aggressive growth maverick) who currently owns Fidelity Magellan might rotate up to a faster-paced product. Similarly, a CGM with QQQs—the exchange-traded funds tracking the tech-heavy Nasdaq 100—should definitely seek out a more cautious path toward his or her long-term objectives. (I might recommend a diversified mutual fund with a higher tech-sector exposure, for example.)

SURVIVAL OF THE FITTEST

Unless you live in a cave, you've probably noticed the hottest turn-of-the-century trend in television—what I call "survival of the fittest TV." Islanders and outbackers in the *Survivor* series weed out the weaker tribe members, one by one, to increase their odds of winning the game. A British import forces a team of contestants to identify and knock off its "weakest link" as the game progresses.

I suggest to mavericks that they apply some of this hard-nosed gamesmanship to their investment choices. Selecting superstar funds involves a process of elimination—knocking off the weakest performers, and investing in those that remain. For instance, here are five steps for choosing a stock fund in your 401(k).

Step 1: Drive out anything that can't achieve 20 percent per year.
   This includes bond funds, balanced bar funds, fixed-income vehicles, and lemons on the Fabian Lemon List. In a typical 16-pack 401(k), there might be three bond funds, three income-related

products, and two lemons. That'll leave you with eight viable candidates.

Step 2: Dismiss anything outside your risk profile.   For instance, if you are a moderate growth maverick, you'll want to avoid aggressive plays, such as sectors, emerging markets, and small-cap tech. You'll also want to bid farewell to conservative value funds that won't have the upside kick you crave. Once again, you've reduced the field significantly, simply by saying goodnight to two aggressives and one conservative. (And then there were five!)

Step 3: Screen out short-term weakness and long-term inconsistency.   Plug in the tickers of your potential picks at your 401(k) administrator's Web site. You'll want to get the three-month and six-month percentage jumps to determine the sharpest gains in the near-term. Plus, if we're in a bull market, you can eliminate those that did not earn 5 percent in the quarter, 10 percent in six months, and 20 percent in the year.

But don't stop there. The near-term is not enough because you also want consistency. The same fund screen will tell you what a fund did over three and five years during bull markets. If it failed to compound at 20 percent in the longer-term, if it underachieved its peer average over those three- and five-year periods, toss it.

Step 4: Reduce the field with "drawdown."   The mainstream media do not provide tools to adequately evaluate downside risk. They tend to provide measures that are either too specific or not specific enough. General Web sites like yahoo! finance sometimes list a single down quarter for a fund. The fairly common "worst three months" stat, for example, might include eight weeks down and five weeks up. (Valuable information may be washed out in that kind of aggregate statistic.) Meanwhile, the equally common "Beta" only gives you price movement relative to an index that is already volatile. (If you're a good math student and understand what "Beta" is, great; otherwise, don't worry about it.) When nothing is pinned down, numbers don't mean much.

Instead, check out a fund's *drawdown*—in other words, the fund's percentage decline from its highest peak to its lowest valley. To do this, get out to BigCharts.com or Quote.com with the three or four funds left on your list. Then measure the funds from the March 2000 high to April 1, 2000—a recent Nasdaq bear period. Get rid of those whose drawdown makes you squirm.

By the end of Step 4, you should only have two or three possibilities left for your portfolio.

Step 5: Assess the 4-, 8-, and 12-week performance.   We've already dumped short-term underperformers, long-term losers, risky products, lemons, anything that can't hit the 20 percent growth goal, and anything that gooses your risk tolerance in an unpleasant way. Now you need the icing on the cheesecake. You want to know what's got *momentum*—what's hot right this second.

To figure that out, you need the 4-, 8-, and 12-week performance numbers. It's difficult to get these numbers, which I call "momentum scores," at conventional Web sites, but you can get momentum scores at fabianlive.com with a Maverick Advisor subscription. You can also use the tables of closing prices at Yahoo! Finance, and compute percentages with your calculator.

These are the "oommph" scores. They represent the sprinters—the funds that are currently running on adrenaline. The one that bolts the fastest is the one you will select.

I'VE SCREENED OUT EVERYTHING!

This five-step "survival of the fittest" approach works for every type of maverick. Consider James in Rockaway.

> I'm fortunate that my 401(k) has more choices than most programs. But I've found myself in a jam. I'm a conservative mav, so I've eliminated tech sector, small-cap growth, and international funds. I've also red-lined two lemons and four bond and fixed-income funds. That leaves me with six choices. Unfortunately, only two of them are conservative and neither one is on track to reach 20 percent annual growth. All I have left are four moderate growth funds, and I'm not sure if they're out of my league. What can I do?

Assuming James is investing in a bona fide uptrend, he can not afford to ignore the progress of the four moderate growth funds. Mavericks must be flexible enough to rotate up or down a risk class when no choices perfectly fit.

In this instance, James needs to screen the four moderate growth funds for: (a) the strongest 4-, 8-, and 12-week numbers, and (b) the "one" fund that gives back the least of its gains in a down cycle (that is, the drawdown). The fund with the lowest drawdown may be the sleep-well-at-night choice that James is looking for.

OUTSIDE THE 401(k)

Rydex, Invesco, T. Rowe, Northern, Firsthand, Slowhand—you may have hundreds or thousands of choices at your fund store. At Schwab, for example, there are more than 1500 no-loads in the databank. How do you pare down such a vast universe?

For starters, don't attempt to evaluate every fund out there. Life is short, and mutual fund lists are long.

Instead, investigate the options at your specific fund family. For example, if you house your stock funds at Janus, you might have two dozen to screen. If you're an Invesco loyalist, you're looking at some fifty alternatives.

If you use a discounter—Schwab, Ameritrade, Fidelity—start by getting rid of entire fund categories. For instance, at the close of the second quarter 2000, 8 of the 15 domestic fund category averages achieved 20 percent annual growth over one, three, and five years. That means seven categories did not, including small-cap value (SCV), flexible portfolio (FX), and multi-cap core (MCC). Eliminate them.

Now you can revisit the criteria in the five-step process:

Step 1: 20 percent potential.   Say no to bonds and lemons.

Step 2: My risk profile.   Eliminate conservative birdies.

Step 3: The short and the long end of my pick.   Ban 5/10/20 offenders and one-, three-, and five-year underachievers.

Step 4: Don't draw me down.   You've got a 45 percent drawdown? Get outta my headlights.

Step 5: Momentum strength.   Those are some pretty sharp-looking 4-, 8-, and 12-week percentages. I think you're the one for me!

SELECTING A WINNER

Rowena from Pasadena writes:

> I'm using the S&P 500 as my large-cap indicator and the current price recently climbed above its trendline. I'd like to commit my remaining cash position to a large-cap fund—one that meets my personal maverick profile (moderate). I'm at Schwab, but the fund screener confuses me; I don't know what criteria to use in my search. Can you help?

Tip 1. Select no-load funds only.   Schwab allows mavericks to separate no-loads (no sales commission) from the load (commission-based) funds. There are few times when you'd ever choose a load fund, and certainly not when you're doing the legwork on your own.

Tip 2. Select funds appropriate for your risk category.   Schwab lets you screen by the type of large-caps—value, blend, or core growth, or all of the above. Since Rowena is a moderate maverick, she would eliminate value-oriented funds that are designed for low-risk, conservative investors. Instead, she would opt for large-cap growth and large-cap blend.

Tip 3. Select all expense ratios and all asset sizes.   Schwab lets you sort by expense ratios and asset size, but I advise against using this feature. Conventional wisdom suggests that low expense ratio funds will benefit you in the long run, or that a small asset base means the fund manager has more flexibility, but there are too many exceptions to these rules. For example, at the end of Q1 2000, as many as 70 percent of the top 20 large-caps and top 20 mid-caps sorted by one-year returns had significantly higher-than-average expense ratios. Rowena therefore should look at funds of *all* expense ratios and asset sizes.

Tip 4. Sort by three-month return.   Schwab lets you sort your performance by three-month return, and also by one-, three-, and five-year performance. While you will want to confirm that your candidate achieved 20 percent over the one-, three-, and five-year time horizons, first sort by the three-month measure. This is roughly equivalent to the 12-week momentum figure discussed earlier.

Tip 5. Show the Top 10.   For example: "Display the top 10 large-caps with a growth and blend style." Reviewing more than 10 is unnecessary.

If Rowena ran this fund screen in May of 2000, she'd want to make a decision between funds like White Oak Growth (WOGSX), with three-month, one-year, and five-year returns of 15.84, 56.92, and 40.26 percent, respectively; and Babson Growth (BABSX), with corresponding percentages of 14.32, 25.3, and 23.4. As a moderate, Rowena might prefer the lower drawdown of Babson Growth.

Please note that we were able to use Schwab's online screening tool to perform the five maverick steps outlined earlier. Why is that important? Because providing good tools ought to put a discounter like Schwab at the top of your short list of potential brokerage house providers.

One of your objectives as a maverick is to locate a Web site that lets you search by asset class (stock, bond, cash), fund style (growth, value, combo), short-term performance (momentum), long-term performance (one-, three-, and five-year numbers) and risk (drawdown). These are the elements of a successful fund screen, and they are good evidence of a solid, service-oriented provider. When you find such a provider, think about giving them your business.

BONUS: MAVERICKS DO IT DIFFERENTLY

Are you relying on stars, bells, and high marks to pick your mutual funds? (If you're not, forget I mentioned it!) Do you listen to columnists who tend to drone on about the importance of choosing a tax-efficient fund? Have you been sold on the idea of low turnover? Low expense ratios?

Forget all that stuff. The truth of the maverick matter is, *we do this selecting thing differently.* We don't pay attention to ratings, because performance and risk are rarely measured in the right way. We don't look for low turnover or low expenses, because the evidence simply doesn't support those approaches. And for the most part, we aren't even hung up on tax efficiency. That's because maverick investors focus their wealth efforts in tax-deferred accounts—where, of course, the efficiency concept is irrelevant.

What do mavericks do? We address performance, cost, and risk directly in the fund-screening process. We define and act on our personal risk-tolerance profile. We use drawdown to gauge a stock fund's downside danger. We use one-, three-, and five-year figures to look at long-term consistency. And finally, we factor in 4-, 8-, and 12-week momentum figures to assess the here and now.

HOW MANY FUNDS DO I NEED?

Are you one of those innocent souls who believes that the more funds you have, the better diversified you are? Have you come to accept the idea that stocks are for trading, whereas mutual funds are for holding? Are you a collector, rather than a mutual fund investor?

One prevailing approach, often cultivated by Wall Street, is to hoard a variety of mutual funds. Over time, you pick up a piece of the S&P 500, and a tech-sector play, and a little bit of the Dow, and a parcel of Europe, and a real estate trust, and a couple of mid-cap blends, a small-cap value, and a partridge in a money tree. Ugh! This is diversification—and of course, buy'n'hold—run amok.

You don't need to go this route. One of the key benefits of a mutual fund is that, as a basket of stocks, it *already diversifies.* What's more, mavericks manage downside risk by knowing when to sell, rather than by owning every type of asset or asset class.

Granted, few people are willing to put millions of dollars into a single mutual fund. But I've known millionaires to do just fine with just three or four.

Here's my rule of thumb: a maximum of two positions for a total investment of $15,000, three for less than $50,000, four for less than $100,000, and between five and seven for less than $1,000,000. There's nothing magic about the number "seven." But in my experience, with seven funds, you can diversify clear across the spectrum. Anything more is very likely to result in overlap.

Remember, *simplicity is a virtue,* in life and investing. The more complicated you make your investing—the more positions you end up tracking—the less likely you are to stick with it. So don't get caught in the hype over the wisdom of diversification. You only need so much of it.

ROTATING UP OR OUT: MAXIMIZING YOUR MID-CYCLE BUYING POWER

On November 17, 1999, in the midst of the hot and (as it turned out) over-hyped Y2K environment, I recommended a Buy on domestic mutual funds and exchange-traded funds. In my list of recs for taxable accounts, I included the large-cap Spiders (SPY).

Three months later, on February 18, 2000, I reevaluated my recommendation. There were other areas of the market performing exceptionally well—areas outside the S&P 500 that were on target to achieve 20 percent annual growth.

As part of my three-month portfolio checkup, I advised clients to sell positions with less than 5 percent growth and rotate up to new strength. By repositioning assets out of the Spiders (SPYs) and into vehicles with stronger growth patterns, my clients were able to kick their portfolios into higher gears.

Stay in touch, and when the opportunity presents itself, *rotate.* Move up. If after three months, you discover a better place for your money—one that is in line with your risk profile—go for it. That's what rotating up is all about!

Another tidbit? Never trade from a position of strength to the highest flyer. In other words, if you earned 5 percent in a quarter, HOLD!

NO MAVERICK GUTS, NO GLORY

What does it mean to be maverick selector? It means doing the unexpected—bucking traditional wisdom with eyes and arms wide open.

Consider Chaz's Fund X experience:

I'm not sure if I should rotate up or not. I have Mid-Cap Growth Fund X. It lost 8 percent in Q2 and is down 2 percent on the year. That's much worse than the average mid-cap growth fund that gained 10.6 percent in Q2. But Fund X is still outpacing the Nasdaq. Isn't that a good sign?

Chaz is comparing pineapples and strawberries. The Nasdaq may be an appropriate benchmark for Science & Tech sector funds, but it is not the yardstick for large-cap value, small-cap core, or, in Chaz's case, Mid-Cap Growth Fund X.

Chaz has to rotate up or rotate out. He can rotate up to an investment that earned 5 percent in Q2, 10 percent year-to-date, and 20 percent over the last 12 months. Or, he can rotate out—that is, raise cash, and be primed for the next great uptrend to emerge.

What if there isn't a suitable mid-cap growth replacement? Then Chaz has several alternatives. He might rotate up to a fund in a higher risk class—one that achieved 5 percent over the last 13 weeks and 20 percent over the year. (Remember that for a given individual, popping up a level may involve an uncomfortable jump in risk.)

A second option is equally viable: rotate out. Chaz can raise cash for a "blue-light special" further down the maverick road.

As I've noted in earlier chapters, cash is not the place to build wealth long-term. Yet there's something exceptionally pure and soothing about having 100 percent of your nest egg in your money market account in stormy weather. When significant market barometers sink beneath their trendlines or struggle to stay atop of them, cash is a wonderful place to wait.

Rotate up or out? Think of it like this: Rotate up to get your money to grow, rotate out so you don't lose the money you already have.

THE W's OF ROTATION (AND THE H!)

It's like the reporters in those B movies from the 1930s used to say: Who, What, When, Where, Why, and How. That's all you need to remember, whether you're thinking about newspapering or about rotation.

Who?   You. Because you're a maverick. Because you choose a more fulfilling, smarter, less traveled road.

What?   Rotating out of an underachiever.

When?   Whenever you've given adequate time for an investment to deliver. Three to six months is adequate.

Where?   At your fund family. But if you need to go to another family to achieve satisfactory results, whether you have service concerns or product concerns, *just do it.* Do what's right for your future wealth.

Why rotate? To manage risk. For example, consider the situation in which tech, large-cap growth, and small-cap growth all experience three months of downward pressure. In all likelihood, there would *not* be an opportunity in this climate to rotate up to an aggressive growth fund. On the other hand, you might find a less risky value play that is conservatively achieving its compounding targets.

Another reason to rotate involves goal achievement. When you're rotating up a risk class, you may be increasing some exposure to downside danger. But you're also minimizing the risk of lost opportunity as you pursue maverick returns.

How?   Transfer assets to your money market account, or transfer them directly into your chosen upgrade. If you go the money market route first, and want to slowly allocate to a new stock fund vehicle, you can purchase incrementally.

For instance, if you're concerned about excessive market volatility, do what I do with "new" money: Use the incremental purchasing plan described in an earlier chapter. I place one-third in the vehicle of choice. I wait for it to rise 5 percent before committing the second third. And I wait for the fund to rise 5 percent more before adding the last third.

But be mindful! When you rotate up to near-term strength in a riskier asset class, you must implement a stop-loss; that is, before you buy, choose a preset percentage "sell" point off the high.

CAN YOU CONCLUDE THIS?

There are scores of lessons that a maverick needs to take home on fund selection. Here's my roundup:

1. **To thine own self be true.**   You gotta know who you are and what you're about when it comes to genuine tolerance for risk.
2. **Make your investments make sense.**   See to it that your stock funds match your growth profile—aggressive, moderate, or conservative.
3. **Make selection fun.**   Don't let the process bore you. (If you do, you'll start avoiding it like you avoid that boring coworker.) Think of

it as a personal quest to acquire your first million. Regard the activity as a survivor challenge—determining which fund will make the final cut. Gain some insight, flush the weak, and smoke out the fittest fund of them all.

4. **Be willing to step apart from the buy'n'hold herd.**   Mavericks like the idea of upgrades and rotating up. We're not dissuaded by the prospect of the occasional bad pick. Why not? Because we know that if we need to sell—if we need to pursue a new opportunity—we will!

   Selling, in fact, is your secret weapon against mediocrity. In the next chapter, we will talk about trending—the third tool in your sell strategy arsenal.

16

Trending to Wealth

Did you ever wish there were a simple way to know whether to be in or out of the stock market? Do you find yourself jumping in at the highs and dropping out at the lows? Do you sometimes feel that you can't sell—that the only way to participate is to hold a stock or a fund forever?

If there's one thing Wall Street won't ever tell you, it's when to sell. Mutual fund companies want to keep your assets "in-house." Financial advisers want the ongoing revenue stream from fees. Analysts won't risk losing access to a company by suggesting that you dump its shares, let alone risk losing their jobs. And the media covet the advertising dollars from investment firms, banks, and brokerages.

Mavericks understand the reasons why the Street works against the Sale. More important, we recognize the benefits of knowing when it's time to sell—when it's time to walk away, even run, from the table.

For example, if you want to avoid unnecessary losses, you need to know when large-cap value stocks are heading into a down cycle. Similarly, if you want to rotate your money into near-term strength, you need to know when small-cap growth is breaking out of a downtrend and into an uptrend.

Mavericks know when to get into or out of specific asset categories. Knowing when to say when—on the buy side and the sell side—is a key to:

1. Capturing fresh opportunities
2. Managing downside risk
3. Extending upside gains

SELLING IS FOR WINNERS

When's the last time a major publication ran a headline, "10 Stocks That Underperform," or, "Why These 400 Mutual Funds Will Ruin Your Retirement Plans." It just doesn't happen.

We can blame Street injustice for part of the buy-side bias. Just to recap my point from an earlier chapter: Of the 33,169 buy, sell, and hold recommendations across 6000 stocks in 1999, professional analysts uttered the word "sell" a scant 125 times. That's less than 0.3 percent! When the ordinary investor never hears the word "sell," he or she tends to think "buy'n'hold."

Yet the maverick mindset must be stronger than that of the herd-follower. Whereas Joe Ordinary thinks of selling as an admission of failure or the front porch to a tax hit, a maverick looks to put new money to work in a better performing asset or fund.

In fact, it's not the number of losses versus the number of gains that separate the winners from the losers; it's the quality, or size, of the gains. It's the ability to grow your portfolio at 20 percent per year.

TIMING IS EVERYTHING

How often have you heard the expression, "Timing is everything"? It permeates every aspect of our culture, from the success of a business venture to a great tennis serve to the effectiveness of a comedian's punch line. And yet, the mutual fund and financial services industries have gone to great lengths to discourage us from "timing the market." For example:

1. Schwab and Fidelity raised their "holding periods" from three months to six months immediately following the bear scare of 1998. What does this mean? It means that if you don't hold your mutual fund for six months, the big discounters slap you with an early withdrawal fee.
2. Legendary indexer John Bogle criticized just about everybody he could lay a glove on—the public, the Vanguard family, and the fund industry in general—for showing interest in funds that trade like stocks. Bogle suggested that exchange-traded vehicles like the QQQs

and the Vanguard Vipers increase investor desire to "time" their buys and sells. Which, of course, he considered to be a bad thing.

3. Fund managers regularly blame "market timers" for underperformance. In fact, one individual—Oscar Castro of Montgomery Global Growth—publicly denounced me when I advised clients to sell international funds in August 1998. Of course, mavericks completely averted the worldwide stock selloff that plagued global markets that year. Slamming investors for being smart enough to defend their own best interests seems like an unwise strategy to me. But maybe that's why I'm not a fund manager.

Nobody can predict the future direction of equity markets, and I would be absolutely the last person in the galaxy to advocate day trading. But mavericks have to take advantage of technical indicators to avoid damage from downtrends. We have to use our (nonemotional) charts and information to dodge down cycles, and to catch the earliest stages of up cycles.

It's really not a question of being "for" or "against" market timing. It's a question of doing the right thing at the right time, to defend your financial interests. Any person who invests with a technical, nonemotional discipline will earn more than one who invests with his or her emotions; any person who uses objective and easy-to-interpret info will enhance his or her chances of buying and selling at the appropriate moment.

TRENDING: THE BEST OF BOTH WORLDS

What is the one thing that all buy'n'holders have in common? Surprise: *They sell.* The problem is that they have no rhyme, reason, or rationale guiding their actions.

Consider these stats. By June 30, 2000, the average diversified stock fund had earned 20 percent over the course of one year. Meanwhile, the S&P 500 showed a gain of only 6.58 percent. Did buy-'n'-hold advocates continue to sing the praises of the S&P 500 index fund? Of course not. Did staunch, died-in-the-wool buy-'n'-holders sell their S&P 500 assets to acquire more tech? Absolutely.

Buy-'n'-holders fail because they buy late and they sell late. They arrive at a hot sector as it's beginning to cool. Then, when the next great investment becomes iceberg cold, they sell out of frustration and disappointment.

Market timers are equally ill-equipped to succeed, because they obsess over short-term fluctuations. They spend countless, arduous hours trying to predict what the market will do on a daily and/or weekly basis, even though it's most often blind luck that gets them their big wins.

Market timers fail because they buy and sell too frequently. They spend too many minutes of the day at this nasty game. They incur unnecessary expenses, and exhaust all of their emotional energy.

Is there a happy medium between the hyperactivity of market timing and the passive inactivity of buy'n'hold? Is there a technique that can tell you when to jump (either in or out) that is sensible, simple, and—most important of all—exceptionally profitable?

Well, sure. That's why I brought up the subject, and devoted this chapter to it. Maverick investors employ a technique that I call *trending*. It is designed to get mavericks into stocks when the long-term trend of stocks is up, and also to get us out when the long-term trend is down.

WHAT IS TRENDING?

Trending is a way to see when a stock, a fund, or an index is experiencing an up or down cycle. Mavericks use trending to make informed decisions for getting in or out of the market—without guesswork, predictions, or emotions.

The basic indicator in trending is a "moving average." We all have experience with averages, from pay scales to test scores to baseball stats. Why are averages so prevalent? Because they give us an unbiased perspective on something that we want to understand.

A moving average graphically portrays the long-term trend of a stock, a fund, or an index. It paints a portrait of a closing price relative to a 10-month trend average. For instance, the chart in Figure 16-1 shows the smooth line, or trendline, that represents a plot of a moving average over time. You'll also notice the jagged movement of the closing prices.

In Figure 16-2, the Vanguard 500 Fund finished the week above its trendline. This is a sign that one should continue to invest in this equity

FIGURE 16-1   Moving Average Example: Invesco Dynamics

FIGURE 16-2   Moving Average Example: Vanguard 500 Fund Closing Above Trendline

position. If Vanguard 500 were to close below its 10-month trendline, it would be an indication that the investment was entering a down cycle (see Figure 16-3).

What makes trending so powerful is the way it lets us see our investments in action. A picture is worth not only a thousand words, but—in many cases—thousands of dollars.

WHY SHOULD YOU TREND? FIVE KILLER REASONS

If you track market trends, you can make your first million in half the time with half the effort. You won't jump in too late. And you won't jump out every time a major index falls 100 points.

FIGURE 16-3   Moving Average Example: Vanguard 500 Fund Closing Below Trendline

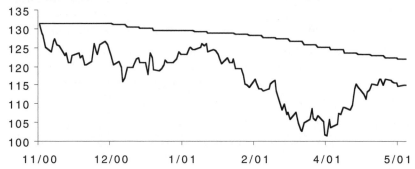

What you have to do as a maverick investor is utilize the long-term trends of your investments and their respective indexes. Here are five killer reasons why this will work for you:

1. Trending is nonemotional.   People tend to get attached to their investments. They also tend to get attached to the decisions behind those investments. We think with our hearts, and we hate to admit that we're wrong.

Trending is the opposite of emotional. It's mechanical. You're not making a bet based upon feelings. You're not wishing or hoping. You're simply following a plan—a plan that'll keep losses to a minimum, and keep you on track to achieve your financial dreams.

2. Trending is performance-based.   Trending doesn't care whether Microsoft wins or loses its lawsuit. Trending doesn't care about Federal Reserve rates, trade deficits, or peace accords. As noted, it merely paints a portrait of a closing price, relative to a 10-month trend average. Trending uses objective data to help you chart your course.

3. Trending has "track."   Over 24 years, my company has employed this simple approach with amazing results. Trending alone has outperformed the S&P 500 index with significantly less risk across four bear markets and a variety of bear scares.

Were we out before the crash of 1987, the bear of 1990, and the scare of 1998? Absolutely—sitting on those sidelines. And believe me, buy-'n'-holders weren't looking to dollar-cost-average into stocks after the 1987 crash.

What about getting into the market? In January 1991, the country was getting ready to go to war with Iraq. We were facing the highest unemployment figures and the worst recession stats in decades. Yet the trendlines told mavericks to buy. The result? Enormous gains over a five-month stretch.

4. Trending lets you be a maverick, getting 100 percent invested at the right time.   When you're a maverick, you've got 100 percent of your money invested 80 percent of the time. But that kind of commitment requires a system for controlling the risk of a down cycle.

Trending is a way to ride the bulls and to avoid the bears. When you put 100 percent into stocks, you *know* that a bear is lurking out there, somewhere. Trending helps you identify the right time to sell.

5. Bottom line . . . it works!   The media are fond of offering up certain dusty old theories—for example, how buying'n'holding the S&P 500 would have earned you a princely 15.30 percent over this specific 25-year period. But buy'n'hold is a myth. It would have worked if you had gotten into it 25 years ago. But the assumption the media are making is that the markets, economy, and funds will act the same in the future. This is a bet I'm not willing to make.

And even if there were some compelling logic to buy'n'hold, I've already pointed out that investing is not a logical game. We humans are emotional critters. This means that when it comes to buy'n'hold, nobody ever sticks to it anyway. For most of us, it turns out to be little more than a short-lived ride on a bad roller coaster.

Trending, by contrast, produces strong performance, while letting you relax during more volatile market moments.

WHERE TO GET YOUR TREND INFO

Online trading, Web charting, Internet searching: Your access to great information has changed dramatically. Before the Net, it would have been a real challenge to get your eyes on a picture of a stock or fund's trendline. Now mavericks can get this info with the click of a mouse.

Oki from Wanskatchawa writes:

> I listened to your Maverick Investing CD recently, and I really like the idea of trending. I love the idea of being to visualize and see the changes in the marketplace. But now that I understand moving averages and have faster access to the Internet, I've discovered all these Web sites with different charts and graphs. I'm not sure who to trust, or which trendlines are accurate or how many days the moving average is supposed to be.

In my 24 years of research and study, nothing is more accurate or easy to trend with than the 39-week, or 200-day, moving average. I've learned that 39 weeks, or about 10 months, is the best measure for evaluating the long-term trend of a stock, fund, index, or market.

There are hundreds of small-time outfits and chart shops on the Internet, many of which will tell you that they've developed proprietary systems and averages for the twenty-first century. These claims aren't even believable enough to pass for Wall Street hype. Ignore them.

On the other hand, there are three charting resources that I like a *lot,* and which I use to generate pictures of market activity. You might want to bookmark these beauties:

- BigCharts.com serves up the vital signs of any stock or fund, and does so graphically. For example, you can see the relationship of

Janus Worldwide (JAWWX) to its own trendline. Simply enter the symbol, click on "Interactive Charting," click on indicators in a 200-day moving average as your indicator, and hit "Draw Chart." You can also save these chart settings to use for future graphs. http://www.bigcharts.com (see Figure 16-4).

- Yahoo! Finance delivers down-and-dirty charts of market indices. It is the fastest way to get a sneak peek. You type in your stock or fund, click on "Chart," then hit "moving average." By default, a 200-day moving average will appear on your screen. http://finance.yahoo.com/. (Figure 16-5).

FIGURE 16-4   BigCharts.com Interactive Charting Feature

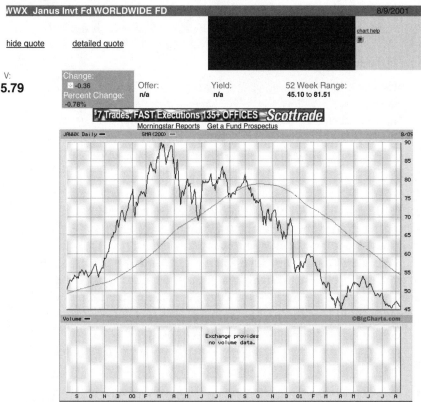

email this chart   printer-friendly format

FIGURE 16-5   Yahoo! Finance Charting Feature

Janus Worldwide Fund
as of 31-Jul-2001

```
90 ┤ ■ JAWWX
80 ┤ ■ 200-day MA
70 ┤
60 ┤
50 ┤
40 ┤
      Jan00      May00      Sep00      Jan01      May01
```

Copyright 2001 Yahoo! Inc.   http://finance.yahoo.com/

TRENDING WITH THE INVESTMENT ITSELF

There are many ways to trend. You can track the big-time benchmarks. You can use an industry index. However, if you own only one or two mutual funds, you may want to trend with the specific investment itself.

Remember that the trendline is a plot of the 39-week average (39WAR) over time. In general, a trendline that is rising is a positive sign, while a descending trendline is negative.

However, the *current price of your investment relative to the trendline* is what dictates your buy, sell, or hold decisions. Specifically, mavericks want to be *invested when the current price is above its 39WA, and out when the current price is below the 39WAR.*

Take a look at the Fidelity Magellan Fund in Figure 16-6. In March 2000, it crossed beneath its trendline. This is when a maverick investor would have transferred his or her assets out of this fund to cash. This may

FIGURE 16-6   Fidelity Magellan Fund Moving Average Example: FMAGX

```
150
140
130
120
110
100
 90
 80
     5/00    7/00    9/00    12/00    2/01    4/01    6/01
```

**FIGURE 16-7   Transamerica Equity Growth Moving
Average Example: TEQUX**

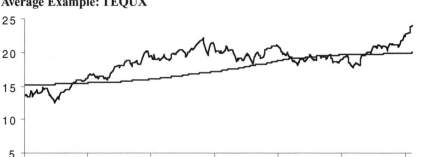

mark the end of this maverick's relationship with Fund FMAGX, or it may not. It all depends on where the next great opportunity is!

In Figure 16-7, we see Fund TEQUX Transamerica Equity Growth crossing above its 39WAR. Assuming this fund has the momentum and track record to achieve maverick returns, this represents a "Buy" signal.

Sometimes a fund hugs its trendline for weeks, maybe months, as is the case with Scudder Growth & Income in Figure 16-8. This is a transitional phase—a yellow alert that signals the likelihood of a change in status. In this instance, Fund SCDGX is a probable "Sell." Therefore, mavericks should be preparing a future "Buy" list to have a candidate on hand to replace this asset.

**FIGURE 16-8   Scudder Growth & Income Moving
Average Example: SCDGX**

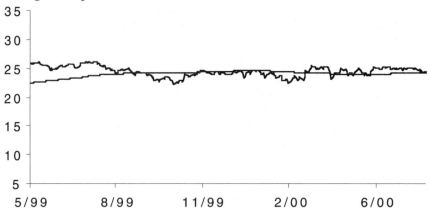

TRENDING WITH THE BIG-TIME BENCHMARKS

How do you know when to get out of a heavy tech position? What should you look for if you want to get into the small-cap arena? What trend indicator will tell you when to get out of *all* stock positions?

When you want to know if an entire segment of the U.S. market is moving higher or lower, then trend with the big-time benchmarks (i.e., Dow Industrials, S&P 500, Nasdaq, Russell 2000, Wilshire 5000). For example, let's say you're checking the charts on large-cap growth. If the current price of the S&P 500, our large-cap growth index, is below its trendline (39WAR), then large-cap growth is trending downward (see Figure 16-9). Similarly, when the price of the Russell 2000, our small-cap growth index, is above its trendline (39WAR), then small-cap growth is trending upward (see Figure 16-10).

Is the technology sector in an uptrend or downtrend? What about large-cap value? How about the entire market?

These are the questions that mavericks ask each Friday. For example, if you have positions in large-cap growth, tech, and large-cap value, you'll want to make sure that the S&P 500, the Dow, and the Nasdaq are still above their trendlines. You'll also want to look at the Russell 2000 and the Wilshire 5000 to see if small-caps and the broader market have completed a down cycle and moved above their long-term trends.

Looking at three to five benchmark charts once a week at Yahoo! Finance is much simpler than scanning a wide variety of positions for several accounts. If it becomes too time-consuming to examine individual positions in a diverse portfolio, stick to the benchmarks.

FIGURE 16-9   S&P 500 Index Moving Average Example

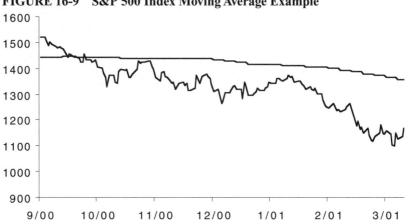

FIGURE 16-10   Russell 2000 Index Moving Average Example

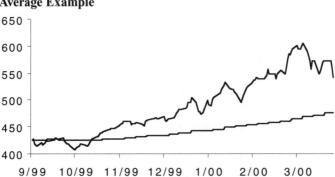

DECISIONS, DECISIONS, DECISIONS

Josephine from Schenectady writes:

> I used to look at the charts of each individual investment. Now, however, I have five accounts—a SEP, my husband's 401(k), 2 taxable, and a Variable Life Policy. It's obviously easier to monitor the big-time benchmarks a few minutes each week. The only problem is, the Net has made it easy for me to occasionally go back and check an individual position. And sometimes I find that a fund is moving contrary to its benchmark. In those instances, do I buy, sell, or hold?

My answer is, *Keep life simple.* When monitoring individual positions weekly becomes more of a chore than a delight, just use the market indexes and stick to the discipline.

When a stock fund is moving completely counter to the trend of its benchmark, however, you might want to take a deeper look into the specific sector weightings or stock holdings of the fund. For example, if the Dow Industrials show that large-cap value is in an uptrend at the same time that your large-cap value fund is struggling at 52-week lows, something's gone awry. That fund could have an exceptionally weak exposure to large-cap technology, or it may have drifted from its prospectus objective.

If you discover a discrepancy, don't be afraid to investigate further. The Net has more information about a stock, fund, or index than any broker will ever confide.

Another option for mavericks is to trend with the specific investment, and use the benchmark as a confirming indicator. Similarly, you could trend with the benchmark, and get confirmation for your buy/sell decision from the movement of the specific stock or fund.

THE BIG THREE COLORS

Mavericks and drivers of hot cars are interested in three colors: red, yellow, and green.

If you're a listener to my radio show, you may have heard me say that "the green light is lit and it's time to buy." Or, you may have heard me issue a "red flag," warning you to get out of the stock waters.

The greens and the reds pop up when a closing price of an index moves above or below its trendline. In contrast, the yellows represent an alert mode—a time when a change of status may occur.

What determines a yellow "alert" signal? The percentage a closing price is above or below its trendline, also known as the *39-week differential* (39WD). When the 39WD is less than 5 percent away from its trendline, either above or below it, this is a transitional period; it is a time when you need to pay greater attention to the marketplace and your positions in it.

The 39WD shows the weakness or strength of a stock, fund, or index in relation to its own trendline (39-week average). A positive 39WD represents an uptrend in progress, while a negative 39WD indicates a downtrend en route.

The 39WD primarily comes into play when there's less than 5 percent difference between the closing price and the trendline. Mavericks use this information to stay on top of any quick developments that may occur.

A 39WD that hits double digits, whether positive or negative, requires a different type of vigilance. It means that the fund or index is either so strong or so weak that trending alone may be insufficient; that is, you give back too much of your gains before selling, or you give up too much lost opportunity before buying.

WHEN TRENDING GETS TOUGH

Is trending an appropriate tool at all times? Is it right for all investments? Will it sit you atop every bull at the very bottom, and get you out at the very top?

No, no, and definitely not. Trending helps you:

1. Get into the market early
2. Keep your nose clean while you're there
3. Lock up the majority of your gains when you exit

Trending is far from bulletproof. Let's face it: There are times when it is easy to make money, and times when it is not so easy. There are times when it's easy to preserve assets, and there are other times when it's more challenging. Specifically:

1. There are times when it's easy to make money.   For example, all of the major indexes in a broad-based bull are moving higher. Trending takes advantage of these broad market moves.

2. There are times when it's difficult to make money—times when it's difficult to detect any direction. The markets are in transition and they're hovering close to their trendlines. Market leadership doesn't seem to be coming from anywhere. Trending will help you prepare for a change.

3. There are times when it's easy to preserve money.   For example, nothing's in favor. Every segment of the economy is experiencing a down cycle. At those times, it's a no-brainer for trenders. You're standing on the sidelines and waiting for the next uptrend to emerge.

4. There are times when it's difficult to preserve assets.   Trending is rendered relatively useless by an incredible bull or incredible bear. For instance, when the Nasdaq was 40 percent above its trendline in February of 2000, how on earth could you trend it? The answer is, you couldn't. That's when you slap on a stop-loss, and hold on to the reins.

TO TREND OR NOT TO TREND: A PERSONAL QUESTION
Jonesy from Jones Beach writes:

> I like "trending" in theory. But I don't like it in practice. It seems that every time I get out of the market because the trend is down, I wind up returning to the stock market a short time later. At times, it is three months. Other times it is two weeks! While this isn't costing me much in my tax-deferred accounts, I'm getting hit hard on my taxable trades. And when I calculate how my funds would have performed if I did nothing at all, I see that the performance is always better if I just stayed put. I think I'm going to buy and hold from now on.

Oh, dear. To me, what's most striking about Jonesy's analysis is that he feels compelled to justify his decision to return to buy-'n'-hold investing. He's almost apologetic.

But what about Jonesy's concerns? Isn't it true that he is experiencing short-term trades that have cost him tax dollars and early redemption penalties? Isn't it true that he has moved to a money market position on several occasions, only to return to stocks several months (or even weeks) later?

Yes, and yes. Indeed, there are times when "trending" is going to feel like it hurts more than it helps. For example, when the market breaks its trendline and demonstrates a likely downturn, it may quickly reverse its course and take you higher. That's called a *whipsaw* (see Figure 16-11).

FIGURE 16-11   Moving Average: "Whipsaw" Example: Janus Fund

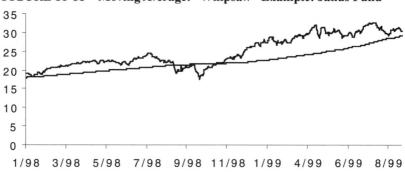

Another problem occurs when the closing price is so far above or below its trendline that trending alone can not protect enough of your gains, or ensure against lost opportunity. The mid-March Nasdaq high, and its subsequent decline, shows how investors gave back most of their gains with trending alone (see Figure 16-12).

Yet what is the alternative to trending? Jonesy has the answer: Buy'n'hold. What Jonesy isn't acknowledging is that buy-'n'-holders gave back all of *their* Nasdaq gains, as well. Granted, buy-'n'-holders don't experience whipsaws, redemption fees, or tax hits in their taxable accounts. But mavericks who trend *never* experience bear markets, or the discomfort associated with not having a clue when to sell. And once again: Selling is liberating (for both you and your asset). When you sell an asset, you get the opportunity to choose a new stock or fund with better performance.

The facts of the trending matter are these: (1) Not everyone can be a maverick; (2) mavericks use trending to buy, and (3) mavericks use trend-

**FIGURE 16-12   Closing Far Above or Below Trendline:
Robertson Stephens Emerging Growth—RSEGX**

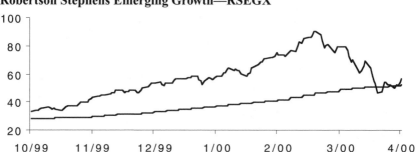

ing to sell. If you do not believe it matters when you buy or when you sell—if you do not think you need to protect against the devastation that a future bear might bring—by all means, buy, hold, and hope.

ENHANCING THE PLAN

Trending is totally maverick because—as with stop-losses and 5/10/20 vision—you're not waiting on the dubious wisdom of a Wall Street analyst. When it's time to buy, it's time to buy. And when it's time to sell—when the closing price of your stock, fund, or index falls below its 39-week moving average—it's time to sell.

Best of all, being a maverick means having the independence to personalize your sell strategy. *You* decide how to make the best use of the 20 percent growth goal, stop-losses, and trending. As long as you stick to the sell discipline that you set for yourself, creating and protecting wealth will be reasonably easy, and exceptionally satisfying.

17

The Art of Selling

A radio show listener named Jeremy recently sent me a thank-you note. At the risk of sounding too full of myself, I have to say that getting a friendly note from a maverick isn't all that unusual. Over the years, lots of people have sent me notes to thank me for giving them the confidence to take the first steps toward financial independence—or, in less happy circumstances, to climb out of the hole that some ill-advised financial strategy has put them in.

But I saved this particular note because it made me feel particularly good. It convinced me that all of my passionate talk in that cramped little studio down at the radio station adds up to something, every now and then.

"I've written down more ticker symbols than McDonald's has french fries," Jeremy wrote. "Web chats, magazine picks, business channels—you name it. My focus was buy, buy, buy. But now you've got me thinking about the *selling,* as well as the buying. That's different! In fact, I've never heard anyone speak so convincingly about the beauty of selling stocks and funds."

Jeremy got the message: *mavericks sell.*

Is that such a hard message to get? Well, no and yes. No, it's not hard to hear, understand, and pay lip service to. ("Of *course* you have to sell.

Everybody knows that!") But in real life, it's easier said than done. When you start thinking about selling an asset, few people will pat you on the back and say, "Go for it!" For example: Your broker is going to try to talk you out of it. If you consult your friends and family, you're likely to hear stories about how if only Aunt Tilly had held on to that phone company stock in 1929, we'd all be on Easy Street today. And when you read disapproving stories in the media about day traders, profit-takers, and short-term thinkers, you may start to wonder if selling your holdings will put you in with these ne'er-do-wells.

What's really going on here? Why is selling so difficult? The answer is, "All kinds of things are going on here." We've already talked about your broker's vested interest, so you can forget about that. The aunt may or may not have ruined the family's fortunes. (That was a long time ago, and we can't relive the past.) What's harder to ignore is what's going on inside your own head—which, if you're like most people, is the *psychology of uncertainty.*

We humans crave certainty. All things being equal, we tend to stick with an unsatisfactory status quo rather than leap into something new. Selling threatens the status quo. It raises disquieting questions: Am I pursuing a better opportunity, or am I simply creating losses in my account? Am I locking up investment gains, or simply paying unnecessary commissions and taxes? Am I reducing my exposure in a situation where the trend lines are negative, or am I getting out at just the wrong time?

So, OK, I'll grant you that selling tends to stir up a whole pot full of emotions. But if you take to heart the maverick outlook—if you recognize that greatness only occurs by traveling an unconventional path—you'll quickly recognize the power that a sell strategy affords you.

MEMORY LANE

Let's look at it from the other side of the Street. Have you ever lost money because someone convinced you not to sell? Have you ever felt like others are in the right stocks while you're holding onto the wrong ones? Has the buy-'n'-hold hype finally shown you its true colors?

Maverick investors know why selling guarantees future wealth. We sell to decrease downside risk; we sell to increase upside opportunity; we sell to stay on target to reach our financial goals.

You're already familiar with the selling tools that mavericks use. First of all, we check the market trends, which tell us when to dump assets that are losing ground. We employ trailing stop-loss percentages, to make sure the dumping process is disciplined. And, of course, we pursue only those investments that give us the ability to reach 20 percent returns (or some other ambitious goal that we set for ourselves).

In fact, because these three tools are so important, I devoted entire chapters to them earlier. They are:

- **Chapter 8: How to Fire Underachievers and Overchargers** (Focusing your 5/10/20 vision and getting rid of lemons)
- **Chapter 13: Stop-Loss Strategy** (Everything you ever wanted to know about setting stop losses)
- **Chapter 16: Trending to Wealth** (The when, what, why and how of tracking stock market trends)

In this chapter, you'll personalize your sell strategy. You'll combine the objectivity of maverick tools with the subjectivity of your unique, individual preferences.

Specifically, you'll get to be on intimate terms with your growth orientation—conservative, moderate, or aggressive. You'll take a look at your personal wiring: for example, whether investing intrigues you, or if it is simply a means to an (important!) end. You'll consider the experience you have, the time you're actually willing to spend, the types of investments you own today (stocks, funds, annuities, ETFs) and the kinds you can expect to have tomorrow.

OIL, WATER, ART, SCIENCE?
Method, procedure, exactness, objectivity: These are words that we tend to associate with the hard sciences, like chemistry and physics. And maybe you've picked up on the fact that maverick investing involves a lot of these same concepts (Mavericks are nothing if not objective). But I've also mentioned earlier that the world of investing is less a logical turf and more a *psychological* turf. So we mavericks have to leave room for some *subjectivity,* along with all that objectivity. And this means that we have to *personalize our selling strategies.*

For instance, an aggressive-growth maverick trading a stock would not use the same stop-loss percentage as a conservative-growth maverick trading a mutual fund (see Figure 17-1). This is true even within a single individual's strategy. For example, a moderate-growth mav wouldn't use the same stop-loss for the QQQs as he or she might for a diversified growth fund.

Selling is an artistic process—a unique blend of science and subjectivity. And a true maverick finds his or her own proper fit.

FIGURE 17-1   Stock, ETF, Fund Stop-Losses

	Stock	ETF	Mutual Fund
AG	17%–20%	15%–18%	12%–15%
MG	12%–15%	12%–15%	10%–12%
CG	10%–12%	8%–10%	8%–10%

CREATING YOUR SELL STRATEGY

As the chapter title suggests, I think of selling as an art. Why? Because it expresses a lot about the kind of person you are. But the art of selling isn't arcane, obscure, or abstract. It's pretty accessible stuff. For example, here is a modest, three-step approach to personalizing your sell strategy:

Step Number 1: Figure out who you are.   Many of us imagine that we are real aggressive characters—that we can handle a great deal of volatile price movement in our investments. And that tends to be true right up until the ship hits the sand.

Remember, your maverick growth orientation is measured on the downside as well as the upside. If you can't handle a 30 percent loss, then you're not as aggressive as you think you are. Paint a new picture of yourself.

And there's more to your makeup than the pursuit of maverick returns (or at least I *hope* there is!). What do you want to be when you grow up? Some individuals would like to retire the minute they've got the cash to Winnebago through Wyoming. Others want to keep dedicating most of their available hours to their ultra-cool careers. Some people are Major Mavs, pushing themselves (and me) to refine the maverick discipline. But others recognize that they are Mini Mavs—consumers of certain tenets of maverick investing, but not necessarily the whole shebang.

Fine by *me,* by the way. I encourage you to decide who you are, and to be perfectly honest about it. This is the first step toward creating a sell strategy that's right for you. In fact, the only sell strategy that'll work is the one that you stick to and believe in.

Step Number 2: Determine the types of investments you have today and might have tomorrow.   Once you know who you are, you're better able to evaluate the investments that you possess. Some will be too conservative—like a high-yield bond fund in a moderate mav's 401(k). (Just say no to bonds!)

Other types of investments are far riskier than people imagine. Just ask the investors who bought'n'held Microsoft or Amazon in the first quarter of 2000. These so-called "sure-bets" dropped 40 and 80 percent, respectively.

Almost from the get-go, you'll find that you're going to want to sell stuff to make your portfolio reflect your personal reality. Maybe you'll need to transfer assets that don't belong in your growth mix. Or perhaps you'll have to rethink where your tax-deferred dollars are compounding—whether they're stuck in an underachieving IRA, an asset-allocating education plan, or an annuity lemon.

Even after you've arranged your taxable and tax-deferred accounts in appropriate ways, you'll probably find that more change—more selling—starts to make sense. For example, as you gain knowledge and confidence, you may develop a taste for more sophisticated vehicles. You may want to get involved in exchange-traded indexing, or enhanced sector funds. The sell strategy you create today should have enough foresight and flexibility to accommodate tomorrow's choices.

Step Number 3: Identify the circumstances under which you will use a specific tool, or tools.   You know who you are. You know what you invest in. Now you need to outline when and how to implement trending, stop-losses, and 5/10/20 vision.

Let's get specific. Imagine an investor—call him Pete—with a fair amount of experience, a typical amount of tolerance for risk, and a reasonably lousy track record with individual stocks. (Sound like anyone you know?) What are Pete's possible remedies? Well, he might: (a) move from individual stocks to exchange-traded funds that trade like stocks, (b) choose a percentage stop-loss that he is willing to give up, and (c) check his investments every three months with the 5/10/20 sell rule. Note that *all involve the art of selling.*

Of course, every Pete is a little bit different. Looking at the table in Figure 17-1, the moderate-growth Pete would select a specific stop-loss between 12 percent and 15 percent. A Pete who was a newcomer to stop-losses should use 12 percent. Granted, this percentage might get Pete out of the market too soon, but it would serve to lock up Pete's gains and/or preserve capital quickly. Plus, as I've said so many times already (and I'm gonna keep right on saying it!), if Pete's asset is not achieving maverick growth of 5 percent every three months, he should sell and pursue a better opportunity.

THE ART OF THE STOP-LOSS

Caroline, who lives in one of my favorite cities, recently wrote:

> Doug, I've been so successful implementing stop-losses alongside trend-lines, I'm wondering if you'd approve. For instance, last year I bought Invesco Leisure. I set my stop-loss at a stingy 10 percent. I hit the stop-loss several times, but I didn't sell because the fund did not drift below its 200-day trendline. This kept me invested for a total portfolio gain of 50% in just 1½ years. Did I do the right thing—waiting for the trendline to confirm a stop-loss?

My answer to her question was "yes," although not necessarily for the reasons she expected to hear. The "right" plan is the one that you'll stick with through thin and thick. The fact is that Caroline exposed herself to greater downside risk by hanging on when her stop-loss hit. (She exposed herself to the risk of losses in excess of 10 percent.) But she managed that risk with a sell discipline that *felt right for her.* In other words, she needed to see more evidence of a true down cycle before unloading her investment.

So when I say that Caroline "did well," I'm not talking only about the fact that she nailed an enviable 50 percent gain. I'm also talking about the fact that Caroline took some good, natural-bristle paintbrushes out of the maverick art-supply closet, and then painted her own picture. She coupled two technical indicators—a 200-day moving average and a 10 percent stop loss—and made some magic.

Sherif had another idea:

> I like the 20 percent growth goal so much, I'm thinking about using a preset stop-gain. What do you think? For example, let's say my equity gains 20 percent in three months. Why risk giving back 10 percent with a stop-loss when I can safely transfer the capital to a money account? I've reached my goal for the entire year!

Interesting, right? Sherif is thinking like a maverick. He is thinking outside the box, with this notion of a "stop-gain." He is absolutely correct in saying that 20 percent in three months is as good as 20 percent in twelve months. And maybe Sherif will go with that particular selling strategy. From my perspective, though, the chances are high that a stop-gain will leave you stuck in cash while the bull is still very powerful. Remember:

Mavericks want to be 100 percent invested in stocks as long as the charge is on.

And let's keep remembering that we mavericks, bright and disciplined as we are, are still humans. We have emotions. We find it difficult, if not impossible, to sit on our hands for extended periods of time. As the bull snorts and stomps all around us, we're going to be tempted to reenter the market in an undisciplined way—for example, disappointingly late in a cycle. And that's when we risk getting whacked.

So, Sherif, there's nothing inherently bad about establishing a "quit-while-you're-ahead" point. But the art of selling is driven by your determination to *stay committed to stocks*. (You might want to read that sentence one or two more times to make sense out of it. It's less obvious than it sounds.) We're not in this game to sell; we sell creatively to play the game well. The best way to ensure commitment is to stay in for as long as the bull's in command, and then to exit the market and hit the sidelines.

THE ART OF THE 5/10/20 RULE

How patient should you be when evaluating your investments? That depends on how active an investor you intend to be. An exceptionally active, interventionist maverick may demand that his or her investment earn 1.67 percent per month or it gets the axe. A more conservative maverick may put a fund on alert for missing 5 percent in a given quarter, but only pull the trigger if the fund fails to achieve 10 percent over six months.

All mavericks seek 20 percent annual growth (or their personal-target equivalent). Each of us steps up our vigilance when investments are not achieving this rate of return. But the day of reckoning—the "put up or shut up" checkpoint—can occur monthly, quarterly, semiannually, or even annually. It really depends on *you*.

Nomar (not the Red Sox shortstop!) writes:

> I discovered your 5/10/20 vision just in time to take advantage of my terrific 401(k). With more than 15 domestic stock funds to choose from, and great online access, I start with 100 percent of my money in the least risky mutual fund that is earning 1.67 percent or greater. If it fails to earn 1.67 percent in a given month, I sell and transfer the assets to the least risky fund that is still on target; I only rotate when my fund doesn't get 1.67 percent and another one does. If nothing's on target, I sell and move to cash. Over three years, I've only moved to cash three times and I've achieved a maverick rate of return of 27.7%. What do you think, Doug?

Hey, Nomar: It's not what I think, it's what I *know*—27.7 percent is a sensational rate of return! And just as cool, you got there with a very personal selling style. Without watching the market more than once monthly, you developed an approach to selling that you're comfortable with—one that obviously works well for you.

No, not everyone is comfortable with the possibility of moving money once a month. Others would rather use a quarterly checkup, or the general trend of the broad market, to sell.

The most important thing to remember about the 5/10/20 rule is *staying the course.* You can't be sloppy or timid. You can't visit one investment quarterly, another one monthly, and another one annually, never really knowing what you'll do until your gut tells you to act. Identify the time frame and the circumstances under which you'll sell, and then . . . *sell.*

THE ART OF TRENDING

What's the one thing that most investors loathe about selling, more than anything else? Easy: *Turning paper losses into real losses.*

Consider a colleague of mine who sold 100 shares of the QQQs at 98. She had purchased them at 102. Her spouse, she told me, was absolutely livid. It didn't matter to him that the Nasdaq 100 was entering a downtrend. It didn't matter that health care was entering an up cycle. In his mind, his wife had lost $400, and she should have hung on to that investment at least until it broke even.

Chapter 2 in this little drama (which you may be able to anticipate): The Nasdaq 100 hibernated over the next six months. The health care sector, meanwhile, soared. My colleague sold her health care fund for a handsome $2548 gain. I'm happy to report that my colleague's husband found it in his heart to express his sincerest apologies. Faced with some pretty powerful evidence, he decided that trend identification was a good thing, after all.

Notice, however, that trending still involves subjective decision-making. My colleague used the 39-week moving averages of the specific investments—the Nasdaq 100, her health care sector fund—to decide when to sell. Others might prefer the big-time benchmarks (S&P, Dow, Nasdaq) when trending. That's your call.

One also must look at where to throw up the "yellow alert" on holding a position. Typically, an investment that moves within 5 percent of its trendline gets a yellow flag from me, indicating that investors should refrain from allocating new money. I've known other mavericks to set their yellows at 7 percent, 3 percent, or even 0 percent—in other words, no cautionary alert at all. (It's personal: At 0 percent, I'm out of my personal comfort zone!)

ADDITIONAL TRENDING TIPS FOR ARTISTS

If you understand moving averages and trend charts, should you expand your technical horizons? Specifically, should you start employing what are called "support lines" and "resistance lines"?

Maybe yes; maybe no. An understanding of support and resistance definitely helps you understand more about the stock market. That said, a trending sell strategy doesn't require this level of mastery, and for some, it may just overly complicate things. Read on. You decide.

Simply put, "support" and "resistance" are price levels at which price movement should, theoretically speaking, stop and reverse direction. Support acts as a floor and resistance acts as a ceiling to future price movements. (See Wilshire 5000 in Figure 17-2).

If you track the closing price of a market barometer, it's not uncommon to see it bounce off its own trendline (39-week average). In this instance, the moving average itself acts as a support level. (See Value Line Composite in Figure 17-3).

In addition to serving as a "reversal of fortune" point, support/resistance levels have another interesting trait. That is, once a support is pierced—once the floor gives way—it changes roles, and becomes a *resistance* level (and vice versa). For instance, the Nasdaq falls below 4000 and

FIGURE 17-2   Wilshire 5000

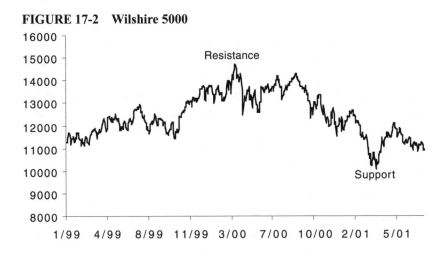

FIGURE 17-3   Value Line Composite

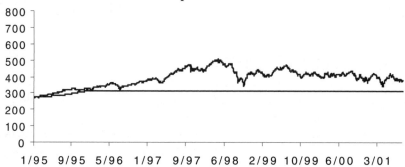

FIGURE 17-4   Nasdaq Composite

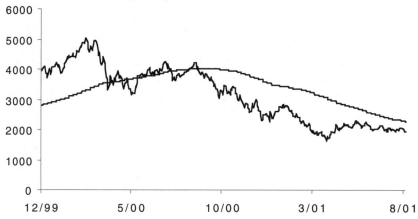

closes below 4000 for several weeks. Now the ability of the index to rise above 4000 is significantly hampered by program trading, online trading, and investor psychology. (See Nasdaq Composite in Figure 17-4).

How might this help your sell discipline? Some technicians note that when a market barometer repeatedly bumps up against a high—a resistance level—and fails to break through on its third attempt, this is a good time to sell. Picture a helium balloon bumping along the ceiling. The third bump is the troublesome one, historically speaking. The good news is that if you get out then, you're likely to get out near the high.

In general, though, mavericks should *not* use support and resistance levels to make their buy and sell decisions. Instead, you should learn about these kinds of technical indicators to improve your overall knowledge of the stock market. Understanding why a particular stock or fund is caught in a trading range should increase your ability to target an investment that is moving forward, rather than stuck in neutral.

WARNING SIGNS: YELLOW-RED FLAGS TO BECOME MORE VIGILANT

Although markets appear to react to social, political, and economic news with warplike speed, long-term changes tend to occur more slowly. That's what trending's all about, and why it's so important to mavericks.

Nevertheless, there are times when a rocket's red glare is so obvious that you simply can't ignore the fireworks. Here are three kinds of flare-ups that ought to prompt the maverick's extra vigilance:

1. Fundamental shifts in management.   When a senior member of management quits, take note. Maybe that guy or gal is a loser, whose departure will only help. Or maybe not. Don't let the inevitably positive spin that will be put on this story keep you from doing your due diligence.

For instance? Dateline, April 2000: Janus does not get to free itself from its parent company, KC Stilwell (later Stilwell Financial). Soon, performance questions begin to surround the Janus crew. Five months later, Jim Craig, the CIO of the third-largest mutual fund company, steps down.

None of these events mark the end of Janus—far from it! In another example, Fidelity experienced a variety of downs and ups following the departure of its superstar Peter Lynch, and recovered quite nicely. Nevertheless, managerial shifts and uncertainty are *really good* reasons to keep your eye on the ball.

2. Drifts and shifts in style.   "Style drift"—slipsliding from one thing to another without much public notice—is pretty common stuff in the fund industry. Companies trying to revive struggling products typically change the names of those products, modify their styles—drift (little) or shift (big) and/or merge the loser into a more popular brand.

If I ran a mutual fund company and had that kind of problem, I might be tempted to do the same thing. But you and I sit on the other side of the fence. We can't get complacent when a brokerage house weaves its soothing yarn. We can't let style shift or drift mess up our well-structured portfolios.

Consider the long-running lemon and repeat offender of the Fabian Lemon List, Fidelity Trend (FTRNX). It has tried to get comfortable in whatever fits, shifting from mid-cap value to large-cap growth. Yet despite manager changes and purchases of the safer, larger companies, FTRNX continues in its D-grade ways.

If a fund feels the need to change its style, you might express your feelings with a sell order. Remember, the best funds prove their worth year out and in, while the worst get caught following the latest fad.

3. High volume swings.   Yes, you want to remain calm and NOT get caught up in the day-to-day volatility of the stock market. But when an unusually high stock market volume (lots of trades) accompanies volatility (rapid up-and-down shifts), someone knows something!

This is about the best circumstantial evidence you'll ever get that insider knowledge dictates movement on the stock market. Why? Because extremely high volume is often indicative of large blocks of program trading—that is, big buy and sell orders by fund managers and/or heavy hitters. Either they're being stampeded by gossip and rumor (always a possibility!), or they know something you don't know.

Don't be quick to see a high-volume down spike as a bargain. Even if shares start to rebound, you could still get walloped by a horrific dose of downward pressure. In other words, stay on your toes.

THE MAVERICK TAKE ON VAGUE ADVICE

What is the greatest injustice to investors? Wall Street's vague advice on selling. Here are three extremely weak ideas that you may have heard somewhere along the financial line. Each has a good idea buried deep within it—but only if you use maverick eyes.

Vague Idea Number 1: Sell if there's trouble in an industry.
Well, *that's* not particularly helpful! How do investors learn that there's trouble in a segment of the economy? Read the newspapers? Watch the tube? Subscribe to a Web-based community of online investors? We've already seen how lame most of those sources are.

Most investors won't discover that an industry sector is hurting until well after the fall. Don't pay attention to hyped-up media commentary, Web "buzz," and analyst downgrades (if you can find one!). If you sell on this news, you're likely to get stir-fried.

Maverick Lesson: Don't sell when the herd is leaving. In all likelihood, a maverick is getting ready to buy!

Vague Idea Number 2: Prune your portfolio when an asset is not performing well.   Great: So how do you know if the asset is underperforming? Do you compare your investment to the S&P 500, the Dow, or the Nasdaq? Do you use similar companies and/or similar funds? And how long should you give a stock or a fund before you decide that it's a loser? Thirty days? Six months? Five years?

Portfolio pruning is a hazy, lazy concept that the media drag out when they run out of things to waste ink on. In contrast, mavericks already know what benchmarks and timelines to use.

Maverick Lesson: Craft your sell discipline in advance. Know what you will do, and under what circumstances, before you put a red cent into the market!

Vague Idea Number 3. Sell when you see a better opportunity.

Are we supposed to wait for new possibilities to bonk us over the head? Or should we go looking for them? If so, when and how often do you go scouting? Once a day, twice a week, three times a year?

Maverick Lesson: Selling is what creates opportunity—not the other way around. Let your winners run with the bull until they hit your sell parameters. Then, seek out new opportunities.

USING ALL OF THE BRUSHES IN THE MAVERICK ART-SUPPLY CLOSET

In the next chapter, we'll use all of the methods and techniques that you've learned in previous chapters to make over a wide variety of sample 401(k) plans. You'll remove lemons, throw out bomb (bond) funds, and eliminate investments that don't have the potential to achieve the maverick growth goal of 20 percent.

Why should you learn to apply maverick tools to 401(k)s? Because there's no single engine that does more for individual portfolio growth than your employee-sponsored, tax-deferred, 401(k) diamond mine.

18

Your 401(k),
the Maverick Way

W hat has the potential to become your most valuable asset, over
time? Forget your real estate holdings, your whole-life insurance
policy, your bond fund, and—yes—even that hand-picked portfolio of individual stocks that you've been working so hard at. The answer
is, your 401(k) has the potential to become your most valuable asset.

The key word here is *potential.* This chapter is about (1) getting *you*
to recognize that potential, and (2) getting your 401(k) to live up to *its*
potential.

With the simple maverick formula introduced in previous chapters
(money + time + compounding = dreams realized!), you *can* accumulate
millions. But *will* you? Unfortunately, most people do not see their 401(k)
as the most golden of geese. Some don't really understand how this wealth-
building tool works. Others think of it as a burden: too many decisions to
make, too many rules to think about, and too many investment choices to
sort through. If any of these describes how you think about your 401(k),
then I have great news. In this chapter, I will retool your perspective, and
set you up to succeed in the Land of the 401(k)s.

I will show you how to get started, or—if you're already started—how
to take your 401(k) to the next level of success. I'll help you avoid some

fairly common mistakes, and encourage you to take the five steps that will make you 401(k) dreams a reality.

Remember: You have maverick dreams. (That's why you're reading this book.) In your 401(k), you have a spectacular tool for realizing those dreams. Let's get there.

WHAT IS A 401(k)?

First things first, for you newbies: What is a 401(k)? It is a government-qualified retirement plan that is administered by your company. Pretax dollars are deducted from your paycheck and placed in a separate account that you are responsible for managing. (Pretax is good, because your take-home pay is reduced by less than the amount you're salting away.) You choose from a limited list of investment options approved by your company, and your account is allowed to grow tax-deferred for the rest of your working life. When you reach retirement age, you are able to make withdrawals, at which point your income from the 401(k) is taxed—but almost always at a *much lower tax rate.* (Your tax bracket is much lower because you're no longer earning that big salary.) Between today and your retirement, you make most (but not all) of the decisions concerning the allocation of your 401(k) assets. The account is *yours,* rather than your company's. If you leave your company, you take the assets with you to your next place of employment, or "roll over" the account into an individual retirement account (IRA).

Imagine having enough money to be able to stop working forever. Congratulations: You've just imagined your 401(k). That's its purpose: to let you live comfortably (even very comfortably) at some point in the future, without punching that clock. This account—and your successful management of it—is your ticket to stop working. It *is* the most golden of geese.

Another bit of definition: Some employers call their 401(k)-like accounts by different names. For example, you may hear about a 403(b), a 457 plan, various kinds of "deferred compensation" plans, and so forth. Sometimes the account is the core element of something called a "variable annuity" (as is true for many teachers around the country). No matter what they are called, all of these vehicles refer to the same retirement section of the IRS tax code, and play by the same rules. All let you put away pretax savings in a separate account to be managed by you for long-term growth.

The words "managed by you" need a little more emphasis. The rules for funding one's retirement have changed dramatically in the last 25 years. Simply put, whether you like it or not, *you're* in charge. Most corporate pension plans no longer exist, at least in their former glory, because companies were having enormous difficulties in funding and managing them. And although Social Security is everybody's favorite political football, kicked first in one direction and then the other, it's fair to say that the Social Security system is no longer the safe bet it once was. So for better or worse, you need to make this retirement thing happen for yourself.

To start making things a little more concrete, let's look at an e-mail from Stephanie:

> Hi Doug, my name is Stephanie and I need your help. I am a 37-year-old married woman with a two-year-old son. We own our home and we own a condo that we rent out. I make $50,000 a year and have worked for the same company during the past five years. I have contributed to the company's 401(k) plan for the past four years. I have maxed out my contribution at 15 percent with a company match of 3 percent. Here are my choices.
>
> - $9226 in Growth fund of America
> - $3800 in New Perspective Fund A
> - $2093 in Fundamentals Investors A
> - $5090 in Smallcap World A
> - Total: $20,409
>
> Please let me know if I have diversified too little or too much. I am looking to accumulate $250,000 in the next 20 years. This I know will put my son through college—and I might have some change left over, if I'm lucky!!

The good news is that Stephanie is already making steady progress toward her goals. On the other hand, she is putting her cart before her horse. She shouldn't be focusing on one investment as opposed to another before she has figured out what different rates of return can do for her. In other words, she is asking a good question at the wrong time. First, she needs to compute her future wealth to see how she should invest.

Here's what we know about her. First, she has accumulated around $20,500. She is saving $9000 per year. She has a goal of $250,000 in 20 years. Let's see where she will wind up, at several different rates of return.

At 5 percent—a most unmaverick of goals!—she will accumulate $375,865 in 20 years and accomplish her goal.

At 8 percent, the figure would be $549,356.

At 12 percent, $933,037.

At 15 percent, $1,404,805.

At 20 percent, $2,811,151.

Once Stephanie understands what compounding can do for her at different rates of return, she can more easily figure out what investment strategy she should follow. If her goal is *truly* to wind up with (only) $250,000, she should invest in a money market fund. There, she'll accomplish her objective with almost no risk.

Maybe you're thinking that she needs to invest for her retirement, too, so she should be reaching for a higher rate of return, right? Well, actually, no; wrong. Stephanie has stated her financial goal. From my perspective, and maybe yours, her goal is not a very maverick one. But hey—! She's thought about it, and she's written it down, and those are the most important first steps toward achieving a goal. I hope and assume that she has her retirement needs covered in some other way.

My feedback to her, by the way, was that she was taking too much risk by investing 80 percent of her 401(k) in the stock market, at least in the volatile state that the market was in at the time. But I also steered her toward the compounded-growth calculations just listed. Once you know where you are going, figuring out what to do next is a whole lot easier.

THE BIG PICTURE: THE THREE STEPS TO 401(k) SUCCESS

Want the big picture on your 401(k)? I'll introduce the three steps to success, and then talk you through each of them:

- Save all that you can.
- Believe in your 401(k)'s potential.
- Invest to achieve your desired rate of return.

Save All That You Can

Whether you are just starting out or have been contributing to your 401(k) for years, the first thing you should do is take a good hard look at how much you *are* saving each month, and how much you *could be* saving each month.

Part of the answer lies in the relative tightness of your monthly budget. In other words, how much can you live without? Remember that we're talking pretax dollars here, and putting away 50 more pretax dollars per month (that's $11.54 a week that gets you $600 per year) *never* means that your take-home pay will go down by that much. Ask your benefits officer to run these numbers for you, and salt away as much as you can stand to. Believe me: When it's deducted from your paycheck in pretax dollars before you ever see it, you won't miss it.

The second part of the answer lies in your company's degree of participation in your plan. Many companies match a portion of your contribution, and you should definitely check this out with your benefits department. An employer's 401(k) match is the easiest money in the world to make. It's like finding money on the sidewalk, except that you don't even have to look at the sidewalk. If your employer matches your contributions up to a certain point—for example, up to 6 percent of your pay—then you absolutely, positively have to establish (at least) 6 percent as your savings goal. You must always *save to the max*.

As we can see from Stephanie's example, "saving to the max" means "maxing" out her 15 percent contribution, and also getting that 3 percent from her company. Never, never, never pass up your employer's match, whatever that percentage might be.

Once you have figured out how much you're going to save, and when you know what's currently in your 401(k)—if anything—then you can start getting excited about your future. And getting excited early is very important. Most people fail to realize the value of *time* in their savings decisions. Each year that you let go by without contributing to your retirement is a savings year lost forever. Don't let this happen to you. At the start of each year, review how much you are saving, and figure out how much additional money you could put away.

Then do it.

Believe In Your 401(k)'s Potential

Some people don't get it (despite my best efforts!). They just don't think about how they are going to provide for themselves in the future. They don't get started with retirement savings when they have the most valuable growth-maker working in their favor: *time*.

Time allows for compounding. The sooner you start wealth-building, the more benefit you will derive from the compounding process. Take the examples of two people who both invest $2000 per year, and achieve compounded growth rates of 12 percent. The only difference between them is that one starts at age 25 and the other starts at 30. How much will they both have at age 65?

Starting at age 25, investing $2000 per year, and compounding at 12 percent annually for 40 years equals **$1,720,284.**

Starting at age 30, investing $2000 per year, and compounding at 12 percent for 35 years equals **$968,926.**

What's the difference that results from getting started five years sooner? The difference is more than **$750,000.**

It is amazing what compounding can do for you over time. All you have to do is *get started,* and then keep saving and managing your money. Still not quite with me on this? Then run your own numbers, and play the "what if?" game. This is the best way to watch compounding do most of the hard work for you. I have included some compounded growth tables near the back of this book (Chapter 21) for reference, but perhaps the easiest way to run your own numbers is to use one of the many wealth calculators on the Web. For example, look at:

• Yahoofinance.Com
• Fabianlive.com
• Quicken.com

Once you've got one of these tools at your disposal, getting the evidence for the power of compounding is easy. Simply answer the following four questions, plugging in numbers as you go:

Step 1: How much money will you be saving on a monthly basis?

Step 2: How much is your 401(k) worth now?

Step 3: How many years before you reach 59.5?

Step 4: What rate of return would you like to project?

For this last step, I suggest that you work with several rates of return. This will become important when we start talking about investment strategies. For now, try out 8 percent, 12 percent, 15 percent, and of course the maverick investing goal of 20 percent compounded (or your ambitious personal equivalent).

Well? Are you amazed at the power of compounded growth? You should be. Albert Einstein called compounding the eighth wonder of the world. Benjamin Franklin, that wily old colonial sage, laid out a scheme in his will whereby the city of Boston—over the course of the 200 years following his death—would turn his bequest of 1000 pounds sterling to that city into 4.6 million pounds sterling. How? You got it: the power of compounding. You don't have 200 years, but you've got plenty of time to do plenty well.

Invest to Achieve Your Desired Rate of Return

Does everyone have to invest in the stock market? No. Can you follow a simple asset-allocation plan to meet your long-term retirement goals? Well, based on what I've written earlier, it pains me to say it, but, "Sure you can." Stephanie, whose case was cited earlier in this chapter, could reach her objective simply by investing in a money fund. That's why you need to run the numbers. It aligns your investment strategy with your goals and risk profile.

This brings up the separate subject of risk. Most investors have been programmed to believe that there is little risk in the stock market, if they're willing to stick it out for the long term. Especially in the wake of the decade-long bull market of the 1990s, people are inclined to believe that if you hold stocks long enough, you will do just fine, because stocks always rise over the long term.

Well, yeah, *if* you're holding the right stuff, and *if* you don't need the money at the bottom of a down cycle, and *if* you don't panic in reaction to a bear market. That's a lot of "ifs," all lined up in one sentence, right? Taking an example from another field: In 1925, owning real estate in downtown Detroit was probably a great thing. Fifty years later, it was a terrible thing. And maybe in the year 2025, it will be a great thing again. (Things seem to be looking up for downtown Detroit, as of this writing.) But what if you had been forced to sell in 1975?

Now think about the opportunity costs of holding that real estate all those years. What if you had gotten out of Detroit real estate altogether in 1925, and pursued a maverick investment strategy for the next 100 years (I like your chances in that scenario!)

Risk can be managed, to some extent, through diversification—that is, not putting all your eggs in one basket (Detroit real estate, tech-sector funds, etc.). Many media pundits start from the assumption that the people they are communicating with are already diversified, and are holding the "right stuff" in their portfolios. Well, this could not be further from the truth, in the case of many of the portfolios that I have reviewed. Either they never were diversified, or they became less diversified over time.

Finally, how will you react if we experience another scary bear market, and the majority of your assets are exposed to risk? Investors' reactions to bear markets have been well documented, and are pretty well understood. Most people don't sell before or even during the bear. It is *after* the decline that investors find themselves in the position of giving up on stocks for the long term.

This is why you need to truly understand how you react to risk. I would rather see someone work with a low stock exposure—even though that will limit their upside gains—if they know for a fact that the prospect of risk will cause them to react negatively.

For that reason, I'm including a "risk questionnaire" in this chapter. This builds on the material presented in Chapter 15, where I introduced the concept of a risk spectrum (ranging from conservative growth maverick to aggressive growth maverick). If you answer the following questions honestly and accurately, you'll know a lot more about how *you* should manage your 401(k)—with the emphasis on the "you." Discovering your true risk quotient will help you select and invest in the right funds. It will go a long way toward keeping you committed to your goals for life, and keeping you and your 401(k) out of trouble.

UNDERSTAND YOURSELF (AND HOW TO MANAGE YOUR ACCOUNT)

There are 65 million participants in 401(k) plans around the country, and no two of these people are alike. Everyone has different dreams and desires. What does this mean for you? It means that at least until you understand yourself—and maybe for a long time thereafter—you shouldn't let anyone tell you how you should invest.

On the next two pages you'll find my risk questionnaire. It's easy, painless, and nobody but you needs to know how it comes out. It will take you, at most, five minutes to fill out. These will be five minutes well spent. When you add up your score, you're sure to find out something new about yourself.

1. **Which of the following statements best describes your investment knowledge?**

   a. I'm clueless, but I want to learn more.

   b. I have a general idea of what is happening when the Dow or NASDAQ moves up or down.

   c. I have a basic understanding of stocks, bonds, and cash, and could explain these different asset classes.

   d. I understand how stock mutual funds work, and I am familiar with different types of funds and different fund categories.

   e. I am extremely knowledgeable. I could explain standard deviation, beta, drawdown, and other risk-measurement concepts.

2. **Which of the following statements best describes the way you first set up your 401(k)?**

   a. I put everything into guaranteed income contracts (GICs) or fixed-income funds.

   b. I chose a mix of stock funds, bond funds, and cash.

   c. I picked the three highest-rated Morningstar funds.

d. I chose stock funds only.

e. I placed most of my money in company stock and the rest in aggressive growth stock funds.

3. **Which of the following statements best describes when you might make changes to your 401(k)?**

a. Never. I basically leave my 401(k) alone.

b. Only when I get a quarterly statement and a fund has gone nowhere in a year.

c. When I see a fund that has three-year returns of better than 20 percent, I move a good portion of my money there.

d. I go online at least once a month to shift my choices a bit.

e. If I'm honest about it, I'm changing things at least once a week.

4. **When would you be most likely to sell a stock fund in your 401(k)?**

a. I won't sell. Even if it's doing badly today, it'll come back when the market shifts.

b. When I can't stand seeing it lose one more dollar.

c. When it's losing money after one year.

d. When it appears on lists of worst stock funds or shows up in the worst 20 percent in its category.

e. When another fund in my 401(k) is doing better.

5. **Your company not only wants to offer you a promotion, but they want to increase your compensation in a way that will make you the happiest. Which of these choices sounds best to you?**

a. A 5 percent raise and a 5-year contract guaranteeing employment.

b. A 15 percent raise and a 10 percent year-end bonus.

c. A 10 percent raise and bonus potential between 10 and 25 percent.

d. A cost-of-living increase with incentives that could range anywhere from 10 to 50 percent of my salary.

e. Stock options worth hundreds of thousands if the company goes public.

6. **How would your spouse or closest friend describe you?**

a. Afraid of your cat's shadow.

b. Cautious.

c. Smart risk-taker.

d. Carefree.

e. Adventurer, even reckless.

7. **How do you feel when you suffer a financial loss?**

a. I don't suffer losses because I don't risk very much.

b. I feel guilty for risking too much.

c. I feel like I failed.

d. I feel bad, but I am determined to learn from mistakes.

e. I feel like I have a brand-new opportunity.

8. **Your 401(k) was worth $40,000 six months ago. It has dropped 11 percent, and you now have $35,600. You think:**

a. Time to move everything to a very conservative investment or group of investments. It's too difficult watching the money disappear.

b. Time to become a bit more moderate. I must be taking unnecessary chances.

c. Time to look at individual holdings and see if there are one or more positions that are dragging the entire portfolio down.

d. Time to be more aggressive and get 100 percent of my money into aggressive growth funds.

e. Time to become bold and put everything into an individual stock or a single aggressive growth fund.

9. **Agree or disagree: One of your most important investment objectives is to beat the Street!**

a. Strongly disagree.

b. Disagree.

c. Neutral.

d. Agree.

e. Strongly agree.

10. **Refer to the Investment Choice table. Which of the following gain/loss combinations is most appealing to you (no mixing and matching!)?**

Investment Choice	Best Case	Worst Case
Stock Fund A	+60 percent	−40 percent
Stock Fund B	+40 percent	−25 percent

Investment Choice	Best Case	Worst Case
Stock Fund C	+25 percent	−14 percent
Stock Fund D	+18 percent	−10 percent
Stock Fund E	+12 percent	−6 percent

a. Stock Fund E
b. Stock Fund D
c. Stock Fund C
d. Stock Fund B
e. Stock Fund A

Scoring:

Score the quiz the following way: For every "a" answer, give yourself 1 point; for every "b" answer, 2 points; for every "c" answer, 3 points; for every "d" answer, 4 points: and for every "e" answer, 5 points.

If you scored more than 40 points, you're an Aggressive Investor, and you should feel comfortable taking on extra risk to attain 20-plus percent annualized compounded growth with your investments. While all fund categories are suitable for your 401(k) portfolio, your most aggressive choices are:

Mid-cap growth

Small-cap growth

Science & technology

Sector funds

Don't worry if you aren't familiar with these terms. Later in this chapter, I'll present a detailed explanation of all of these choices. For now, just file the list away.

If you scored between 21 and 39 points, you're a Moderate, comfortably taking on some risk to attain 17 percent+ annualized compounded growth with your investments. Fund categories suitable for your 401(k) portfolio include all moderate and conservative growth choices, but you would eliminate the aggressive choices from your selections. For example, you'd be most comfortable with:

Large-cap growth

Mid-cap core

Small-cap core

Small-cap value

Multi-cap growth
Global
Global flexible
International

If you scored between 10 and 20 points, you're a Conservative Maverick, comfortable with attaining 15 percent-plus annualized compounded growth on your investments with limited risk. You would eliminate both the aggressive and moderate risk categories. Fund categories with suitable growth for your maverick 401(k) portfolio include:

Large-cap core
Large-cap value
Mid-cap value
Equity income
Multi-cap core
Multi-cap value
Flexible portfolio
Balanced

To sum up: Knowing whether you are aggressive, moderate, or conservative in terms of your risk tolerance will help you in choosing the appropriate investments for you. As noted, there are about a zillion choices out there, and a great company 401(k) menu may include dozens of fund choices. When you are choosing investments, you have to be able to eliminate some the choices right off the bat. Work with these lists, based on your self-profile, and you'll have a good jumping-off point.

BE AN ACTIVE MAVERICK MANAGER OF YOUR 401(k)

Here's where mavericks part company with many of their fellow investors. As I've already noted, almost all of the advice and counsel you receive will recommend that you invest in stocks for the long haul, and not trouble yourself about intervening ups and downs. (Buy'n'hold!) Then—as this conventional wisdom goes—as you get closer to retirement, you start to back away from equities to keep risk at bay. Financial planners often call this strategy "age-based asset allocation." The assumption behind age-based asset allocation is that returns and risks both increase with increased stock-market exposure, according to the following formula:

• No exposure to stocks: potential rate of return is 5 percent
• Minimal exposure to stocks: 7 percent

- Some exposure to stocks: 8 percent
- Mostly stocks: 10 percent
- All stocks: 12 percent

As you know very well by now, asset allocation is *not* the maverick way. Mavericks are seeking extraordinary returns. Therefore, we must use unconventional means to attain them. We have to be more active in our investment allocations than those who play the asset-allocation game.

Managing your 401(k) actively is an *absolutely critical part* of the maverick strategy. This means investing in a timely way, and also disinvesting in time to capture gains. Consider the following e-mail from a youngish listener named Tim:

> Doug, I need 401(k) HELP! I lost about $200,000 after having most of my money in company stock and a mutual fund. I am now waiting for a buy signal. My choices are blah, blah, and blah. I am 39 years old, and plan on working another 15–20 years.

Here is another story plucked from the annals of bear markets. Think about what that last bear market cost Tim ($200,000!). Even worse, think what would have happened to Tim if he had been 20 years older when the bear bit him, and he lost 66 percent of the value in his retirement account! That planned retirement would have been postponed indefinitely. Don't let this happen to you—but at the same time, don't retreat to the passivity of age-based asset allocation. Instead, invest your 401(k) assets in stocks appropriate for your risk tolerance when the market is in an uptrend, and retreat to the money funds when a bear market is in control. Be active!

One more yellow flag that's raised by Tim's story: While he doesn't provide a breakdown as to how much of his money is in company stock, this is an issue that I always try to follow up on. Some 401(k) investors work for companies that are publicly traded, that offer company stock as an investment option, and that offer incentives for the purchase of that stock. This is a generally well-intentioned idea that can be fraught with peril. Although I think it's all well and good for people to be invested (at least psychologically) in the company they work for, company stock can be a true retirement-killer. I've had way too many people call the radio show and tell me about how their company stock holdings have dropped by 50 percent or more. "Now what?" they ask. But at that point, there's no great answer.

My rule of thumb? *No more then one third to company stock, ever.* Or almost never. If you must go above 33 percent initially to get the company match, take a deep breath and do it (unless you have no faith in your com-

pany's near-term prospects, of course, in which case you need to ask why
you're working there). Then sell down your position as quickly as you can
reasonably get away with it, and don't ever get overexposed to your company stock again.

DECODING THE JARGON

Mavericks are like Willie Sutton. "Why do you rob banks?" he was asked.
"Because that's where the money is," he answered.

We mavericks don't rob banks, but we *do* go where the money is. As
we've learned in previous chapters, the only investment choices with any
chance of getting us to our growth rates are the equity options. So for the
401(k) investor, any employer-offered fund that invests 90 percent of its
portfolio or more in stocks should be considered a potential buy for mavericks, and monitored accordingly.

Unfortunately, mutual fund companies (and sometimes even 401(k)
plan administrators) tend to make identifying stocks funds a little difficult.
Fund companies give their funds unrevealing names—in some cases, I
think, to keep their "shift-n-drift" options open. They use marketing gimmicks that obscure, rather than illuminate, exactly what's for sale here.

So in the interest of illumination, let's review what's for sale here. All
stock funds are (or should be) described by (1) the *style* that the manager is
using, and (2) the *size of company* that he or she is investing in, most often
expressed in terms of the company's capitalization (how much all of its
stock is worth on the market).

There are two basic styles—*growth* and *value*—which can refer either
to the manager's personal style (a "growth orientation") or to the kind of
stock favored by the fund (a "growth stock"). Growth stocks are shares of
those companies that have prospects for significant growth in the future.
Value stocks are shares in companies that have been around for a while, that
have underlying value, and that are producing earnings.

Stocks (like mavericks) come in different sizes: small cap (for capitalization), medium cap, and large cap.

Blend them together and you get the universe of funds. For example:

- Small-cap blend
- Mid-cap value
- Large-cap growth

Understanding the following working definitions for the Lipper fund
categories currently used in *The Wall Street Journal* will make managing
your 401(k) a lot easier. They are:

Large-cap growth (LCG).   Funds that, by portfolio practice, invest at least 75 percent in large-cap companies. (Large-cap companies are those that the stock market values at more than $5 billion.)
Large-cap growth funds typically invest in companies with earnings that are expected to outpace industry and index peers.

Large-cap core (LCC).   Funds that, by portfolio practice, invest at least 75 percent in large-cap companies. Large-cap core funds have a wide flexibility with the stocks they invest in, whether they are rapid earners or beaten-down bargains.

Large-cap value (LCV).   Funds that, by portfolio practice, invest at least 75 percent in large-cap companies. Large-cap value funds go after companies that are underappreciated and oversold. Fund managers will acquire stocks with below-average p/e ratios and below-average growth figures.

Mid-cap growth (MCG).   Funds that, by portfolio practice, invest at least 75 percent in mid-cap companies. (Mid-cap companies are those that the stock market values between $1 billion and $5 billion.) Mid-cap growth funds typically invest in organizations with earnings that are expected to outpace industry and index peers.

Mid-cap core (MCC).   Funds that, by portfolio practice, invest at least 75 percent in mid-cap companies. Mid-cap core funds have a wide flexibility with the stocks they invest in, whether they are rapid earners or beaten-down bargains.

Mid-cap value (MCV).   Funds that, by portfolio practice, invest at least 75 percent in mid-cap companies. Mid-cap value funds go after companies that are underappreciated and oversold. Fund managers will acquire stocks with below-average p/e ratios and below-average growth figures.

Multi-cap growth (MLG).   Funds that, by portfolio practice, invest in a hodge-podge of market cap ranges; that is, they do not concentrate 75 percent of their equity assets in any one particular market capitalization. Multi-cap growth funds typically invest in companies with earnings that are expected to outpace industry and index peers.

Multi-cap core (MLC).   Funds that, like MLGs, invest in a hodge-podge of market cap ranges; that is, they do not concentrate 75 percent of their equity assets in any one particular market capitalization. Multi-cap core funds have a wide flexibility with the stocks they invest in, whether they are rapid earners or beaten-down bargains.

Multi-cap value (MLV).   Funds that, like MLGs and MLCs, invest in a hodge-podge of market cap ranges; that is, they do not concentrate 75 percent of their equity assets in any one particular market capitalization. Multi-cap value funds go after companies that are underappreciated and oversold. Fund managers will acquire stocks with below-average p/e ratios and below-average growth figures.

Small-cap growth (SCG).   Funds that, by portfolio practice, invest at least 75 percent in small-cap companies. (Small-cap companies are those that the stock market values below $1 billion.) Small-cap growth funds typically invest in companies with earnings that are expected to outpace industry and index peers.

Small-cap core (SCC).   Funds that, by portfolio practice, invest at least 75 percent in small-cap companies. Small-cap core funds have a wide flexibility with the stocks they invest in, whether they are rapid earners or beaten-down bargains.

Small-cap value (SCV).   Funds that, by portfolio practice, invest at least 75 percent in small-cap companies. Small-cap value funds go after companies that are underappreciated and oversold. Fund managers will acquire stocks with below-average p/e ratios and below-average growth figures.

Equity income (EI).   Funds that, by portfolio practice, seek relatively high income by investing 65 percent or more in dividend-paying securities.

Global (GL).   A fund that invests at least 25 percent in securities trade outside the United States. May own U.S. securities, as well.

International (INTL).   A fund that invests its assets in securities with primary trading markets outside of the United States.

Science & technology (ST).   You don't need to ask. A fund that invests 65 percent of its equity portfolio in science and tech stocks.

Balanced (BAL).   Weak-performing, asset-allocating, principal-conserving funds with a stock/bond ratio around 60 percent/40 percent. (This is, of course, a maverick-influenced definition; the one in the paper reads a little different.)

Flexible portfolio (FX).   Talk about names that deceive the eye with special effects. This one invests across a variety of asset classes and market capitalizations with its own unique philosophy. Best description: Anything goes!

Global flexible (GX).   This one also invests across a variety of asset classes and market capitalizations with its own unique philosophy. At least 25 percent of its portfolio is invested in securities traded outside of the United States.

OK: there you have it. All the jargon you need to understand in order to match your risk profile with appropriate fund choices in your company's 401(k) menu. All we have left to do is keep you away from serious 401(k)-related mistakes, and you'll be on your way to Easy Street.

THE FEROCIOUS FIVE: 401(k) MISTAKES YOU DON'T WANT TO MAKE

I'll wrap up this chapter by running through what I call the Ferocious Five: that is, the five things you really don't want to do (or fail to do) to your 401(k).

Mistake Number 1: Not investing in the plan at all.   I know, I know: It's easy to get snared in the relentless grind of day-to-day finances. There's rent or mortgages, property taxes, car loans, soccer uniforms, schooling, groceries, utilities—and so on, and so on. Studies have shown that almost everybody in the galaxy, no matter what their income level, feels like they're about 20 percent short in their operating budget. ("If I could just take home 20 percent more . . . !") So when our new employer asks us if we want to contribute to a 401(k), many of us decide that we can't afford to. But the truth is that *we can't afford not to.*

Remember, starting with a minimum contribution (even if it's as little as 1 percent of your salary) is just that—a start. Once you see the zeros in your account multiply, parting with more of your paycheck gets easier. (In addition, your 401(k) contributions are pretax, which means less reportable income for the taxman to latch onto.) And don't forget all that compounding: A 30-year-old who contributes just $100 per month will amass nearly $4 million by the time he or she reaches age 65.

Plus, if your employer matches any amount of your contribution—let's say 50 percent of every dollar you salt away—you receive an automatic 50 percent return on your investment. This is the best guarantee you'll ever find in the financial industry. That's an additional *$2 million return* on that $100 monthly contribution!

Mistake Number 2: Taking out 401(k) loans.　I also know how hard it can be to keep your hand out of that 401(k) cookie jar, especially when you've got that BMW brochure sitting on your lap and retirement is still many years away. And according to some figures I've seen recently, an alarmingly high percentage of Americans are dipping into the cookie jar.

Resist that temptation! First of all, you won't like the negative compounding consequences of yanking 401(k) money out for frivolous reasons. (It can set you back hundreds of thousands). But more important, draining your retirement fund today may leave you in the lurch when you finally hang up those working shoes.

Exhaust every other option—like opening an equity line of credit, or visiting your credit union, or begging a family member—before you tap into your retirement for short-term gratification. If you can't talk your rich uncle into it, then it's not a good enough reason to loot your 401(k).

Borrowing hurts your compounding. Let's say you've saved $50,000. Now you decide you want to borrow $10,000 for five years. If you stuck a lump sum of $40,000 in a mutual fund account and let it sit in an S&P Index Fund for five years and didn't touch it, and it grew at an annual rate of, say, 12 percent, you would wind up with $71,000. But a $50,000 investment, assuming that same rate, would mushroom to $88,000. (And of course, both those numbers and the difference between them would be considerably higher if you used maverick strategies.) Hands out of that cookie jar!

Mistake Number 3: Investing too conservatively.　Lots of investors are given the remarkable opportunity of enjoying tax-deferred growth in a company-matched 401(k) with great investment options—and then they throw that opportunity away by keeping the money in money markets, guaranteed investment contracts (GICs), or bond options.

Let me go back to where I opened this chapter. This money is among your most important assets. It's what you're going to use to support yourself for as long as 30 years after you retire. That's why you want to invest 100 percent of it in stock funds. Consider that a $10,000 annual contribution growing at a buy-n-hold clip of 14 percent will be worth over $2 million in 25 years—more than enough for a comfortable lifestyle. But at 20 percent, you'd be looking at more than $5.5 million. Which number do you like better?

Only about 45 percent of the $1.72 trillion in 401(k) plans today is where it should be: in stock funds. Forget the money-market accounts, forget the bonds. Go where I've already told you to go so many times before—stocks!

Mistake Number 4: Owning too much company stock.   I touched on this earlier. The good news is that your company has a matching provision for its 401(k) program. The bad news is, it's in company stock.

Don't get me wrong: Free money is always good, in my book, and a company that antes up for its employee's retirement years is doing right by those employees. But the fact remains that company stock may not be the best option for you. We've talked about your risk profile. Company stock is an aggressive holding, and should be grouped as such for your account. I don't care if you work for a startup Internet firm or a solid blue-chip company; there's no reason to pin all of your financial dreams on just one stock.

I know someone personally who works for Raytheon, and had some serious six-figure cash tied up in Raytheon stock in his 401(k). We're talking about a stock that traded at $70 back in July 1999. The picture since then hasn't been too pretty. Dogged by troubled defense programs and delays with a new business jet, the number 3 U.S. defense contractor has traded as low as $18 per share—in other words, a 74 percent nosedive. As of this writing, my acquaintance had lost nearly half of his retirement savings— some $200,000—because he was way overexposed to company stock.

Go into company stock if your company makes it worthwhile. If you have to let that holding drift above 33 percent of your portfolio in order to get matching benefits, fine—but sell as soon as possible to get that percentage down to one-third (or lower, if possible).

Mistake Number 5: Not asking for more options.   It's often said that you can't fight City Hall. In that spirit, many people just figure they have to live and lose with the funds currently being offered in their 401(k) plans. Year after year, they plop their hard-earned money into funds that undercut their ability to grow that million-dollar portfolio.

But you have *every right* to request a change in the menu offered by your company. In fact, your company has what the lawyers (if we would let them into the room) would refer to as "fiduciary responsibility," meaning that the law *strongly encourages* them to give you the necessary tools to make the best possible investments in your retirement plan.

Hey, who wants a disgruntled employee filing a suit claiming that better funds would have given them a bigger nest egg? And from the company's perspective, it's really just a matter of filling out some paperwork. And finally, the chances are good that the person or people at your company responsible for these decisions are good guys who want to do the right thing. All you have to do is help them *get* there.

Here's how.

If you haven't already researched and come up with suggestions for some new fund choices, do so. That's your first step. Once you have a solid proposal, write it down. Be succinct. In the fewest words possible, explain how it will be beneficial to both the company and its employees.

As soon as you've got a solid plan, run it by your coworkers. Call them, e-mail them, organize a meeting. Get the word out. Even if a small percentage of employees requests a change, that will be a powerful catalyst.

Meanwhile, find out who at your company is responsible for making these kinds of changes. Is it the benefits manager, a benefits committee, or a plan administration committee? If you don't feel comfortable going to the top, try presenting the plan to your boss. After all, he or she has a stake in this, too. Encourage coworkers to do the same. Make some noise; create a buzz in the office.

Keep in mind, too, that this reassessment should be an ongoing process. (In fact, this is something you should consider sticking in your proposal.) Funds thrive, and then they fail to thrive. Take the PBHG Growth Fund, for example. Over the years, it has been one of the most popular 401(k) funds, compounding at nearly 20 percent per year between 1992 and 1997. In 1999, it returned 47 percent. But today it's a lemon, losing 22 percent in 2000 and underperforming its mid-cap growth peers over 1, 3, and 5 years. Why stick with it?

In your conversations with your company, be both patient and persistent. Recognize that most of the time, managers are engaged in fire fighting. They put out the scariest fire, and move on to the next one. You have to get a nice warm glow going behind your cause, but you don't necessarily want to set fire to headquarters. Strike the balance.

So there you have it: the Ferocious Five, and how to solve or sidestep them. In the next chapter, we'll look at some more exotic ways of building wealth. But never, never, never forget the power of the 401(k)!

19

New Growth Vehicles

In Chapter 3, I presented the 10 principles of maverick investing. The last principle on this list—as I'm absolutely *sure* you'll recall—was that *mavericks are adept at recognizing useful investment-related innovations, and quickly capitalizing on them.* In that context, I talked about the Internet, "$50, $5, $0 Investing," and something mysterious—"funds that trade like stocks"—that I promised to return to later in the book.

"Later" is now. In this chapter, I'm going to talk about some of the new growth vehicles that exist out there—vehicles that can help you live up to your advance billing as an investor (a *maverick* investor!) who spots and capitalizes upon innovations.

But first, a review of a few of the basics. Every investor is faced with the strategic decision as to *what* he or she will invest in: individual stocks, or funds? I believe strongly that you need to make this call for yourself— but I believe equally strongly that 90 percent of all investors should use diversified investments versus individual stocks.

By extension, of course, one investor in 10 out there can and should make money by buying and selling individual stocks. It's a scary life, for steely-looking characters with nerves of iron. Maybe you're one of them. I know I'm not!

I run into a lot of people who *think* they're in the 10 percent, but aren't (or shouldn't be). Many seem to indulge in individual stock transactions as a way to be cool, an insider, a player. When they do so, they seem to think they are *way cooler* than the mutual fund crowd.

Well, fine, if you have the nerves, skill, and luck to pull it off. Most people don't. Most of the poseurs learned something about themselves in 2000, when they saw their portfolios—which were not well diversified, for the most part—plunge farther and faster than the general market. Bear markets, it turns out, are the great levelers. They whack the *way cool* crowd much harder, and much meaner, than they whack mavericks like me.

The moral? Professional management is a good thing, if you can (1) find it, and (2) buy it inexpensively enough. The same is true for diversification: Done right, and done efficiently, it's a wealth-generator and wealth-protector. A good mutual fund—or a mutual-fund-like vehicle—gives you these valuable attributes at an affordable price.

In that spirit, let me introduce to you the latest mutual-fund-like innovations from Wall Street. They are cheap, they perform, and they are easy to buy and sell. They give you the ability to customize your portfolio as you see fit, grow your portfolio at desirable rates, and provide lots of investment options for the changing times ahead. And just as good, these three kinds of investments are a lot of fun to own. Once you get a taste for them, you may never be tempted to buy an individual stock again.

The three new growth vehicles are called *exchange traded funds, enhanced index funds,* and *sector funds.* Each provides unique advantages to the maverick investor. Each gives you the ability to be either conservative or aggressive. All can help you achieve maverick-sized returns.

EXCHANGE TRADED FUNDS (ETFs)
If you follow the financial news, chances are you've read about exchange traded funds (ETFs), and the odds are you are going to keep reading about them.

ETFs come in lots of different flavors, with hip names like Cubes, Diamonds, Spiders, Webs, VIPERS, and iSHARES. In all cases, they are a cross between stocks and mutual funds. They have features that appeal to long-term investors, as well as short-term, rapid-fire traders.

Exchange-traded funds (ETFs) are the fastest growing asset-grabbers in the investment world. Why? Because they are less expensive to own than mutual funds, more diversified than individual stocks, and easy to buy and sell.

WHAT ARE EXCHANGE TRADED FUNDS?

ETFs are funds that seek the returns of a broad market index or a sector index. Unlike traditional mutual funds, however, ETFs may be bought or sold throughout the trading day. That's why many people call them "funds that trade like stocks."

Like stocks, ETFs are extremely liquid; that is, you can exchange your ETF for cash, or cash for an ETF, at the exact moment that you want. Similarly, you can execute your purchase or sale at an intraday price; you do not need to wait for the market to close, as with traditional mutual funds.

ETFs also enjoy the benefits of index mutual funds. For example, when you acquire a "basket" of stocks, you are diversifying and reducing the likelihood of getting hurt by a single company's misfortunes. Also, because the managers of ETFs are not picking stocks, the expenses of operating an ETF are extremely low. Most important, your basket will cover an established index like the S&P 500 or the Nasdaq 100. That means your ETF gives you the exposure to a particular market segment, size, or style, at the time and in the form that you need it.

Although the American Stock Exchange (AMEX) introduced the first ETF in 1993, the investing public did not begin embracing the concept until recently. That's in part because many investors only became aware of these interesting new options when they began to explore online trading.

Today, investors pour billions of dollars into these stock baskets every quarter. Diamonds, Spiders, Vipers, iShares, and Holdrs: ETFs suddenly seem to have exploded onto our computer screens and into our financial accounts. The truth is, though, that they've been around for the better part of a decade.

ETFs VERSUS INDEX MUTUAL FUNDS

ETF owners have equity in a pool of securities, just like the owners of traditional index funds. Both instruments give you broad market exposure—or, if you like, more specialized sector exposure—at a low cost and with a high degree of diversification.

Unlike traditional index funds, however, ETFs give you the opportunity to change the direction of your portfolio when you want, more or less instantaneously. Forget about worrying about what the net asset value (NAV) of your mutual fund will be at day's end, especially when the market's in a one-day tailspin! And say "goodbye" to those onerous redemption fees. You want out? Push the button, and you're out.

Simply stated, ETFs give you greater control over your money. With a single trade, ETFs allow you to buy or sell a well-known and infrequently altered basket of stock—any time that the market is open.

FIVE KEYS TO ETF INVESTING

There are five basic things you need to know about ETF investing. They are:

1. Great Profits, Less Risk!   Most people can easily grasp the terrible danger inherent in betting their retirement on the fate of a single stock. Simply put, we don't want the value of our shares to plummet from $150 per share to $20 per share overnight!

That's why we diversify our stock assets. Diversifying in ETF baskets is a terrific way to pursue the maverick compounding goal of 20 percent per year.

While ETFs are similar to mutual funds (both are "baskets of stocks"), ETFs have several advantages over their older, more established counterparts. They're less expensive, more tax-efficient, and more flexible than any other basket.

Saving money is always a good thing, of course, but it's particularly good in terms of investments. When you save money on costs and taxes, you have more money with which to build future wealth. And when you're able to sell on your own terms, you can lock in your profits intraday; you don't have to wait for a closing price that may have fallen several percentage points by the close of market.

2. Tiny Expenses!   I mentioned the low-cost appeal of ETFs. ETFs are the kings of low-cost "baskets." For instance, the average annual expense for a mutual fund is 1.1 percent. ETFs range between 0.10 percent and 0.65 percent.

Many index fund providers argue this point, explaining that their S&P index fund carries a mere 0.30 percent ratio. However, equivalent ETFs like the Amex Spider (SPY) and the iShares S&P 500 (IVV)cost 0.12 percent and 0.09 percent, respectively.

No matter how you slice or dice it, ETFs are less expensive to own. But they're not appropriate for dollar-cost averagers because of the trading costs at your brokerage. Even $8 a trade can add up.

3. Sorry, Uncle Sam!   ETFs most often represent an established benchmark in the industry. For instance, you might be interested in the S&P 500, the Nasdaq 100, the Dow Jones Healthcare Index, or the S&P Financial Subsector Index.

Since indices have much lower turnover than the overwhelming majority of actively managed funds, capital gains distributions are negligible. In fact, you barely have to think about them.

This does not mean that ETFs won't distribute any capital gains to shareholders—because they will. Big-time composites do, on occasion, change their underlying stocks. Still, the tax-efficiency benefit is attractive for mavericks accumulating wealth in their taxable accounts.

4. Savvy Investing in a Fraction of the Time!   Do you spend countless hours hunched over your computer, scouring the details of insider trading reports, balance sheets, and analysts' recommendations? If so, my question to you is, *Why?*

You can spend half of your waking hours investigating the everchanging attractiveness of 10 to 20 individual companies on a quarterly basis. In all probability, you still won't outperform an established broad market benchmark or appropriate sector index. Alternatively, you can spend 10 minutes a week inspecting key info on the universe of ETFs (i.e., uptrend, downtrend, and recent momentum). They number about 100, but they cover virtually any style, sector, or market cap on the books.

5. Simply, Very Flexible!   Ready for some deep Wall Street jargon? ETFs can be shorted, margined, and optioned(!). I mention this because it's simply another indicator of how flexible these investments are. But don't worry if that jargon baffled you. Mavericks can take advantage of the flexibility of ETFs without engaging in any complex stock strategies.

What aspects of ETF flexibility do we enjoy? In addition to being able to buy or sell ETFs at any point in the trading day, we like the choice of choosing any style, sector, or market-cap size. For example: Want exposure to small-cap value stocks? Try the iShare IWN for coverage of the Russell 2000 Value Index. Thinking this is the year for big-time banks and financial service firms? The S&P Select Financial Spider (XLF) may be your ticket.

At the same time, though, if you're going to play the ETF game, it's critical that you understand intraday trading. In particular, sectors move very quickly and you have to treat them in the same way you'd treat an individual stock—that is, put a 10 percent stop-loss underneath your investment. That way, you can get out before a disastrous plunge destroys your profits.

A MAVERICK APPROACH TO ETF PROFITS

If you're new to ETFs, you may want to begin slowly. There's no better way to get into the game than to peel off a portion of your total portfolio and put what you're learning in this chapter into action.

Your first stop on the Web is AMEX.com. This is the Web site for the American stock exchange. Click on "exchange traded funds" in the tool bar at the top of the page. When the new screen comes up, you'll have in front of you detailed information on every ETF that is available for purchase that day. You will be provided with the ticker symbols, charts, volume, and the underlying securities for each ETF.

In the resource section (Chapter 21) of this book, we have included a list of all ETFs (as of April 2001) and their respective risk categories. Think back to the previous chapter, in which you defined your own risk profile. As you begin building a portfolio with these new tools, you need to keep in mind the universe of choices that are appropriate for your risk profile.

Next, consider starting with your taxable investment account, preferably one with online access. Schwab, Fidelity, Datek, Ameritrade—they all feature the online order procedures that are needed to purchase ETFs.

For example, let's assume you have $1000 in cash and you'd like to put it to work in small-cap growth. You've selected small-cap growth because it has shown real short-term strength, which is one of our criteria for identifying top performers. Next, you check the trend charts and see the Russell 2000 index is breaking out above its trendline. The Russell 2000 and its iShare (IWM) have entered a new uptrend. Therefore, you'd go to the order field of your account, and—assuming that IWM is trading at around 100— you'd buy 10 shares of IWM.

You can probably guess what I'm going to say next: *Always maintain a sell discipline when using ETFs.* When you monitor your ETF holdings each week, you also want to see if there's been a change in status. Has your position fallen below its trendline (moving average)? Have you hit a stop-loss?

Remember, when 100 percent of your assets are in stocks, you absolutely have to control the downside. If an ETF hits a stop-loss or crosses below its trendline, then *sell.* Be diligent. You'll want to monitor more aggressive positions closely, and execute your own sell order if you are close to your stop-loss percentage price. Personally, I use a 10 percent stop-loss—in other words, a point that is 10 percent below the high that my ETF reaches from my date of purchase.

Remember, you're able to move your money quickly with ETFs. That's a positive feature when you need to get out of a volatile sector like tech, telecom, or energy.

Some people find that ETFs move too rapidly for their tastes. If you find yourself feeling that way, or if you find that they're chewing up more of your time than you like, don't feel obligated to use them. You can pursue the maverick target of 20 percent compounded growth in actively managed mutual funds. Or, you can use some combination of ETFs and mutual funds that you find comfortable. It's up to you!

THE WORST MISTAKES ETF INVESTORS CAN MAKE

In the last chapter, I listed five mistakes that people can make in the management of their mutual funds. Here, I'd like to list four mistakes for ETFs.

Mistake Number 1: Buying-n-holding 'em.   Buy'n'hold stock investors got the shock of their lives in 2000. Those who held individual issues of tech stocks witnessed declines of 50 percent, 60 percent, and 70 percent, even in the big names like Dell, Intel, and Apple. Many dot-com gamblers lost 90 percent or more on popular names like e-Toys and Priceline. Even mutual fund investors who thought their basket of stocks meant less risk discovered that they, too, could lose 40 percent in value, just like the Nasdaq.

It's dangerous to hold ETFs as well, particularly if you're concentrating on a single sector. So you need to have a sell discipline in place *before* you make your first purchase. Whether you use the trendlines, stop-losses, the 20 percent growth goal, or some combo as a guide, know when you're going to sell.

Mistake Number 2: Too much trading.   Transaction costs can whittle away at your portfolio's total return. With ETFs you are buying a diversify investment, not an individual stock, so you should not be day-trading these vehicles. They're a great way to build a focused portfolio, or to get exposure to a board sector. But don't own too many EFTs. The same ratios mentioned earlier in the book for the number of funds to size of your portfolio more or less apply to ETFs. For example, if your portfolio is in the $50,000 range, you need to own 2 or 3 funds, but not 6 to 10.

A related mistake is buying and selling on emotions, rather than according to a specific set of rules. If you give in to fear or greed, you may find that trading costs are eating up your gains, and the only one getting rich are the stock exchanges themselves.

Mistake Number 3: Too aggressive . . . again??!!!   Perhaps this mistake doesn't need much highlighting. While many people like the fact that they can go short on ETFs, buy them on margin, or trade them all week long, I would argue that this type of activity detracts from a maverick's long-term objective—20 percent annu-

alized compounded growth, or the personalized equivalent
thereof.

In other words, you don't need to try and hit the home run
with 100 percent of your ETF allocation in a sector. If you do,
you'll probably find yourself watching that sector all the time.
I've said it before: You don't need to spend that much time doing
this investing thing. (Go outside and smell the roses.) You don't
need to bet the farm on a single country ETF or sector when there
are other, more diversified choices with better risk-reward ratios.
Be sensible.

Remember, mavericks tend to their investment affairs for 10
minutes at the end of each week. That's it. If you're spending
more time than that, you're probably getting bogged down.

Mistake Number 4: Falling in love.   You can fall in love all you
like; just don't fall in love with things like new investment vehicles. ETFs are simply tools for the pursuit of our goal. They are
not objects to fall in love with.

For example: Even after the tech bear of 2000–2001, people
are still hooked on the QQQs. This is an ETF that represents
exposure to the NASDAQ 100, which are the largest stocks in

FIGURE 19-1   Chart of the QQQs from December 1999 to June 2001

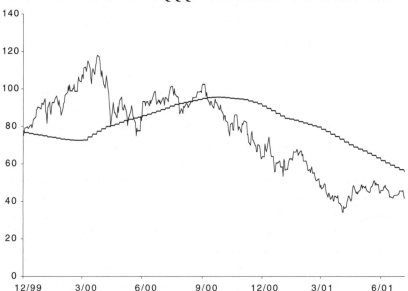

terms of market cap on the over-the-counter exchange. Many investors are hoping that these brand name companies will return to their former glory. Maybe they will; maybe they won't. Letting go of the past and focusing on achieving your goals is the essence of maverick investing. So don't fall in love with any ETF or other investments. Take it from me: They won't reciprocate your love (see Fig. 19-1).

ENHANCED INDEX FUNDS (EIFs)

This is the second of our three categories of new growth vehicles. Enhanced index funds, or EIFs, are a new kind of mutual fund that combines the diversification of a single index with the power of leverage to enhance performance during up markets. EIFs were first introduced in 1995 by the Rydex fund group. The idea was simple: Let's take the concept of indexing and add a performance component to it.

Many people have shied away from basic index funds because active fund investing is more profitable and exciting (at least in a bull market). Now, through selective use of EIFs, you can get both performance and diversification in an index fund. The fund managers use futures and options of the underlying stocks indexes to achieve their results.

ENHANCED INDEX FUNDS CAN TURBO-BOOST YOUR PORTFOLIO

Just for a minute, let's think of investing in terms of automobiles. (In love and investing, metaphors are always risky.) Like cars, mutual funds have different styles. The middle-of-the-roadsters—for example, Accords and Camrys—provide comfort and reliability. Assuming good maintenance and reasonably low mileage, they'll get you from point A to point B without a hitch. Sensible? Yes. Boring? For sure.

Corvettes and Porsches, by contrast, are thrilling beasts that go from 0 to 60 mph faster than the average space shuttle. Higher maintenance than your typical Camry? You bet. Riskier than your average Accord? Yep. Popular? Without a doubt. (And they'd be a lot more popular if anybody could afford them.)

Just about every guy, especially those in the midlife-crisis phase, dreams about turning in his minivan for a hot ragtop with a tight stick shift and a radar detector and escaping down the coast. Well, switching back to market-speak, enhanced index funds can give even the most conservative investor a turbo-boost. There's nothing quite like the sheer rush you get from watching a portion of your portfolio earn at time-and-a-half, or even double time.

Traditional index funds, like Vanguard's Index 500, seek to match the exact stocks held by the corresponding composite and mirror performance as closely as possible. But enhanced index funds, like Profunds UltraBull or UltraOTC, allow you to routinely beat the index, employing futures and options to supercharge returns.

So when the S&P or NASDAQ 100 gains 10 percent, your active portfolio surges close to 20 percent. With a beta of 2.0, UltraBull and UltraOTC are specifically designed to outpace the average in an up market. Enhanced index strategies bring together the best aspects of active and passive management, offering the possibility of outperforming a benchmark while at the same time providing tight tracking.

Keep in mind, though, that trying to double returns on the upside can lead to doubled losses on the downside. When the market dips 5 percent, in other words, you're quickly down 10 percent. A 15 percent market pullback translates to a 30 percent personal meltdown.

That's why you need to move fast and trade actively. If that sounds daunting to you, use a more conservative investing vehicle.

Anyone who uses enhanced index funds needs to employ a highly structured, risk controlled approach—that is, set a stop-loss–designed to prevent the swoops and swoons that naturally accompany these more aggressive and active approaches.

Here are some fund profiles from enhanced index families:

1. **ProFunds** currently offers 7 enhanced index funds and 12 enhanced sector funds, including:

- Bull fund. Tracks the performance of the broad-based S&P 500.
- UltraBull. Seeks 200 percent of the performance of the S&P 500.
- UltraOTC. Seeks 200 percent of the performance of the Nasdaq 100.
- UltraSmall-Cap. Seeks 200 percent of the performance of the Russell 2000 index.
- UltraMid-Cap. Seeks 200 percent of the performance of the S&P 400.
- Ultra-Japan ProFund

   Reach them at:

   Profunds c/o Bisys Fund Services
   3435 Stelzer Road
   Suite 1000
   Columbus, OH 43219-8001
   1-888-PRO-FNDS/1-888-776-3637

2. **Potomac** currently offers 7 index and 2 enhanced sector funds, including:

- OTC Plus. Seeks to achieve 125 percent of the return of the Nasdaq 100.
- Small-Cap Plus. Seeks to achieve 125 percent of the return of the Russell 2000.
- US Plus. Seeks to obtain 150 percent of the return of the S&P 500.
- Dow 30 Plus. Seeks to obtain 125 percent of the return of the Dow Industrials.

Reach them at:

The Potomac Funds
C/o Firststar Mutual Fund Services
P.O. Box 1993
Milwaukee, WI 53201-1993
1-800-851-0511

3. **Rydex** currently offer 13 enhanced index funds, including:

- Titan 500. Seeks 200 percent of the performance of the S&P 500.
- Velocity 100. Seeks 200 percent of the performance of the Nasdaq 100.
- OTC. Seeks to mirror the performance of the Nasdaq 100.
- Nova. Seeks 150 percent of the performance of the S&P 500.
- Mekros. Seeks 150 percent of the performance of the Russell 2000.

Reach them at:

Rydex Series Funds
9601 Blackwell Road
Suite 500
Rockville, Maryland 20850
Customer Service Department:
Phone: 1-800-820-0888
Fax: 301-296-5101

SECTOR FUNDS

Last but not least in our list of new investment vehicles is an updated version of a not-so-new idea: the sector fund. In its most classic form, the business cycle involves a recession giving way to modest growth, then stronger growth. Eventually, growth reaches a peak, and a slowdown begins, leading to recession and a completion of the cycle.

The reality, of course, is a lot lumpier than that. Certain parts of the economy roll over sooner than others; some bounce back quicker than others. These parts, called *sectors,* include things like health, leisure, energy, technology, financial services, biotech, and so on. Some sectors (like financials, for example) depend largely on interest rates and consumer spending, whereas technology might stay out in its own little orbit, working counter to interest-sensitive funds and sometimes even to the entire broader market.

If your crystal ball could always keep you in the hottest sectors all the time, you could get rich quick. But it can't, and once again, opportunity comes hand-in-hand with risk. Because sector funds have narrow, industry-specific focuses, investors need to keep their radar screens tuned to the push and pull of economic and business cycles.

Now that you're a budding maverick, I bet you can anticipate the two key questions I want you to ask about sector funds before you take the plunge. First, what are the parameters under which I will buy? And second, when circumstances changes—as they surely will—when will I sell?

USING SECTOR FUNDS

When it comes to investing in a single segment of the economy, some people follow the dinosaur herd. They'll buy a biotech fund after it has risen to the moon. This usually means that it's at or near the end of its run, which means in turn that the hapless newcomers who paid top dollar get to watch their new baby fall like a meteor from the sky.

For example: Latecomers who poured their money into biotech, tech, and/or the Internet during the first quarter of 2001 soon found themselves experiencing losses of 30, 40, and even 50 percent. They bought late, and had no plan for when to sell.

Knowing *when to buy* is particularly critical in the aggressive sector arena. Mavericks get in early. We look to diversify across three to four rising segments of the economy, well before they get that "subway buzz." (If you hear somebody in a restaurant or on public transportation talking about a hot sector, you can pretty much be sure it has already run its course.) A maverick buy discipline tells us when to get into a specific industry. For example, you might use the 50-day moving average–a trendline that's readily available on the charts section of Yahoo! Finance or bigcharts.com.

Let me walk you through a specific case. In October of 2000, most sectors of the economy were feeling the pain of the technology slide. Yet Fidelity Select Chemicals (FSCHX) crossed above its 50-day trend-

FIGURE 19-2   Fidelity Select Chemicals (FSCHX) with 50-day Average

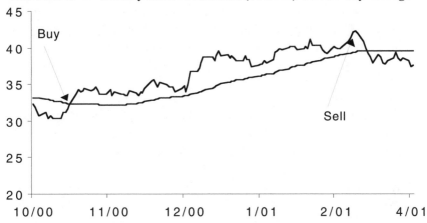

line in late October at a price of $33. This was an indication to "buy" chemicals.

Knowing *when to sell* is equally critical, when you're in the sector game. Sectors are far too volatile to rely solely on "trending." I employ a trailing stop-loss of 7 percent. In other words, if my investment falls 7 percent from the high point it reaches from the date of purchase, I sell.

Let's look at Fidelity Select Chemicals (FSCHX) again. It reached a high of $42.51 in the first week of March 2001, then began falling rapidly. In just four trading days, the price hit my trailing stop-loss of 7 percent (approximately $39.50) when it closed at $39.42. I sold the next day at $38.77, locking in a 17.5 percent gain in less than five months (see Fig. 19-2).

Again, aggressive mavericks investing in sectors must be pigheaded about sticking to both their buy discipline and their sell discipline. When do you buy? When the sector fund and an index of the sector itself both eclipse their respective 50-day trendlines. When should you sell? When the fund hits your predetermined stop-loss of 7 percent. Be pigheaded—a more colorful word for "disciplined"—and you can't go wrong.

THE TEN WORST MISTAKES A SECTOR INVESTOR CAN MAKE

Maybe you've noticed by now that I love nothing better than a good list. Well, here's another good list: the 10 real bonehead moves a sector investor can make:

1. Rely on emotions to make decisions.   Fear, greed, regret, eupho-ria—four different emotions, all with the ability to make investors act on impulse, rather than logic. By letting your heart, rather than your head, dic-tate buy and sell decisions, you can cause wounds to your portfolio that may never heal. (But nearly 20 chapters into this maverick world, you already knew that, right?)

The tech wreck—and the whole myriad of emotions it brought on—has severely scarred modern-day investors. Maybe you got greedy and poured all your money into tech. Maybe you got scared at the prospect of missing the train completely, and jumped in determined to make up for lost time.

Can't say I blame you. Talk of triple-digit gains, and of how easy this "investing thing" was, lured even the most conservative investors from their secure S&P corner to chase a piece of the tech dream. In 1999, we saw a one-year, 130 percent-or-greater surge in both Fidelity Technology and Invesco Telecommunications. As the stampede increased, the Vanguard 500 S&P 500 fund experienced the first net outflow in its history in March of 2000—which happened to be the same time that the Nasdaq hit its 52-week high of 5048.

What did this fear and greed get investors? A big, fat ulcer. Those who couldn't resist the temptation saw their tech assets lopped in half in less than eight months. An unrealistic analysis that "the New Economy couldn't keep falling" led to a severe portfolio pounding for zillions of investors. Lesson? Emotionality causes big blunders, and *sector plays greatly mag-nify the consequences of such a blunder.*

2. Chase top performers.   Didn't learn your lesson with biotechnol-ogy in 1995, energy in 1996, or technology in 2000? Fell for health care's one-two punch in 2000, and figured it would knock investors dead in 2001? Those are some pretty tough lessons. The only consolation is that you're hardly alone in this school of hard knocks.

Chasing top performers at the worst possible time—that is, after a long, hot run—is a big-time goof. Health care is a perfect example. In 2000, while many investors clung to their technology holdings for dear life, health funds gained an impressive 55.4 percent. If not for a mediocre last quarter in which the category slumped 3 percent, they would have ended the year even higher.

Investors soon took notice, pouring money into these offerings. But the Dow Jones Health Index was soon down more than 20 percent.

3. Fall in love with a fund.   Are you painfully clinging to Janus Global Technology, down 52 percent from its high? If you find yourself so *in awe of, so enamored of, so in love with* a fund that you'll do anything to own it and keep it forever—hey! Snap out of it, and come to your senses. Love hurts.

Technology sector funds come to mind. (Holding on to one of these?) Technology funds today are like the once-lofty tulip. Don't follow me? In seventeenth-century Holland, the red-and-white-striped tulip became a status symbol. Lust for tulips mounted to a frenzy, and the cost of a single bulb reached the equivalent of 15 years' salary for a skilled laborer. As demand soared and prices rocketed skyward, investors began selling "futures" on crops not yet grown or harvested.

The seemingly invincible tulip market crashed in 1637. Investors (belatedly) realized that outside the confines of a garden, the tulip was, well, not very valuable. Today, you can purchase just about any 10-bulb pack of tulips for $4.95 (plus shipping) at www.tulips.com.

As I said, today's Internet funds are a whole lot like yesterday's tulips. People lived and breathed the Internet in 1999, until analysts and investors began to wonder out loud about why companies that had yet to turn profits were so valuable. The answer: *They aren't.* As of this writing, a share of Internet retailer Buy.com—once a "steal" at $26—sells for 21 cents.

4. Don't sell.   So, you've thought about selling Invesco Technology many times, but the problem is, you never did it. Thinking and doing: two human activities divided by a chasm of emotions, inertia, laziness, and what-have-you. But when it comes to sector investing, selling often means the difference between locking in profits and losing principal.

Maybe you fell for the "hope rallies" the market delivered time and again in 2000 and into 2001. You jumped on the bottom-calling bandwagon, and figured that we were in for a tech revival. After all, Invesco Technology gained 144 percent in 1999. It was just a matter of time— wasn't it?—before it scratched and clawed its way back to those levels.

Wrong. The shakeout since March 2000 has been relentless. Say you bought Invesco Technology back on March 3 at $109.75. When it dropped 30 percent the week of April 7, you hung onto it. When it wound up down 22 percent for 2000, you clung to it. When it gained 8.98 percent in January 2001, you celebrated. And, now that it's down 45 percent from its high, you're scratching your head wondering what to do.

Just to break even from a 45 percent loss, that fund will have to grow nearly 85 percent. Get real. When do you think that will happen?

5. Put all your eggs in one basket.   Tell me you're not like one radio listener, who called the show to say she had put $50,000 (100 percent of her portfolio) into Fidelity Select Technology when the fund was trading at $200+ a share—only to see it shrink to $19,000.

Allocating 100 percent of your actively managed portfolio to *any* sector—be it financial services, health, consumers, or technology—is just a bad, bad idea. And it's probably worse than you know, if you're not paying attention to all your holdings. When a sector catches fire, fund managers dump their cash into that sector. So if you plunged on a technology sector, and your growth-fund manager was out doing exactly the same thing without you noticing, you had one big bet going on technology.

At the end of last year, the average big-cap growth fund—the largest and most popular fund category in recent years—had more than 40 percent of its assets invested in tech stocks, compared with 23 percent for the Vanguard 500 Index fund, which tracks the S&P 500. Yes, this can boost returns. But it can really knock your teeth out when that sector cools off—as many of us learned, painfully.

6. Buy funds based on published past performance. Let's say you've been living under a rock. Out you pop, somewhere toward the end of the year 2000, looking for a cool investment. You decide on the Monument Digital Technology fund, because a bar chart on its Web site showed a *272 percent return* in 1999. Wow! Hot stuff! Unfortunately, you don't pay much attention to that little footnote that discloses the fund's negative 10 percent return from July 1 through Sept. 30, 2000. And because you spent all that time under that rock, you have no idea that the footnote skipped over the fund's 0 percent and −22 percent returns in the first and second quarters of 2000, respectively, and failed to mention the fund's 57 percent decline for the year.

I certainly don't mean to imply that the Monument Digital Technology fund is the only such purveyor of, uhm, *selective* information. Three weeks into 2001, *not one* of 14 sample online prospectuses for Internet funds yet included 2000's horrific performance results.

I learned very early on in my investing life that I should never believe everything I read. Unfortunately, this is particulary true with regard to funds. While the SEC requires that fund performance in fund ads be current as of the most recent quarter, marketers will do whatever they can to embellish the good and hide the bad. If you buy based on self-descriptions, you are going to be sorry you came out from under that cozy rock.

7. Fall for bad ideas. Remember when the Internet frenzy got so out of hand that it spawned a Web site on which a movie-star monkey picked

Net stocks? (Please don't call in to the radio show and tell me that the chimp made you money.)

I often wonder what some fund managers are thinking. I often wonder about those investors too, who fall prey to less than rational investments. In the infancy stages of the Internet craze, for example, there were five funds: Amerindo Technology, WWW Internet, Munder NetNet, Monument Internet, and the Internet Fund. Then, in December 1999, along came the Goldman Sachs Internet Tollkeeper Fund to jump on the bandwagon. Mind you, this was after Internet retail funds already showed signs of weakness. But *this* fund—said Goldman's marketing materials—was unlike those other generic internet funds. *This* one specialized in "infrastructure." Uh huh. It tanked three months later, along with the rest of the dot.coms.

Now there are 24 Internet funds, and apparently, the broad Internet funds weren't enough. Managers began slicing and dicing the broad funds into ever-smaller pieces. For instance, Munder Funds offers three different tech funds, including two internet funds, and Kinetics Asset Management offers five funds that carve up the Internet into different slices. Here's a fund that's suffered from anorexia: Launched in May 2000 (how's that for timing?), the Amerindo Internet B2B Fund holds just 12 stocks, and has 15 percent of its assets pegged to eBay. It's down 62 percent year to date as of September 4, 2001.

Jacob Internet, Potomac Internet Plus, and Firsthand E-Commerce. All down, down, down. Down more than 80 percent, measured from March 2000 through September 4, 2001.

8. Use funds with high fees/surrender charges.   Are you the type of person who thinks that the more you pay for a product, the better it is? Well, when it comes to funds, that's what the brokers want you to believe. But it's simply not true. In fact, according to fund-tracking firm Morningstar, no-load (i.e., cheaper) funds have historically outperformed load funds.

Surrender charges stink, too. For example, if you own Amerindo Tech (ATCHX), you are a victim of that fund's policy that requires investors to hold it for at least one year or pay 2 percent of the purse. (And it was 3 percent until the SEC changed the rules.) Now, I'm sure you didn't give it a moment's notice when Amerindo Tech was the hottest fund in America. After all, what's a measly 3 percent, when your money is doubling in one year?

Over the last 12 months, however, ATCHX has lost 73 percent of its value. That type of drawdown unmasks the true purpose of the 3 percent redemption: a cheesy way to lock investors up—even through a horrific bear market downtrend.

You can, and should, do much better than that.

9. Ignore tax ramifications. Let's say you were still recuperating from the 32 percent losses you suffered from Fidelity Technology at the end of Y2K. Then one day, the mailman came to the door and delivered a Form 1099, reporting capital gains on the fund. This meant that you were looking at a tax bill on a losing fund! I'd like to be able to tell you that it's an impossible notion, but it's not.

Some fund managers sold stocks bought in previous years to secure gains and reshuffle their portfolios. Fair enough. And shareholders are required to pay taxes on distributions, no matter whether the distributions are paid out or reinvested.

Here are a couple of examples: Fidelity Select Computers wound up down 31 percent for 2000, with year-end distributions representing 25 percent of its value. Similarly, Fidelity Developing Communications took a 29 percent beating, and handed out a 31 percent distribution to fund owners.

Some investors even hold onto lagging funds to avoid paying taxes. Rather than shelling out a couple hundred bucks on their gains and locking in profits, they watch a fund lose 40 percent, 50 percent, or 60 percent. It's a pretty ridiculous way to get a tax break.

Who's spared this double-whammy? Investors who trade sector funds in qualified plans, like a 401(k), IRA, or annuity.

10. Pick bad managers and sour funds. Let's just hope you didn't hop on the tech train holding either of these two tickets: AIM Global Telecom and Tech (GTTCX) or Monterey Murphy Tech (NMWTX). They're big yellow lemons, in maverick speak.

The average tech fund (according to Lipper Analytical Services) lost 37.84 percent in one year, gained 22 percent over three years, and 17 percent over five years. Well, the AIM offering fared fairly well in 1 year—losing "only" 38.86 percent—but it's only gained 14.55 percent over three and 12.35 percent over five years. The Murphy offering? Even worse. If you held this puppy in 2000, you lost 58.55 percent. And it only averaged 9 percent in three years, and lost 6.66 percent over five years. Would you have guessed that *no* technology fund could have run in the red over that period of time? Guess again.

Maybe you think I've got nothing nice to say about any sector funds. Well, Fidelity Select Technology is up 39 percent over three years and 28 percent over five. Invesco Telecommunications gained 36 percent and 31 percent in the same periods. These are two fund families with managers who know how to pick 'em, and whose expertise lies in sectors.

TAX STRATEGIES USING EIFs AND SECTOR FUNDS

It's a fact. If you invest in enhanced index funds (EIFs) or sector mutual funds, you are going to be trading more frequently. That's a primary reason for using tax-advantaged accounts for these vehicles—so you don't have a taxable event when you buy or sell.

The two tax-shelter alternatives—in addition to your qualified choices such as your IRA or 401(k)—are variable annuities (VAs) and variable universal life policies (VULs). Both are insurance products with investment components. And because both are either unknown to or misunderstood by most of the public, few investors reap the rewards of using them.

For the most part, the media have written off the variable annuity as a commission-heavy tax shelter with limited investment choices. In recent years, however, some VAs have begun offering more than 40 mutual funds, including sector mutual funds. Some annuities, moreover, feature low management fees, no commissions, and no surrender charges.

For example, I've discovered an annuity offered through Ameritas Direct that simply runs away from all of the bad press. This annuity features 46 investment options, including sector funds and enhanced funds from ProFunds. No commission or surrender fees, and you're allowed 20 free trades per year.

Variable universal life (VUL) is another vehicle that baffles the media skeptics and rewards the tax-oppressed investor. The VUL was designed for investors with changing insurance needs to acquire coverage with both flexible premium payments and flexible investment choices.

The knock on VULs has been very similar to VAs; that is, surrendering them costs too much, the sales people charge too much in commissions, and the management expenses are too high.

Well, a while back, I came across a variable universal life product from the Ameritas Life Insurance Corporation that sets itself apart from the competition. Not only does Ameritas offer a commission-free, no-surrender-fee product with reasonable management expenses, but the "trending"-friendly portfolios have terrific sector fund and EIF choices.

Specifically, there are enhanced index funds from Rydex that tie to the S&P as well as the Nasdaq 100. There's even a precious metal alternative for sector enthusiasts. Invesco's four top sector choices are included, too: Health care, technology, financial, and telecom.

Ameritas Direct
5 Greeenway Plaza #1400
Houston, TX 77046-0503
Phone: 1-800-555-4655
Fax: 713-621-8531
E-mail: direct@ameritas.com

In the next chapter, I will explain how these alternative tax-deferred choices can make a huge difference in helping you achieve your goals, and much sooner than you might think.

20

Financial Freedom, Maverick Style

What does financial freedom means to you? Enough money to send your kids to the college of their choice? That get-away-from-it-all sailboat? A home in the outer suburbs, a great space in the downtown loft district, or a vacation hideaway? Or just that great feeling of finally being out of debt, with no fear of going back in?

Financial freedom means different things for everybody, of course. But there are two aspects of financial freedom that are part of just about everybody's vision:

1. **Being free from worry**
2. **Being able to choose how to spend your time**

These are interrelated, but let's look at them separately.

First of all, if you are constantly worried about money, you aren't free. As one of my long-term subscribers recently put it in a letter to me, money can't buy love, but it *can* buy freedom from worry:

> Wealth cannot buy happiness. What wealth can do is make us more comfortable and remove hardship and worry that comes when one does not have wealth. Wealth simply improves our quality of life, not because of the material things that we can buy, but because of the freedom from worry it helps us experience.

And if you are free from worry, you get the big pay-off: *more free time.* Think about it. Isn't your free time your scarcest and most valuable asset? Free time—along with the resources to use that time effectively—adds up to freedom. Freedom to do what you choose with your day. Freedom to travel. Freedom to start a new business. Freedom to spend time on the things that you love to do.

For me, my free time—*not* my brokerage account, or my 401(k)—is my most valuable asset. Freedom to spend more time with my wife and kids. Freedom to spend time with my buddies. Freedom to exercise more, to surf, ski, fish, sail, golf, or whatever. If you could add one thing to you life, wouldn't it be the ability to spend more time doing the things that you love to do?

Lots of people disagree with this statement, the first time or two they hear me say it. "No, Doug," they say, "Why don't you take the time, and I'll take the money?" Well, OK, but I don't think there's much of a distinction, here. What I say back to them is, "Assume you get that money. Are you really going to keep your life exactly as it is today? Are you really just going to pull out those bank statements or quarterly portfolio summaries, sit back in that Barcalounger, and smile a lot? Or are you going to change something about your life?" At that point, most people agree that they would spend the money to change something. And very often, that change sounds a whole lot like more time, and more freedom.

Here's another thing people often say to me, when I start talking about financial freedom: "Hey, Doug—that's what retirement is all about." In other words, if they delay gratification, if they punch the clock long enough and carefully enough, they'll be able to enjoy themselves 10, 20, or 30 years down the road.

Big mistake, fellow mavericks! Don't think about financial freedom in terms of retirement. Think about increasing your freedom, and your free time, starting *today.*

When you think about financial freedom in terms of both time *and* money, you can begin to see that you have a certain amount of freedom— time and money—right now. If you're able to buy and read this book, you have more freedom than most humans on the planet, and far more than that enjoyed by previous generations. I saw a great bumper sticker recently on a pickup truck in Boston. It read, "Union labor: We brought you the week-end." It's worth reminding ourselves that our great-grandfathers worked 12-hour days, six days a week.

So in a very real sense, you already have it good. Now your goal should be to *have it better*—both in the short term and the long term. In this chapter, as I take you through the process of building a plan to attain financial freedom, I want you to keep in mind that this is not something that you are hoping to enjoy 30 years from now. If you do the planning and investing right, you can have more free time quickly, as well as the resources to enjoy that free time. You'll reduce the level of stress in your life, improve the near-term quality of your life, and maybe even extend your life span.

Let's face it: Life is stressful, and stress kills. The stress begins in high school with worry about relationships, wrestling with body image, trying on new characters, fighting for grades, and going through the cruel trials of college admissions. And then stress continues in college, as you strive to either get into graduate school, or to prepare yourself for your first real, full-time job. (Oh, yeah—and those relationship and self-image issues haven't quite gone away yet, either.)

Then comes marriage and kids for some, or a career focus for others. Then it's your first mortgage, bills, and probably some level of debt. And then, before you know it (and often belatedly), you have to start worrying about your own retirement.

Ugh. A big, slow-moving, but still life-threatening river of stress. Sometimes it seems like the pressure is everywhere, and relentless—so much so that even when you *do* have some free time, you aren't able to enjoy it. You're too stressed-out to enjoy yourself, or your family, or that house you worked so hard (and took on so much debt) to buy.

Is any of this sounding familiar? Well, with a little work, we can change all that.

HOW TO CREATE A MAVERICK FINANCIAL FREEDOM PLAN

Why do some people go through life stressed out all the time, while others seem to breeze along?

I'm convinced that it helps to pick rich grandparents (although inherited wealth and position can also be a burden). Failing that, I think I've actually met a few people whose brain chemistry somehow inoculates them against stress. They see stress the way I see a good cup of java: just the little push I need to get started in the morning.

But most people who minimize stress successfully do so by developing and pursuing a life plan that they believe in.

Stress comes from doubt. Doubt comes from fear—fear of the unknown, fear of failure, fear of loss, and so on. Remove the doubt, and the fear and stress start to go away. Many people are stressed out in life simply because they don't really know where they are going—and if you don't know where you're going, it's very hard to tell where the next threat will be coming from.

Do you have a plan? Do you know where you are going? Or are you in the same boat as 90 percent of the population, sailing down that river of life with absolutely no idea of what your destination is?

If so, let's *change* that. Let's fix it. Let's discover your destination. Let's draw the map. Then, once we have the plan, we can *work* it. Check it. See if it is on track. Adjust it, if need be.

Drawing up a plan for the rest of your life may seem like a lot of work. The truth is that it's a lot like maverick investing: Once you understand the rules of the game, building your life's plan is easy. (It involves little more then answering a series of questions about yourself and your family.) And thinking about the possibilities and opportunities of your life can be an exciting and rewarding experience.

"So"—I'm hearing you ask—"this is easy, exciting, and rewarding. If that's true, why do so few people actually do it?"

Three answers, I think. The first is that people don't want to face the possibility of change. The second is that they don't want to risk failing. And the third is that they don't want to invest the time needed.

None of these is a good reason. Do you hate change? Well, you should have a plan that controls the scope and pace of change in your life. Afraid of failing? Then devise a plan that increases your chances of succeeding. Don't have the time? Then come up with a plan that will give you *more* time.

Again: Building this plan is going to create benefits *today.* It will give you more free time, and greater peace of mind. And once you begin to see these short-term rewards, the longer-term process also starts to look more interesting and exciting.

My "Maverick Financial Freedom Plan" involves three steps: (1) assessing where you are today, (2) getting motivated to get started, and (3) applying assets to goals. At the end of the chapter, I'll introduce some new tools for boosting your returns, and making your dreams more likely to be realized.

STEP NUMBER ONE: ASSESSING WHERE YOU ARE TODAY

This is how you pull together the Big Picture. It involves adding up your assets and liabilities, creating a financial statement, and seeing your net worth on paper. This will start to make your situation clearer and more real to you.

For those of you who have never gone through this exercise, this will be the least fun part of the Maverick Financial Freedom Plan. It might even be a little scary, if the result is that you realize that you are not in very good financial shape. It's a little bit like visiting a personal trainer and having your body fat measured for the first time: There is nowhere to hide. But someday—honest!—you will look back with pride on your decision to take this step.

Now is the time to fill out your first worksheet (*see next page*). This is the financial assessment worksheet, designed to get a read on your current finance state. When you've finished completing this form, you will know exactly where you stand. And that's a big step. Once you know where you stand, you can begin to create the path you will follow to reach your goals.

STEP NUMBER TWO: GETTING THE MOTIVATION TO GET STARTED

What's next? What's next is getting motivated to take action. This is not all that hard to do, and it's critically important to your future success.

Let's imagine that you've just finished filling out the financial assessment worksheet, and I've just walked into your living room. Why? Because we are going to go through your numbers and see where you are.

But don't be afraid, or embarrassed. I'm just like that trainer with the body-fat calipers: I'm not going to make any judgments about where you are today, or how you got there. I only care about *where you are going*. I only want you to take advantage of the opportunity to attain your life's goals. I only want the best for you and your family. I only want to help.

Trust me. Hey: You don't even have to show me your numbers. Let me just ask you a few questions, as *you* look over those numbers:

- What will you feel like when you achieve a million dollars of net worth?

- How will you think about yourself when you are totally debt-free?

- How will you feel when you are in the audience of your child's college graduation?

- How will you feel about yourself and your life when you move into your new home?

- What will you do with your time when you attain financial freedom?

- What will you do when you retire?

We live in a land of enormous opportunity. There is no better place to live on the planet. Dream a great dream, and you can make it come true, if you develop a plan to get there and begin to make the right choices in your day-to-day life. So start dreaming!

Net Worth Worksheet

Today's Date

Assets:

Real Estate $_____

Investments (Brokerage & Mutual Fund Accounts) $_____

Savings (banks, CD's & checking) $_____

Retirement Accounts (IRA's, 401k, 40BB, etc.) $_____

Business Interest $_____

Personal Property $_____

Other Assets $_____

                                    Total Assets: $_____

Liabilities:

Mortgages $_____

Auto Loans $_____

Student Loans $_____

Personal Loans $_____

Credit Cards $_____

                              Total Liabilities: $_____

        Assets – Liabilities = Current Net Worth: $_____

This is important enough to repeat and emphasize, as we start to build our plan. In order to get out of any situation you are in now and move towards your goals, you must believe that it is possible. This is the power of positive thinking. You must believe—and you *will* believe, once you have a plan. Believing is an outcome of the plan. That's why it's important to ask and answer the kinds of questions listed above. They help you visualize a desired future, and inspire you to work toward that future.

STEP NUMBER THREE: APPLYING OUR ASSETS TO OUR GOALS

Now it is time to start taking the actions necessary to reach your financial freedom. It is time to settle upon your life's goals, and apply the assets you already have to those goals. Those great dreams you just dreamed won't happen unless have a plan to get there.

Specificity is very important. You need to be as specific as possible when describing where you want to end up. Every goal must have a clear description, and a date by which you wish to attain it. This is relatively easy to do with money goals, which usually involve a specific number that we are trying to hit within a certain time period. It's more difficult with quality-of-life goals, but you need to go through that exercise, all the same.

What is the most important goal in your life right now? Is it financial independence in retirement? Is it home ownership? Is it getting out of debt?

Here's an interesting experiment. Decide *right now* what your highest priority is. Don't think a lot; just write down the candidate that speaks with the loudest voice:

The most important goal in my life right now is:

_____

_____

In my experience, there is a limited range of answers that people provide in response to that question. When you think about it, that's not too surprising. We are all engaged in the "circle of life" (to quote the movie *The Lion King*). We are all going to grow old and die. So are our kids, and their kids. We don't want to be poor or dependent on others in our old age. We don't want to pass away leaving behind loose ends, or expenses for others. On the off-chance that we are unfortunate enough to die young, we want to have taken certain steps to protect and provide for our families. (Did you write down one of these?)

In between there, while life is going on, we want to provide the best for ourselves, and especially for our children. A safe place to live, a good education, travel, vacations, recreation—all are important. We want to avoid debt, and live within our means. (Did you write down one of these?)

Here are some examples of the Big Goals that have been repeated over and over again on my radio show. You may find yours here. Even if you don't, you may find it helpful to think through each goal. At the end of each section, I've provided a worksheet to help you think through this particular goal.

Financial Independence at Retirement

I have yet to meet anyone that has said to me that they want to be poor or financially destitute when they stop working. Everyone wants financial independence at some point in his or her lives. So build a plan for this goal, you would begin at the end. Since our tax-deferred accounts (TDAs) are our savings vehicles for this objective and we cannot access them prior to age 59.5 without severe penalties and taxes, let's start there.

Always remember that *building a plan is answering questions.* Think about the answers to these questions: How many years until I am 59.5? How much money do I have in my TDA accounts now? How much money can I save annually? What rate of return am I striving to attain? Once these questions are answered, then we turn to the compounded growth tables to project our wealth building potential.

Financial Freedom at Retirement

Date: _____

What age do I wish to retire? _____

How many years until I retire? _____

	Tax Deferred Accounts	Current Balance
How many tax deferred accounts do I currently have?	_____	$ _____
(IRA, 401K, Annuity, etc.)	_____	$ _____
	_____	$ _____
	_____	$ _____
	Total Current Balance:	$ _____

How much can I save next year for this goal? $ _____

Is that amount greater or less than 10% of my gross pay? _____

Current Gross Pay: $_____ (Annually)

This years projected annual contribution. $_____

	10%	*15%*	*20%*
Value in 10 years	$ _____	$ _____	$ _____
Value in 20 years	$ _____	$ _____	$ _____
Value in 30 years	$ _____	$ _____	$ _____

Can you move a portion of your taxable assets over the tax deferred assets? (V/A, IRA, VUL) _____

This is the most basic long term financial goal everyone should be saving & investing to attain. By maximizing tax deferred savings options and investing for growth. Project the power of compounding at 10, 15, 20%.

The Permanent Home

It's the American Dream: People want to buy their homes. There is nothing better then to stop paying rent and to stop living by someone else's rules. (Did you ever have a landlord whom you really loved? Me, neither.) There are also significant incentives for home ownership in the tax code. And finally, there is just that great feeling of independence when you finally move into your own pad.

So how do you get there? Again, you begin again at the end. See the worksheet at the end of this section. How much money do you need for a down payment? What can you afford in monthly payments that include interest, principal, taxes, and insurance? When do you want to purchase? How much do you have now? How much can you save each month towards the down payment?

For a goal such as this—that may have a time horizon of between three and five years—I don't recommend aggressive investing in the stock market. But the process for getting to the goals is the same: *Start at the end, and answer questions.*

Home Ownership

My goal is to purchase a home in _____ years.

I/We desire a home in the price range of $_____.

This will/could require a down payment of _____%.

Our interest rate if we purchased today would be _____%.

Our down payment lump sum will be $_____%.

Our mortgage, taxes, insurance cost monthly will be approximately _____%.

Our goal is to purchase this home in _____ months. (12, 20, 60 months)

We have saved $_____ towards this goal.

We can save $_____ monthly.

Our lump sum and savings accumulates to $_____ by our goal date, at a rate of return of 5%.

We are $_____ short of our goal.

Our action steps to work towards this goal:

1. _____

2. _____

3. _____

4. _____

5. _____

College Education for the Kids

For many people, this is the most important goal in their lives. They want the best for their kids, and they believe that a college education relatively unburdened by debt is the greatest gift they can give. There are some tax-deferred options here, such as the Education IRA and the state-sponsored 529 college savings accounts, that can be helpful. And if you start early enough, the power of compounding can go a long way towards accelerating the value of your nest egg.

So answer the questions: When do you need the money? How much money will you need? How much do you have now? How much can you save monthly or yearly? What rate of return are you striving to attain? What options are available to you?

College Education Worksheet

Child's Name:_____

Age:_____

Years he/she will finish high school._____

Our objective is to accumulate $_____ for his/her college.

We want to send them to a _____ institution. (private or public?)

We will use the following tax deferred savings options:

1. Education IRA

2. Roth IRA

3. 529 College Savings Plan

4. Variable Universal Life (VUL)

We will save $_____ towards this goal monthly.

By _____ (date), our savings will amount to $_____ at no interest.

at 5%	*at 10%*	*at 15%*	*at 20%*
_____	_____	_____	_____

(Use the compound interest tables to approximate your savings over the same time period at different rates of interest.)

Early Retirement
Here's a dream that will *only* become a reality if you take the proper steps along the way. I can't begin to tell you how many young investors were

telling me in the late 1990s that they were going to become 401(k) million-aires by the time they reached 45, and they would quit working when they reached their magic number. The problem, of course, is that before age 59.5, you can't access the money in your retirement accounts without severe penalties and taxes. So if this is your goal, you need to create liquidity outside of the TDAs until you can access them. You want to create the bridge income that will sustain you from your early retirement date until 59.5.

Here are the questions you need to answer if this is your goal: When do I want to stop working? How much money will I need to bridge the gap between my target date and age 59.5? How much do I have now? How much can I add to this goal monthly or yearly?

Early Retirement Worksheet

I/we desire to reach financial freedom at age: _____. We are _____ years old now.

I/we have _____ years to save/invest for this goal.

I/we desire to accumulate a nestegg of $_____ and expect it to last _____ years.

This amount will bridge the gap between our goal date and age 59.5, when we can access our qualified T.D.A.s.

We currently have $_____ saved for this goal.

We can add $_____ monthly.

We can add $_____ annually.

Our current savings and future contributions will compound to a lump sum of

in 5 years	*in 10 years*	*in 15 years*	*in 20 years*
$_____ at 5%	$_____ at 5%	$_____ at 5%	$_____ at 5%
$_____ at 10%	$_____ at 10%	$_____ at 10%	$_____ at 10%
$_____ at 15%	$_____ at 15%	$_____ at 15%	$_____ at 15%
$_____ at 20%	$_____ at 20%	$_____ at 20%	$_____ at 20%

Our action steps to start working towards these goals:

1. _____

2. _____

3. _____

4. _____

Getting Debt-Free

Here's a life goal that many people just don't want to talk about. The average credit card balance as of June of 2001 was $7000, and most Americans have *at least three cards*. Americans have been spending more then they make for years. The sad thing is, I'd bet that most people couldn't even say what they spent all that expensive money on.

Brace yourself: There is *no way* you are going to accomplish the goal of financial freedom if you are carrying any consumer debt. Sorry to be the bad-news guy, but that's the way it is. Get out from underneath all consumer debt. (I exclude car loans from this category, because in most places, cars are an essential, and you have at least some kind of an asset with the car itself.) You cannot be financially independent and attain financial freedom if you're carrying credit card debt. Remember: If you are paying interest to someone else so you can live your life in the present, you are making someone else financially independent.

Once again, the process is the same. Where are you today? How much debt do you have? How much can you pay against this debt on a monthly basis? What can you do to reduce the interest rates you're paying?

Getting Debt-Free Worksheet

Total Debt $_____ (includes credit cards, personal loans, 401(k) loans)

Your goal: Eliminate this number!

	Type (Visa)	Amount	Interest Rate
Credit Cards:	_____	_____	_____
	_____	_____	_____
	_____	_____	_____

Department Store: _____

_____

_____

Personal Loans: _____

_____

401(k) Loans: _____

_____

TOTAL $_____

Simple steps to begin:

1. Post the total debt on the bathroom mirror with room to keep this goal in the front of your mind.
2. Use savings to pay down the highest-interest-rate balances.
3. Review your budget and seek to increase your monthly payments to the highest-interest-rate cards.
4. Reduce 401(k) contribution to the level of the company match.

TOOLS FOR ACCELERATING THE PROCESS

OK, so now you've been through some or all of these worksheets, and you're probably wondering how you can possibly get to there from here. (It's like that first hour after the personal trainer tells you that body-fat percentage.) To help answer that question, and more generally keep you inspired and moving forward, I want to introduce you to two important types of tax-deferred accounts, which you can use to accelerate the compounding process. If you have longer than a seven-year time horizon, these tools can help you reach your goals sooner than is the case if you pay current taxes along the way.

Both of these investment products are from the insurance industry. There are two of each type, and their name refers to how you can invest in them: *annuities,* and *universal life insurance.* They are either a "fixed" product, which means a fixed rate of return that is usually around 7 percent—not very maverick!—or they are "variable" products, meaning they give you a choice of different mutual fund–like accounts in which you can invest. Forget the fixed stuff: It's this variability that gives you the opportunity to seek maverick returns. The variable annuity allows you to play catch-up with your savings towards retirement only. If you find yourself with little money in your TDA accounts and more assets in your taxable accounts, then the variable annuity will allow you to transfer money over to the tax-deferred side of the ledger. This works well for those who receive a windfall sometime in their life—for example, an inheritance or a large bonus. The drawback of the annuity is that you must follow the same rules for withdrawals as for any other tax-deferred retirement account. If you put it in there, don't plan on taking it out early!

The variable annuity is a catch-up vehicle for those who have not taken advantage of investing in IRAs and 401(k)s over their working lives. The one problem you must avoid with this tool is not using the money in retirement. If you pass on with a variable annuity in your estate, it can be taxed as much as 75 percent in value when combined estate and income taxes are calculated. If you use a V/A, make sure you spend the money.

The second option for mavericks who have a time horizon of more than seven years and want access to their money prior to age 59.5 is the variable universal life account (VUL). Yes, it's a mouthful, but its unique features and benefits can really help you pursue high growth potential, retain access to your money, and protect your family as well.

This product makes sense for those who desire to retire early, plan for estate taxes, or save for starting a new business. I talk about the VUL all the time on the radio program, and I use it myself. Let me introduce it briefly here, and encourage readers to learn more about it at www.fabianlive.com or from my radio archives.

The VUL may be the only tool that can help you fully fund future tax liabilities, invest for long-term goals, allow for withdrawals along the way, and protect your assets from merciless taxation. For years, investors correctly equated VULs with huge commissions, surrender charges, and a very short stack of acceptable funds, all of which made them a bad choice across the board. Now, though, insurance companies are providing fund choices within this product that meet or exceed maverick standards for annual performance.

Sounds bizarre, eh? Being a maverick by buying insurance! Strange as it may sound, it's true. Once the insurance industry eliminated the objectionable features that had kept many investors at bay, the VUL became the industry's best-kept secret.

The key to getting the benefits of a VUL is to use this vehicle as a part of your financial freedom plan. Here's how it works. Life insurance (in general) has specific tax benefits. You are able to accumulate cash value within a policy. You are able to withdraw your principal payments at any time, for any reason, without tax consequences. The future growth and interest can also be withdrawn from a policy through the loan provisions allowing you to access more of your nest egg. The death benefit of a life insurance policy is also a tax-free event. All these benefits are valid as long as the policy remains in force.

You can invest and save monthly or annually with a VUL. Once your account is established, you are able to self-direct how the cash value will be invested, similar to a 401(k). Contracts allow for tax-free exchanges among many fund choices.

One drawback of policy ownership historically has been high fees and expenses. These fall into three categories: (1) annual policy expenses called "M&E fees" (mortality and expense), (2) the cost of the insurance itself, and (3) the fund management fee. Total expenses should run around 3 percent per year, so beware of commission-heavy products with annual expenses as high as 5 percent. A tip: Always ask what the surrender charge is for any policy you consider. This is an indication of the commission paid to the broker selling you.

As noted, the decision as to whether to own a VUL product has to be linked to your overall plan. If you need a vehicle to help you retire early, this is the only one that allows for early withdrawals (i.e., prior to age 59.5). If you need a desire to shelter more of your monthly income, and if you also have a need for insurance, then the VUL is a fabulous tool.

In order to both buy a VUL and stay a maverick, you want to find an insurance company that will allow you to make multiple trades per year, and which gives you access to an assortment of funds that provide a long-term boost to your portfolio's growth engine. The more you put in, the more you can take out. If circumstances do force you to abandon a savings plan, you'll still have an active insurance policy, albeit one with limited (non-maverick) growth potential.

The noncommission product I recommend—which as you might have guessed is the one with the most maverick investment options—is the Ameritas Universal Variable Life Contract. There are 40 investment options, which include enhanced index fund and sector funds. In addition, the policy has low expenses. To get more information, go to www.builditkeep.com or contact Ameritas-Direct at 1-800-555-0577. Phone 1-800-555-4655, Fax 1-713-621-8531, e-mail: direct@ameritas.com

So there you have it: the maverick way of getting to financial freedom by combining your dreams with (1) inspiration, (2) discipline, and (3) good tools.

In the next chapter, I'll describe some resources that will give you more help in getting to your destination.

21

Maverick Resources

Which resource would you guess is most important to your maverick wealth-building efforts? In an age of cell phones, satellites, and search engines, you might be surprised by my answer. Your most important maverick resource is your favorite national (or major regional) newspaper.

The New York Times, Chicago Tribune, Los Angeles Times, The Wall Street Journal, USA Today, and so on each gives you timely and accurate quarterly mutual fund information that no maverick can do without. So for around a dollar, four times a year, you get much of what you need to be a maverick.

What, exactly, is that? As I've explained in previous chapters, you need the ability to scan three-month, year-to-date, one-, three-, and five-year numbers every quarter. The easiest and fastest way to uncover these percentage performances is to use the alphabetical listing in your newspaper's quarterly mutual fund review. Quarterly reviews typically arrive ten days after a calendar quarter closes—in other words, April 10, July 10, October 10, and January 10.

Granted, there are Web site databases that'll churn out annualized gains any day you need them. But you may find that you waste a lot of time searching for ticker symbols on the Web. Worse yet, you may not be able to get tables of quarterly performance for the Lipper fund category averages, or for the big-time benchmarks (S&P 500, Dow, Nasdaq, Russell 2000, Wilshire 5000).

That's where your newspaper shines. Not only are you able to look at thousands of funds in a single-page format, you can quickly see how a mid-cap value fund did versus the mid-cap value average. You can rapidly eye-ball how your small-cap growth choice stacked up against the Russell 2000.

And who said print was dead?

In this chapter, I'm going to summarize more resources that mavericks can't do without. These include both financial institutions and electronic resources.

BUILDING RELATIONSHIPS

Let's talk about your point of entry into maverick investing: relationships with people and institutions. How and where do you start? Some people clip the name of an online broker out of a magazine ad. Others dial the phone number at the bottom of a television screen. Still others ask financial talk show hosts for a hard and fast recommendation.

The truth is, deciding where to keep your investment dollars is one of the most important decisions you'll ever make. This is your money, and these are your dreams. Don't get off on the wrong foot by entering into the wrong relationship.

The three most important things in selecting your brokerage house are the investment vehicles they offer, the fees they charge, and the customer service they provide. For example, virtually all discount brokers let you trade stocks online. But how many let you buy and sell a wide variety of mutual funds? What choices are available? What are the fees, expenses, and/or commissions associated with those funds? Are there penalties for redeeming your shares within 90 days or 180 days? Can you reach a live person by phone if you run into trouble at their Web site?

Full-service brokers like Paine Webber, Morgan Stanley Dean Witter, and Merrill Lynch still control most of the country's money. Good for them; they've been at it a long time. But mavericks should be looking in the direction of the major discount brokerages. These include:

Charles Schwab & Company

Mutual Funds Department, 101 Montgomery Street, San Francisco, CA 94104. Phone: 1-800-435-4000, Fax: 415-395-6060, Web site: www.schwab.com

Charles Schwab is the daddy Mac truck of discounters—hands down. Not only does Charles Schwab offer more than 1000 no-transaction-fee (NTF) mutual funds, but its customer service rivals the so-called full-service firms. In fact, when it comes to investment vehicle quantity, quality, and a friendly shoulder to lean on, Schwab may very well be the best in the business.

So what's the downside to choosing Schwab as an online and offline brokerage? This one-stop megamart charges a premium for its services. Individual stock trades, margin rates, option charges, transaction-fee mutual funds, short-term redemption penalties—just about everything you care to do as a maverick may cost a little bit more. In fact, Schwab costs more to do business with than any of the other four companies that I will profile.

Nevertheless, beginning mavericks may indeed want to work with the people at Schwab—particularly those who plan to stick to NTF mutual funds. Not only do you have a wide range of choices, but 24/7 service from the best-trained reps in the business is a difficult perk to beat.

Fidelity Discount Brokerage

82 Devonshire, Boston, MA 02109. Phone: 1-800-544-7272 or 1-800-544-6666, Web site: www.fidelity.com

Fidelity Discount Brokerage boasts an equally impressive resume when it comes to investment choice, 24/7 representative access, and Web site quality. In fact, while Charles Schwab may have been the first to cater to the do-it-yourself crowd, Fidelity has built a solid reputation in NTFs and active fund management. (They may have twice as many mutual fund offerings in their arsenal.)

If Fidelity has active fund management expertise, more investment vehicles to choose from, and comparable customer service, why wouldn't all mavericks choose Fidelity over Schwab? For one thing, Fidelity's fee structure is more complex; when it comes to competitive cost advantages, a lot will depend on what you trade and how often you trade it. Second, Fidelity wants its clients to buy Fidelity mutual funds; that is, an individual may feel pressured to choose funds within the Fidelity family rather than use the brokerage as a hands-off discounter.

If there's one area where Fidelity consistently receives praise, it's for Web site comprehensiveness and ease of use. Fidelity has an extremely flexible fund screener, a visual map of the market, online money transfers, real-time quotes and an ability to view non-Fidelity accounts through the proprietary FullView service. New features like bill paying and check writing only add to Fidelity's Web site appeal.

TD Waterhouse

100 Wall Street, New York, NY 10005. Phone: 1-800-934-4448, Web
site: www.tdwaterhouse.com

Waterhouse, which recently acquired Jack White, has more NTF funds and
more mutual fund offerings than either Schwab or Fidelity. It's less expensive to trade stocks or mutual funds at Waterhouse than at Schwab or
Fidelity. And this number three big-time discounter offers as many as five
free redemptions on funds held for less than a year.

Customer service? Waterhouse usually gets high marks on helpfulness.
Variety of product? No problem. In fact, with Waterhouse, you can trade
nearly everything from options to commodities to ETFs; you can even buy
life insurance and annuities.

Waterhouse's biggest problem seems to be its latecomer status in the
marketplace. It behaves a little bit like Burger King in its perennial pursuit
of McDonald's, or like Avis gunning for Hertz ("we try harder, and you can
see us sweating"). And a little more concretely, I've heard some people
complain about the difficulty in getting trade confirmations; Web site navigation; and phone rep responsiveness.

These gripes may all fall into the category of growing pains. The recent
acquisition of the west coast Jack White by the east coast Waterhouse may
be to blame. Nevertheless, if you are new to maverick investing, but you
have a fair amount of general knowledge in the investment arena, Waterhouse may be your port of call.

Ameritrade

*Ameritrade, Inc., 1005 N. Ameritrade Place, Bellevue, NE 68005.
Phone: 1-800-454-9272, Fax: 816-243-3769, Web site:
www.ameritrade.com*

No brokerage house has more mutual fund offerings than Ameritrade. This
should be appealing to mavericks, because it means that Ameritrade's customers have access to the greatest number of top performers. Ameritrade
may also be the low-cost leader for investors who purchase individual stocks
as well as mutual funds; the fee structure is straightforward, transaction-
based, and economical.

If Ameritrade falls down anywhere, it's in the customer service arena.
Service ratings are generally higher than at other online-only services, but
the service being rated here is still more of a unilateral, thanks-for-filling-
my-order, financial relationship.

Aggressive growth mavericks with a reasonable amount of experience need not be afraid. Ameritrade is a dominating market share competitor with the potential to be an online force for decades. It's a member of the National Association of Security Dealers (NASD) and carries Securities Investor Protection Corporation (SIPC) coverage, providing up to $500,000 protection for your investments.

Datek

Phone: 1-800-823-2835, Web site: www.datek.com

Datek offers thousands of mutual funds and charges the same low fee that it does for an individual stock—$9.99. But let's be honest here. Datek was designed with the active, individual stock trader in mind. In fact, Datek specializes in immediate trade execution and instant account updating.

Unlike other online brokers, Datek does not send trade orders to the floors of major exchanges. Instead, the company matches buyers and sellers via computerized networks only. In the absence of a true middleman, your individual stock or option order may get filled at a better price with Datek.

Real-time quotes, streaming quotes, Nasdaq Level II quotes—this is the stuff stock-trader dreams are made of. Bear in mind, though, that Datek has *not* won any awards for its non-online services, such as opening accounts, transferring cash from other accounts, or just enabling you to speak to a representative.

INDIVIDUAL FUND FAMILIES

In general, I recommend that anyone with $15,000 or more to invest should choose one of the five discount brokerage firms just described. But if you're just starting out, or if you want a child to get his or first exposure to the market, or if you're an aggressive maverick needing specific access to a company's sector funds; you're going to want an account at an individual fund family. My favorites are:

Invesco Funds Group

P.O. Box 173706, Denver, CO 80206-4923, Web site: www.invesco.com

Denver-based Invesco is one of the oldest mutual fund companies in the country; nevertheless, it is also one of the most innovative. In 1986, for example, they began offering some of the first no-load sector funds. They're also one of the earliest pioneers of online investing.

Perhaps the firm's greatest appeal, however, comes from its extensive menu of offerings. Many of the dozens of actively managed, no-load funds offered by the company have appeared at the top of best performer lists. This, more than anything else, explains why Invesco rides herd on some $50 billion in assets.

Invesco is by no means a "trader-friendly" firm, so aggressive sector investors ought to think twice before signing up here. There are redemption penalties for leaving diversified stock funds within six months. The company even limits no-load sector trading to four times a year, making them expensive choices for investors who may need to rotate positions frequently.

Janus Group of Mutual Funds

100 Fillmore St., Suite 300, Denver CO 80206-4923, Phone: 1-800-525-8983, Web site: www.janus.com

One thing that Janus does well is stick to their style. With an eye for advances in health care, telecommunications, and technology, Janus led all of its peers in capitalizing on the late 1990s bull market surge on large- and mid-cap growth stocks.

Unfortunately, they rode the bear down as well. And while the company's mutual funds never drifted away from the style each explained in its prospectus—which, as I've explained, is actually a good thing—Janus also never developed a more diversified line of products. And that's a bad thing.

The problem with specialization is that when large- and mid-cap growth funds suffer, a Janus client isn't able to put money to work in small-caps or value stocks. Janus is now looking to expand its coverage, but it may take a few years to see the results of the company efforts.

Nevertheless, mavericks with less than $15,000 and interest in only one fund should consider Janus. Its active management team on 17 or more stock mutual funds is exceptional. (One note of caution: Many individual funds at Janus are closed to new investors. Make sure that the one you're interested in is available to you.)

Vanguard Group

Inc. 455 Devon Park Drive, Wayne, PA 19087. Phone: 1-800-662-7447, Web site: www.vanguard.com

Vanguard created the industry's first index mutual fund in 1976, but it wasn't until a few decades later that passively managed index funds became hot. Today, Vanguard offers more than 50 of them, and they've made the company's reputation. But what many people *don't* seem to know about Vanguard is that they have dozens of actively managed funds, as well. Vanguard Health Care, Explorer, and Selected Value are just a few examples.

While Vanguard emphasizes the tax-efficiency and cost-effectiveness of its products, mavericks need to focus on what matters to them most. Will owning a Vanguard mutual fund through the Vanguard mutual fund family help you achieve *your* maverick growth goal? If the answer is "yes" and the customer service meets with your approval, consider opening an account here.

T. Rowe Price

P.O. Box 89000, Baltimore, MD 21289-1500. Phone: 1-800-541-8803, Web site: www.troweprice.com

Thomas Rowe Price Jr. founded his management firm in 1937. Today, this Baltimore-based giant is one of the nation's largest, no-load mutual fund providers, both for individual investors and for corporate retirement plans.

Six decades of experience isn't too shabby. Plus, individual and institutional clients have access to more than 75 T. Rowe stock, bond, and money market funds; no fund type or risk classification is overlooked.

T. Rowe also has a discount brokerage arm for stock traders and mutual fund investors. You can invest in thousands of no-loads—many of which carry the same NTF benefits as at Schwab or Fidelity—as well as commission-based load funds.

Rydex, Potomac, ProFunds

All three of these fund families are short-term-trade-friendly firms with no redemption fees, no matter how long you hold an investment. Each offers a range of regular index funds as well as enhanced index funds (EIFs). As explained in Chapter 19, EIFs are leveraged funds designed to achieve 1.5 to twice the returns of a particular index on the upside. (Remember that they lose by the same multiplier on the downside, so be careful!)

ProFunds also carries leveraged sector funds—targeting interest in areas like pharmaceuticals, semiconductors, and wireless. ProFunds' UltraSector funds have built-in leverage of 50 percent, so aggressive investors can make more money—or lose more money—than the index being tracked.

Unlike Janus, Invesco, T Rowe or Fidelity, the minimums to open an account here are rather pricey. ProFunds requires $15,000, and Rydex wants $25,000 to get your account set up.

INVESTING WEB SITES

Throughout this book, I've sung the praises of online explorations and investing by mavericks. In fact, I told you early on that getting wired was an *absolute prerequisite* to being a maverick. Let me remind you why I believe this so strongly, by describing some wonderful Web-based investing sites. Oh, yes; I'll include my own site in here, too, which I think holds its own pretty well alongside the big boys.

Yahoo! Finance

Web site: www.@yahoo.com

There are so many things to love about Yahoo! Finance—the breadth and depth of investment info, portfolio tracking, quick-look charts, fund comparisons, even company insider trading. In fact, if you have little more than a vague idea of a mutual fund name, there's no better search engine than the "symbol lookup" at Yahoo! Finance.

How do mavericks get the most out of this site? They start with the "Profile" link on a mutual fund of interest. Here's where you'll get an immediate snapshot with the fund category, objective and manager, three-month, one-, three-, and five-year returns, as well as management expenses and investment minimums. You name it; it's probably in the profile.

The next maverick must-see is the charting feature. You have a variety of time frames you can check out, but I recommend selecting on one or two years. Then you can get a short-term (50-day) and long-term (200-day) trendline picture, just by clicking on moving averages.

Another feature to use in your quest for info is the "Holdings" link. Get an idea of the fund's sector weighting, as well as a quick feel for the types of stocks in your fund. Keep in mind, though, that the SEC only requires investment companies to disclose what stocks they have once a quarter, so the info will be dated.

Yahoo! Finance is also the best place to track your portfolio for free. You can view returns by each security or by account. You can choose from a variety of preset views, or select a custom view on dozens of potential parameters. You can check out your performance across a period of time, and even enter stop-loss alerts for stocks or funds of interest.

Big Charts

Web site: www.bigcharts.com

Most financial sites include a charting feature, and many include an assortment of popular technical indicators. But Big Charts clicks and compares your stocks or mutual funds against any other stock, mutual fund, or index with a ticker. It's extremely helpful to be able to hold up your own small-cap growth fund against the Russell 2000—or more specifically, the Russell 2000 Growth index.

But the *real* value here is with the "Interactive Charting" button. Click it, and then plug in various criteria on the left-hand navigation bar. Choose your time frame, index, or security for comparison, and moving average choice. (Mavericks use the simple moving average option—either a 200-day or 39-week for the long-term trend.) This is a maverick sandbox, and one of the best.

American Stock Exchange

Web site: AMEX.com

You can buy a basket of biotechs in a single trade. You might short-sell an entire industry. Or perhaps you want to rotate out of retail to give your portfolio a jolt of the electric utilities.

ETFs, described in Chapter 19, are the hottest investment vehicles on the market . . . iShares, Spiders, Holdrs . . . and now AMEX.com tracks more than 100 of them. Click on Exchange-Traded Funds link in the middle of the navigation bar and you'll find yourself at the ETF home page. From there, you can decide whether you want to look at broad-based, diversified ETFs (e.g., SPY for the S&P 500), economic sector ETFs (e.g., IYH for the Dow Jones Health Care index) or a variety of international ETFs (e.g., EWJ for Japan).

But here's the really cool part. Once you find the ETF that you're interested in and click on its hypertext symbol, you get a comprehensive one-shot view with performance, expense ratio, and holdings. Most important, since an index rarely changes its makeup, you can get a very clear idea of the exact holdings in your exchange-traded basket.

The AMEX site also covers "HOLDRs" in depth (the Merrill Lynch equivalent of the ETF). With ETFs, what you actually own is shares in an investment company whose fund owns the stocks of a particular index. With HOLDRs, you must purchase a round-lot of 100 shares, and you actually have an interest in the underlying securities of the index.

No matter! The AMEX site's got this variation covered. Whether its biotech, pharmaceuticals, or semiconductors, find out what stocks you own by clicking on the HOLDR of interest.

Fabian Live

Web site: www.fabianlive.com

At the risk of tooting our own horn, this is the site to keep in touch with maverick investing day or night. You can listen to a live radio broadcast on Saturdays, or an archived show any time of the week. You can lemon-proof your portfolio every quarter. You can even check the "trend" charts on Friday evenings.

"Trending" is easy with the big-time benchmarks—Dow Industrials, S&P 500, Nasdaq, Russell 2000, Wilshire 5000. These indicators tell you when a segment of the U.S. market is moving higher or lower.

For example, let's say you're checking the small-cap marketplace. If the current price of the Russell 2000, our small-cap index, is above its trendline (39-week average), then small-caps are trending upward.

At FabianLive.com, you can also review a variety of special reports on 401(k)s and IRAs, read editions of my weekly e-letter—the *Maverick Investing Flash*—and take the Mav Quiz to find out if you are an aggressive, moderate, or conservative maverick. (Of course, you've now done this, so steer a friend toward the Mav Quiz.)

NASD Regulation, Inc. the independent subsidiary of the National Association of Securities Dealers

Web site: www.nasdr.com

Have you ever been ripped off, as an investor? Or have you heard stories about someone who has? If so, you're understandably wary about sending your hard-earned dollars off to be cared for by unknown people.

But there is a way for you to avoid the scam artists. The National Association of Securities Dealers (NASDR) has a Web site, NASDR.com, that is devoted to a singular purpose—protecting you!

For example, NASDR.com regularly publishes "Investor Alerts" about the latest schemes. The NASD, alongside other regulators, can help you file complaints and in some cases, help you retain a lawyer and get your money back.

The thing I like most about NASDR.com, though, is the comprehensive background check that it enables you to run both on brokers and brokerage firms. Before you invest, you can find out whether an individual or a company has violated rules of conduct in the past, and thereby avoid entering into a bad financial relationship.

PERSONAL FINANCE WEB SITES

Mavericks do not create wealth by investing alone. We shift the financial risk of damages by paying affordable premiums to insurance companies.

We exercise individual rights and family responsibilities by reducing taxes. We even seek ways to transfer wealth to our loved ones.

Investing, taxation, insurance, estate planning, retirement planning: These are some of the major categories of personal finance. And while no Web site replaces the tax knowledge of a talented accountant (CPA) or the legal expertise of an estate lawyer, there are several Web sites that can expand a maverick's financial horizons.

Quicken

at Quicken.com

Mavericks might be surprised by my interest in Quicken.com—a megafinancial site with buy-n-hold investing bias. But it's not the investing tips that intrigue me.

Quicken has the widest range of personal finance tools you'll find anywhere on the Internet, whether it's planning debt reduction, analyzing your auto insurance coverage, getting a term life quote, evaluating future tax liabilities, or uncovering potential deductions.

Go to the home page and head for the major topic headings. Click "Insurance" to get to the Auto Coverage Analyzer and the Term Life Needs Analyzer. Hit the "Saving and Spending" link for the Debt Reduction Planner. And although you'll have to scroll beyond a seashell collection of Turbo Tax ads (the company's bread-and-butter software), quicken.com's Tax Estimator and Deduction Finder are worth the effort.

Mavericks should take special advantage of the Debt Reduction Planner. Begin by entering auto, home, credit card, personal loans, and other interest-bearing payments that you make. The program will then identify your total debt, the interest you will pay, and the date when you will be debt-free (in most cases, not for the faint of heart). Ultimately, you can develop an action plan with specific targets to reduce your overall debt sooner.

Bankrate

at Bankrate.com

When we talk about "investing the maverick way," we're talking about a lifetime pursuit; we're talking about a fundamental change in the way we think about achieving our goals.

Sometimes, this change of thinking requires a new way to look at debt—and getting out of it! Other times, we're looking for the best offer on a credit card or a home mortgage.

Enter bankrate.com. Auto loans, refinancing, CDs, mortgages: Use this site's pull-down menu for the product that interests you. If you're looking for a bricks-and-mortar financial relationship, select a location of the country as well. Within seconds, you'll have a listing of the best rates available—local or nationwide.

Equally impressive at bankrate.com are the financial calculators you can use to manage your finances. Auto, home, investing, credit card—answer your questions in a flash.

For example, what is the real cost of your credit card debt? Or, what will it take to save for college education? And, which is better on the purchase of your new car—a cash rebate or dealer financing?

The Dollar Stretcher

at stretcher.com

The Dollar Stretcher is a resource for daily living that actually lives up to its tagline. The editors present online features in one-page, easy-to-scan text—stories on everything from budgeting, credit repair, debt management, and retirement savings.

This is *not* the most intuitive site on the Web—for example, you'll have to journey halfway down the home page to find the Dollar Stretcher Library. But once you do, you'll gain access to the Web's largest collection of free money-saving articles.

Click on "Debt" in the Dollar Stretcher Library, for example, and you'll see more than 50 articles on topics such as which debt to go after first, what to do about your credit report, taking advantage of lower interest rates, and the pros and cons of consolidating loans.

The Dollar Stretcher doesn't barrage you with endless, intrusive, or annoying advertisements. However, they do link up with bankrate.com to help those who are looking to avoid credit card company tricks and to obtain the best deal. Now that's free info that every maverick should read!

ETFs—"FUNDS THAT TRADE LIKE STOCKS"

Here's a complete listing of exchange traded funds, as referenced in Chap. 19.

Exchange Traded Funds

Name	Ticker
Diamonds Trust	DIA
S&P Midcap 400	MDY
Nasdaq 100	QQQ

Name	Ticker
Name	**Ticker**
Spiders (SPDRS)	SPY
iShares Nasdaq Biotechnology	IBB
iShares Cohen&Steers Rlty Majr	ICF
iShares Goldman Sachs Tech Idx	IGM
iShares DJ US Utility Index	IDU
iShares DJ US Cnsmr Cyclical	IYC
iShares DJ US Chemical Index	IYD
iShares DJ US Energy Index	IYE
iShares DJ US Finance Index	IYF
iShares DJ US Financial Servcs	IYG
iShares DJ US Health Care	IYH
iShares DJ US Industrial Index	IYJ
iShares DJ U.S. Non-Cyclicals	IYK
iShares DJ US Basic Material	IYM
iShares DJ US Real Estate	IYR
iShares DJ US Internet	IYV
iShares DJ US Technology	IYW
iShares DJ US Total Market	IYY
iShares DJ US Telecomm	IYZ
iShares S&P Europe 350 Index	IEV
iShares S&P Midcap 400 Index	IJH
iShares S&P Mdcp 400/BARRA Val	IJJ
iShares S&P Mdcp 400/BARRA Gth	IJK
iShares S&P Small Cap 600 Indx	IJR
iShares S&P SmCp 600/BARRA Val	IJS
iShares S&P SmCp 600/BARRA Gth	IJT
iShares S&P/TSE 60 Index	IKC
iShares S&P 500/BARRA Val Indx	IVE
iShares S&P 500 Index Shares	IVV
iShares S&P 500/BARRA Growth	IVW
iShares S&P 100 Global Index	IOO
Spiders S&P Basic Material	XLB
Spiders S&P Energy	XLE
Spiders S&P Financial	XLF
Spiders S&P Industrials	XLI
Spiders S&P Technology	XLK
Spiders S&P Consumer Staples	XLP
Spiders S&P Utilities	XLU
Spiders S&P Consumer Services	XLV

Name	Ticker
Spiders S&P Cyclical Transptn	XLY
iShares Russell 1000 Index	IWB
iShares Russell 1000 Value Idx	IWD
iShares Russell 1000 Gwth Indx	IWF
iShares Russell 2000 Index	IWM
iShares Russell 2000 Value	IWN
iShares Russell 2000 Growth	IWO
iShares Russell 3000 Index	IWV
iShares Russell 3000Value	IWW
iShares Russell 3000 Growth	IWZ
iShares MSCI Australia Index	EWA
iShares MSCI Canada Index	EWC
iShares MSCI Sweden Index	EWD
iShares MSCI Germany Index	EWG
iShares MSCI Hong Kong Index	EWH
iShares MSCI Italy Index	EWI
iShares MSCI Japan Index	EWJ
iShares MSCI Belgium Index	EWK
iShares MSCI Switzerland Indx	EWL
iShares MSCI Netherlands	EWN
iShares MSCI Austria Index	EWO
iShares MSCI Spain Index	EWP
iShares MSCI France	EWQ
iShares MSCI Singapore Index	EWS
iShares MSCI Taiwan Index	EWT
iShares MSCI UK Index	EWU
iShares MSCI Mexico Index	EWW
iShares MSCI South Korea Index	EWY
iShares MSCI Brazil Index	EWZ
iShares MSCI EMU Index	EZU
iShares MSCI Malaysia	EWM
iShares MSCI EAFE	EFA
Biotechnology HOLDRs	BBH
Broadband HOLDRs	BDH
B2B Internet HOLDRs	BHH
Internet HOLDRs	HHH
Architechture HOLDRs	IAH
Internet Infrastructure HOLDRs	IIH
2000+ HOLDRs	MKH

Name	Ticker
Oil Serv HOLDRS	OIH
Pharm HOLDRS	PPH
Regional Bank HOLDRs	RKH
Semiconductor HOLDRs	SMH
Software HOLDRS	SWH
Telecommunication HOLDRs	TTH
Utilities HOLDRs	UTH
Wireless HOLDRs	WMH
Europe 2001 HOLDRS	EKH
streetTRACKS DJ Global Titians	DGT
streetTRACKS DJ US Sm Cap Gwth	DSG
street TRACKS DJ US Small Cp VI	DSV
streetTRACKS DJ US Lrg Cap Gwt	ELG
streetTRACKS DJ US Lrg Cp Valu	ELV
streetTRACKS Mrgn Stnly Intrnt	MII
streetTRACKS Mrgn St High Tech	MTK
streetTRACKS Wilshire REIT Index	RWR
Fortune e-50 Index	FEF
Fortune 500 Index	FFF
Varnguard Total St Mrk VIPERS	VTI

COMPOUNDED GROWTH CHARTS (pages 288–291)

Compounded Growth: Time + Money + Rate of Return = Wealth. There's only one element that's fixed: Time. That's why you have to make the most of it, pursuing extraordinary growth as soon as possible.

Approaching the Maverick Finish Line

Congratulations! You've plowed your way not just through a chapter that was little more than a glorified list, but also through an *entire book* that was permeated by the likes of me. Good job. I feel like I should reward you by setting you free. But I also feel the need for one more short—very short!—chapter to tie a few things together.

5% Annualized Compounded Growth

Monthly

Deposit	5 Years	10 Years	15 Years	20 Years	25 Years	30 Years	35 Years
$25	1,702	3,875	6,648	10,186	14,703	20,467	27,824
$50	3,404	7,750	13,295	20,373	29,405	40,934	55,647
$100	6,809	15,499	26,590	40,745	58,811	81,868	111,294
$200	13,618	30,998	53,180	81,490	117,622	163,735	222,588
$300	20,427	46,497	79,770	122,235	176,432	245,603	333,883
$400	27,236	61,996	106,360	162,980	235,243	327,470	445,177
$500	34,045	77,495	132,950	203,725	294,054	409,338	556,471
$600	40,854	92,994	159,540	244,470	352,865	491,205	667,765
$700	47,663	108,494	186,130	285,216	411,675	573,073	779,060
$800	54,472	123,993	212,720	325,961	470,486	654,940	890,354
$900	61,281	139,492	239,310	366,706	529,297	736,808	1,001,648
$1,000	68,090	154,991	265,900	407,451	588,108	818,675	1,112,942

Yearly

Deposit	5 Years	10 Years	15 Years	20 Years	25 Years	30 Years	35 Years
$250	1,450	3,302	5,664	8,680	12,528	17,440	23,709
$500	2,901	6,603	11,329	17,360	25,057	34,880	47,418
$1,000	5,802	13,207	22,657	34,719	50,113	69,761	94,836
$2,000	11,604	26,414	45,315	69,439	100,227	139,522	189,673
$3,000	17,406	39,620	67,972	104,158	150,340	209,282	284,509
$4,000	23,208	52,827	90,630	138,877	200,454	279,043	379,345
$5,000	29,010	66,034	113,287	173,596	250,567	348,804	474,182
$6,000	34,811	79,241	135,945	208,316	300,681	418,565	569,018
$7,000	40,613	92,448	158,602	243,035	350,794	488,326	663,854
$8,000	46,415	105,654	181,260	277,754	400,908	558,086	758,691
$9,000	52,217	118,861	203,917	312,473	451,021	627,847	853,527
$10,000	58,019	132,068	226,575	347,193	501,135	697,608	948,363

Lump Sum

Deposit	5 Years	10 Years	15 Years	20 Years	25 Years	30 Years	35 Years
$2,500	3,191	4,072	5,197	6,633	8,466	10,805	13,790
$5,000	6,381	8,144	10,395	13,266	16,932	21,610	27,580
$10,000	12,763	16,289	20,789	26,533	33,864	43,219	55,160
$20,000	25,526	32,578	41,579	53,066	67,727	86,439	110,320
$30,000	38,288	48,867	62,368	79,599	101,591	129,658	165,480
$40,000	51,051	65,156	83,157	106,132	135,454	172,878	220,641
$50,000	63,814	81,445	103,946	132,665	169,318	216,097	275,801
$60,000	76,577	97,734	124,736	159,198	203,181	259,317	330,961
$70,000	89,340	114,023	145,525	185,731	237,045	302,536	386,121
$80,000	102,103	130,312	166,314	212,264	270,908	345,755	441,281
$90,000	114,865	146,601	187,104	238,797	304,772	388,975	496,441
$100,000	127,628	162,889	207,893	265,330	338,635	432,194	551,602

10% Annualized Compounded Growth

Monthly

Deposit	5 Years	10 Years	15 Years	20 Years	25 Years	30 Years	35 Years
$25	1,929	5,036	10,040	18,099	31,078	51,980	85,644
$50	3,859	10,073	20,081	36,199	62,156	103,961	171,287
$100	7,717	20,146	40,161	72,397	124,312	207,922	342,575
$200	15,434	40,291	80,323	144,794	248,625	415,844	685,149
$300	23,151	60,437	120,484	217,191	372,937	623,766	1,027,724
$400	30,869	80,582	160,646	289,588	497,250	831,687	1,370,298
$500	38,586	100,728	200,807	361,985	621,562	1,039,609	1,712,873
$600	46,303	120,873	240,969	434,383	745,874	1,247,531	2,055,447
$700	54,020	141,019	281,130	506,780	870,187	1,455,453	2,398,022
$800	61,737	161,165	321,292	579,177	994,499	1,663,375	2,740,596
$900	69,454	181,310	361,453	651,574	1,118,812	1,871,297	3,083,171
$1,000	77,171	201,456	401,615	723,971	1,243,124	2,079,218	3,425,745

Yearly

Deposit	5 Years	10 Years	15 Years	20 Years	25 Years	30 Years	35 Years
$250	1,679	4,383	8,737	15,751	27,045	45,236	74,532
$500	3,358	8,766	17,475	31,501	54,091	90,472	149,063
$1,000	6,716	17,531	34,950	63,002	108,182	180,943	298,127
$2,000	13,431	35,062	69,899	126,005	216,364	361,887	596,254
$3,000	20,147	52,594	104,849	189,007	324,545	542,830	894,380
$4,000	26,862	70,125	139,799	252,010	432,727	723,774	1,192,507
$5,000	33,578	87,656	174,749	315,012	540,909	904,717	1,490,634
$6,000	40,294	105,187	209,698	378,015	649,091	1,085,661	1,788,761
$7,000	47,009	122,718	244,648	441,017	757,272	1,266,604	2,086,888
$8,000	53,725	140,249	279,598	504,020	865,454	1,447,547	2,385,014
$9,000	60,440	157,781	314,548	567,022	973,636	1,628,491	2,683,141
$10,000	67,156	175,312	349,497	630,025	1,081,818	1,809,434	2,981,268

Lump Sum

Deposit	5 Years	10 Years	15 Years	20 Years	25 Years	30 Years	35 Years
$2,500	4,026	6,484	10,443	16,819	27,087	43,624	70,256
$5,000	8,053	12,969	20,886	33,637	54,174	87,247	140,512
$10,000	16,105	25,937	41,772	67,275	108,347	174,494	281,024
$20,000	32,210	51,875	83,545	134,550	216,694	348,988	562,049
$30,000	48,315	77,812	125,317	201,825	325,041	523,482	843,073
$40,000	64,420	103,750	167,090	269,100	433,388	697,976	1,124,097
$50,000	80,526	129,687	208,862	336,375	541,735	872,470	1,405,122
$60,000	96,631	155,625	250,635	403,650	650,082	1,046,964	1,686,146
$70,000	112,736	181,562	292,407	470,925	758,429	1,221,458	1,967,171
$80,000	128,841	207,499	334,180	538,200	866,776	1,395,952	2,248,195
$90,000	144,946	233,437	375,952	605,475	975,124	1,570,446	2,529,219
$100,000	161,051	259,374	417,725	672,750	1,083,471	1,744,940	2,810,244

15% Annualized Compounded Growth

Monthly

Deposit	5 Years	10 Years	15 Years	20 Years	25 Years	30 Years	35 Years
$25	2,182	6,568	15,382	33,094	68,687	124,989	283,953
$50	4,365	13,137	30,764	66,187	137,374	249,978	567,907
$100	8,730	26,273	61,528	132,375	274,747	499,957	1,135,814
$200	17,460	52,546	123,055	264,749	549,494	999,914	2,271,627
$300	26,190	78,819	184,583	397,124	824,241	1,499,871	3,407,441
$400	34,919	105,092	246,111	529,499	1,098,989	1,999,828	4,543,255
$500	43,649	131,366	307,639	661,873	1,373,736	2,499,785	5,679,068
$600	52,379	157,639	369,166	794,248	1,648,483	2,999,742	6,814,882
$700	61,109	183,912	430,694	926,623	1,923,230	3,499,698	7,950,696
$800	69,839	210,185	492,222	1,058,997	2,197,977	3,999,655	9,086,510
$900	78,569	236,458	553,750	1,191,372	2,472,724	4,499,612	10,222,323
$1,000	87,298	262,731	615,277	1,323,747	2,747,471	4,999,569	11,358,137

Yearly

Deposit	5 Years	10 Years	15 Years	20 Years	25 Years	30 Years	35 Years
$250	1,938	5,837	13,679	29,453	61,178	124,989	253,336
$500	3,877	11,675	27,359	58,905	122,356	249,978	506,673
$1,000	7,754	23,349	54,717	117,810	244,712	499,957	1,013,346
$2,000	15,507	46,699	109,435	235,620	489,424	999,914	2,026,691
$3,000	23,261	70,048	164,152	353,430	734,136	1,499,871	3,040,037
$4,000	31,015	93,397	218,870	471,240	978,848	1,999,828	4,053,383
$5,000	38,769	116,746	273,587	589,051	1,223,560	2,499,785	5,066,728
$6,000	46,522	140,096	328,305	706,861	1,468,272	2,999,742	6,080,074
$7,000	54,276	163,445	383,022	824,671	1,712,984	3,499,698	7,093,420
$8,000	62,030	186,794	437,740	942,481	1,957,696	3,999,655	8,106,765
$9,000	69,784	210,143	492,457	1,060,291	2,202,408	4,499,612	9,120,111
$10,000	77,537	233,493	547,175	1,178,101	2,447,120	4,999,569	10,133,457

Lump Sum

Deposit	5 Years	10 Years	15 Years	20 Years	25 Years	30 Years	35 Years
$2,500	5,028	10,114	20,343	40,916	82,297	165,529	332,939
$5,000	10,057	20,228	40,685	81,833	164,595	331,059	665,878
$10,000	20,114	40,456	81,371	163,665	329,190	662,118	1,331,755
$20,000	40,227	80,911	162,741	327,331	658,379	1,324,235	2,663,510
$30,000	60,341	121,367	244,112	490,996	987,569	1,986,353	3,995,266
$40,000	80,454	161,822	325,482	654,661	1,316,758	2,648,471	5,327,021
$50,000	100,568	202,278	406,853	818,327	1,645,948	3,310,589	6,658,776
$60,000	120,681	242,733	488,224	981,992	1,975,137	3,972,706	7,990,531
$70,000	140,795	283,189	569,594	1,145,658	2,304,327	4,634,824	9,322,287
$80,000	160,909	323,645	650,965	1,309,323	2,633,516	5,296,942	10,654,042
$90,000	181,022	364,100	732,336	1,472,988	2,962,706	5,959,059	11,985,797
$100,000	201,136	404,556	813,706	1,636,654	3,291,895	6,621,177	13,317,552

20% Annualized Compounded Growth

Monthly

Deposit	5 Years	10 Years	15 Years	20 Years	25 Years	30 Years	35 Years
$25	2,468	8,607	23,885	61,900	156,489	391,852	977,495
$50	4,935	17,215	47,770	123,799	312,979	783,705	1,954,990
$100	9,870	34,430	95,540	247,599	625,958	1,567,410	3,909,979
$200	19,740	68,860	191,081	495,197	1,251,915	3,134,820	7,819,959
$300	29,611	103,290	286,621	742,796	1,877,873	4,702,230	11,729,938
$400	39,481	137,719	382,161	990,394	2,503,831	6,269,640	15,639,918
$500	49,351	172,149	477,702	1,237,993	3,129,788	7,837,050	19,549,897
$600	59,221	206,579	573,342	1,485,592	3,755,746	9,404,460	23,459,877
$700	69,092	241,009	668,783	1,733,190	4,381,704	10,971,870	27,369,856
$800	78,962	275,439	764,323	1,980,789	5,007,662	12,539,280	31,279,835
$900	88,832	309,869	859,863	2,228,388	5,633,619	14,106,690	35,189,815
$1,000	98,702	344,299	955,404	2,475,986	6,259,577	15,674,100	39,099,794

Yearly

Deposit	5 Years	10 Years	15 Years	20 Years	25 Years	30 Years	35 Years
$250	2,232	7,788	21,611	56,006	141,594	354,564	884,502
$500	4,465	15,575	43,221	112,013	283,189	709,129	1,769,005
$1,000	8,930	31,150	86,442	224,026	566,377	1,418,258	3,538,009
$2,000	17,860	62,301	172,884	448,051	1,132,755	2,836,516	7,076,019
$3,000	26,790	93,451	259,326	672,077	1,699,132	4,254,774	10,614,028
$4,000	35,720	124,602	345,769	896,102	2,265,509	5,673,032	14,152,037
$5,000	44,650	155,752	432,211	1,120,128	2,831,886	7,091,289	17,690,047
$6,000	53,580	186,903	518,653	1,344,154	3,398,264	8,509,547	21,228,056
$7,000	62,509	218,053	605,095	1,568,179	3,964,641	9,927,805	24,766,066
$8,000	71,439	249,203	691,537	1,792,205	4,531,018	11,346,063	28,304,075
$9,000	80,369	280,354	777,979	2,016,230	5,097,396	12,764,321	31,842,084
$10,000	89,299	311,504	864,421	2,240,256	5,663,773	14,182,579	35,380,094

Lump Sum

Deposit	5 Years	10 Years	15 Years	20 Years	25 Years	30 Years	35 Years
$2,500	6,221	15,479	38,518	95,844	38,491	593,441	1,476,671
$5,000	12,442	30,959	77,035	191,688	476,981	1,186,882	2,953,341
$10,000	24,883	61,917	154,070	383,376	953,962	2,373,763	5,906,682
$20,000	49,766	123,835	308,140	766,752	1,907,924	4,747,526	11,813,365
$30,000	74,650	185,752	462,211	1,150,128	2,861,886	7,121,289	17,720,047
$40,000	99,533	247,669	616,281	1,533,504	3,815,849	9,495,053	23,626,729
$50,000	124,416	309,587	770,351	1,916,880	4,769,811	11,868,816	29,533,411
$60,000	149,299	371,504	924,421	2,300,256	5,723,773	14,242,579	35,440,094
$70,000	174,182	433,422	1,078,492	2,683,632	6,677,735	16,616,342	41,346,776
$80,000	199,066	495,339	1,232,562	3,067,008	7,631,697	18,990,105	47,253,458
$90,000	223,949	557,256	1,386,632	3,450,384	8,585,659	21,363,868	53,160,141
$100,000	248,832	619,174	1,540,702	3,833,760	9,539,622	23,737,631	59,066,823

CHAPTER

22

The Final Go-Round

OK: So maybe it *is* a cruel world out there, full of opportunists, bad advice, and bond salesmen.

The question is, as an investor, *what are you going to do about it?* How are you to create your own advantages? How are you going to keep the bad guys out of your portfolio, and out of your life?

How are you going to react when you experience a setback? What kind of example will you set for your children, in terms of managing money today in order to create a better future for themselves?

And even more broadly: Are you able to strike a balance in your life? Are you living in the present, as well as providing for the future? Are you smelling the roses, as well as minding your money?

Like most authors, I hope that you've found my book interesting and challenging, the first time through. I also hope that you'll find it a useful guide and a helpful companion for years to come. You've heard a lot of individual voices in the previous chapters, and seen references to a large number of specific funds, companies, and investment vehicles. These people, institutions, and instruments have been introduced to illustrate the larger points I've been trying to make. Ten years from now, or maybe even two years from how, lots of those names will sound quaint or antique. The

Nasdaq meltdown of 2000–so fresh in our minds as I was writing this book!–will sound like a page from ancient history.

But the larger points–the things that go into being a maverick investor–will endure. So let me restate a few of those larger points, and hope that in 5 or 10 years, you'll find that they still have relevance and power. And since I'm talking about *you, your money,* and *your dreams,* I'm willing to bet that they will.

First, *the easiest thing for an investor to do is to lose money.* Don't ever forget this. Hold on to your nest egg as tightly as you can, whenever you start to hear about the "next sure thing." Losing money happens far more often than we'd like to admit. Think you're the only one who made a stinko investment? You're not; it's just that nobody wants to talk about the experience. Bear markets, bad advice, bad analyses, and bad timing—all kinds of bad things can make an investment go sour. So keep your guard up every time you find yourself listening to someone else's advice, and every time you place a "buy" order.

And by the way: Don't kick yourself around the block when you make a mistake. Learn from it. (Mavericks learn from their mistakes.) Get over it. Move on. Enjoy life.

Another key point: *There are zillions of people out there who would be only too happy to drown you.* In information, I mean. Just about every media outlet has decided that you are in need of financial advice, and that they are the ones to sell it to you. Television, radio, newspapers, books, and the Internet are just some of the portals through which information will come your way. In the face of this flood tide of information, most of it bad, you need a compass, a strainer, a hype detector—something to help you sift through things and filter out the nonsense.

I think a personal philosophy, translated into a lifestyle, is the best possible filter. If you hold everything up to a standard you believe in—if you *live* your philosophy—you're unlikely to get gulled, hoodwinked, or drowned. You'll be able to spot both opportunity and opportunists. This is what maverick investing is all about: adopting a lifestyle that puts you in control.

What else? Oh, yes: *Wall Street is out to get your money.* That's how they make *their* money. Remember that Wall Street is selling more than they are telling. Even if that salesperson you're talking to is just about the *nicest possible* guy or gal in the world, you've simply got to ask the kinds of tough questions that will give you a basis for decision-making and action. Like, What are the annual expense charges? What rate of return should I expect if things go well? What if things go poorly? How much of *your* money is in this program or product you're recommending? If I want my money back, what are the surrender charges or penalties? Asking questions is not a sign of weakness; it's a sign of self-confidence. Ask!

Never forget this: *The media are always behind the curve.* Let's look at just one example. In 1979, *Business Week* published a cover story called "The Death of Equities." The gist of this article was that stock prices would underperform hard assets and cash over the next 20 years.

Hmmm. What was going on, here? The *Business Week* writer made the classic mistake of both generals and pundits—he fought the last war. Drawing on his impressions of the 1970s (in which equities did indeed underperform), he extrapolated from the high interest rates and inflation that characterized that era and predicted that those conditions would continue. I assume that he (and worse, everybody he misled) missed out on the greatest 20-year equity growth period in history.

Oh, what the heck: Let's indulge ourselves and revive a second, more recent example. The March 2000 issue of *Smart Money* included a cover story on the best technology companies—the hot-tech stocks that every investor absolutely had to own!!! *(Exclamation marks added!)* Well, as of this writing, those stocks are trading at discounts of 80 percent from their breathless highs. When it comes to forecasting the future—which mavericks never do, by the way—the media are always hopelessly rooted in the past. And don't forget that the people who write these articles don't have significant money to invest. If they did, they wouldn't be writing these articles.

Remember, too, that *the world is changing at a pace never before experienced in history.* Technology is changing people's lives every day. Advances in health care are extending our lives. Improved telecommunication are giving us vastly better access to information.

So what? Well, dramatic changes create opportunities to profit as investors. As mavericks, we prepare for any and all change that the future will bring our way. We welcome change.

At the risk of stating the obvious, *human beings are emotional, impressionable, and herd-oriented.* As individuals, we are overly influenced by what we read, what others say, and how our stomach feels. We're herd animals: We want to convince others to do what we're doing, and at the same time we want others to convince us to do what they're doing. This explains, in part, all the crazy stock-market stampedes over the decades. In the late 1990s, for example, the herd embraced the indexing of the S&P 500. Then, for a brief period, it was those cool tech stocks that *Smart Money* and all the others were talking about. Life in the herd feels good because it builds confidence. (If I'm in the middle of this big crowd, how wrong can I be?) But herds stumble, panic, and break up under even minor pressure. Think of those nature shows where the lone big cat terrorizes the huge herd of zebras, wildebeests, or whatevers. So much for safety in numbers!

I could keep going with the Big Ideas, but I think you get the point. Be skeptical, but also be open to new ideas and great advice. Ask. Listen. Be disciplined if you see good reason to venture into new territories. Be principled, but not rigid. Don't steer by your wake, and don't consult the crystal ball. Be maverick!

Hey—the time has come. The moment of truth is here. This is *it:* the perfect time to make the commitment to your future wealth. You know it's time for you to get in gear, to create the wealth you desire. You know that it's time to change.

I'm talking about changes in terms of your investments, your dreams, and your attitudes. Changes that will help you get more out of life. No, you don't have to do 20 new things starting today. But you *do* have to commit to following the maverick principles, which by now should be pretty familiar to you:

1. I take full responsibility for my financial future
2. I invest for clear-cut, attainable goals
3. I strive for extraordinary portfolio growth (personally, I shoot for 20 percent annualized compounded growth)
4. I maximize all of my tax-deferred investing opportunities
5. I put 100 percent of my money in stocks
6. I track the performance of the stock market, my holdings, and my choices
7. I know when to buy and sell every asset in my portfolio
8. I pursue growth in stocks throughout my entire life
9. I never predict the direction of stock prices
10. I capitalize on market change and investment innovation

TALES FROM THE FRONT LINES
If I were you, at this point I'd probably be saying something like the following:

> Hey, Doug. Even though you're a reasonably young guy, you seem to have been at this for a while. And if I understand you right, your dad was espousing many of the same principles for a decade or so before you got there. So shouldn't there be a bunch of mavericks out there who have been

at this for, say, 20 years? How are *they* doing? "Just the facts," as you like to say!

The answer is that there are lots of successful long-term mavericks out there, happily pursuing their maverick strategies. Let's look at just two examples. These are real people who have been living the maverick lifestyle for the past 20 years. They've given me permission to reprint their unsolicited comments—thanks, Ron and Dave!—and I do so in the following pages. You'll read these two letters just as they came to me. You'll notice that the first letter is addressed to my dad, and that the second is addressed to both my dad and me.

Dear Mr. Fabian,

Some time back in 1983–84, after watching my savings going nowhere with my first attempt at investing with a full-service broker, I decided I needed to spend some time at the library to see if there was a better way to invest. I just felt that I could do as good as a job as my broker, which would not take to much work to beat.

I don't remember which book it was, but from some place, I found your name. I'm not sure how long I waited, but I finally decided to try your newsletter. It was $20.00 for your book, or one free newsletter, or something? It's been too long. For some reason, the only thing I could relate to was the rock and roll singer "Fabian" who was the competition for Elvis. I just wasn't sure you could do me any good, but the library didn't answer my question and I felt like I might learn something for my $20.00 investment. Little did I know that you knew everything.

After learning your concepts I decide to try a subscription. Then came all the special reports, the videotapes, the cassette tapes, the books, and even a picture of you and your wife. Each week that went by I learned more and more. I listened to the tapes over and over again, reviewed the reports over again, read every book that you told me to read, and learned that keeping your emotions in control, and having a goal, was 95 percent of the battle. I listened to your every word and believed in everything that you taught. Even today I continue to learn from your son.

In just a few more months I will retire. I am 55. We will enjoy our country in a motor home, and visit with friends and family, and help other people, and fish, and hike, and camp in as many other countries as we can visit. This will take place because of you. My family is prosperous because of you. My children will be successful because of you. I have never in my entire life had a person who has made such an influence on me as you have.

Not only taught me how to be financially secure, but how to maintain a good emotional balance and not become sidetracked just because some days or weeks didn't go my way. You are without question my mentor. I can't begin to tell you all the things that I have learned from you. All this knowledge is being passed on to my loved ones, so that the "library" will continue for generations to come.

My parents were not well educated. My dad came from Russia and could not read or write. He passed away when I was in my early teens. We always got by but were poor. We were in the land of opportunity but didn't have a mentor to guide us in any direction. Our goal in life was to become better educated than our parents, so we could obtain better jobs with higher income. My daughters have both fulfilled this goal for another generation. The big difference in their lives is they had you for a mentor. You planted the seed that started the trusts for their college education. You planted the seed that opened their first IRA at age 17. You planted the seeds to have goals. You planted the seeds to be responsible for your debts. They graduated from college debt-free. Their retirement plans are a non-issue at this very young time in their lives. All this success, all this knowledge, all this prosperity, all this education, all been achieved because of what you have taught us. It is truly an honor for this family to have you as our mentor. In one generation, from illiterate immigrant to Masters in Education.

I still have every tape you have ever sent, and the picture of you and your wife still remains on my office shelf. My daughters started learning by listening to you. I laugh when I hear Doug say something about the learning sessions that he had with you as a kid. I've been on that road with my daughters also. My daughter has told me that she has great difficulty finding an adult that understands or has taken advantage of the basic ideas that we have learned from you, let alone someone her own age.

You should feel extremely proud of how your son Doug has continued in your footsteps. We are so blessed to have Doug continue with the endless energy that he generates in keeping us educated and on the right track. I have not missed a single show from day one. I look forward to recording each weekly show from the Web. Not only am I interested in how the plan is doing for the week, but also I really enjoy listening to Doug. He can come up with some extremely funny things to say. I can only imagine what goes on during the commercials. He can be just hilarious. Sometimes I wish I could relate to some of those callers just how well your plan has worked for us. Just get over it and subscribe to the newsletter, it will change your life. People procrastinate. I have heard some people call in who started with you long ago. You have helped change many people's lives and outlooks. Doug is doing the same.

One thing that you always taught us was there is no such thing as a free lunch. So, if you could find the time for some personal words of wisdom from the "master," I would appreciate some words of encouragement to my daughter Christine inside a copy of your new book. I will be more then happy to send you a payment for whatever cost is involved with sending this book. Just enclose a bill. Her birthday is on March 7th and I couldn't think of a better gift then a personal message from the person who has changed her life forever.

I hope that you will feel complimented by what I have expressed in this letter. It is truly my most sincere feelings for all that you have taught us and all the tremendous results we have had by listening to you. This letter and a free lunch are long overdue. I hope as you (and Doug if he is along) enjoy your lunch, you both realize how many people you have helped to under-stand and take advantage of all the opportunity our country offers. I have never come so close to finding a better method while still enjoying life. Sending that $20.00 was the best.

I just finished with the tapes of last week's show. Doug said that in next week's show, you would cover how to get children started and involved with investing. It usually takes until the next Wed-Thurs for me to finish with the previous week's show.

I have enclosed a copy of Christine's year-end worksheet for her retire-ment plans. We got her started saving for her first IRA at age 16. Gave the kids matching dollars as a carrot to keep them on their set goals. They had a hard time believing that this could really happen to them, coming from an ordinary family background. Today we do not have any more discussions about saving. On Jan 2 of each year the full contribution is at the Schwab office. Again, another example of your influence and teaching.

Christine listens to Doug each week also.

Sincerely,
Ron T.
Englewood, CO

And here's the second letter:

Dear Dick and Doug:

My name is Dave L., and I'm the one who called the radio show today as "Dave from Phoenix." (I actually live in Scottsdale.)

This note is overdue personal "thank you" to both of you, and especially you, Dick, for creating the original *Telephone Switch Newsletter* and the Fabian Investment Plan. Though you don't even know me, you've been my virtual financial godfather for the past 20 years.

You may enjoy reading the details below, but the bottom line of my story is that starting with about $20,000 at age 33, I'm now 53 with a portfolio worth nearly $2,500,000 before taxes.

My (rather long) Fabian story:

I graduated college in 1970 with a degree in engineering, and started my career with Bell Labs in New Jersey. Almost immediately, stock brokers began calling me, and for 10 years I made investments under their so-called "guidance." At the end of that time, I had barely broken even. They had made money, but I hadn't!

In late 1980, while riding a bus to work, a friend handed me someone's newsletter (I don't remember whose) that had a short summary of the Fabian algorithm. There was just enough information there to get me interested. I remember wondering if it could really be that simple. I also remember being impressed that you actually shared the investment algorithm openly with anyone—even nonsubscribers—and that there were no backroom secret formulas. That gave me the means to check it out further.

As you described on the radio show last week (or perhaps the week before), I too trudged off to the library and started going through back issues of *The Wall Street Journal* on microfiche. I gathered the DJIA Friday closing values as a surrogate for mutual fund prices. With about 10 years' worth of data in hand, I wrote a trading simulation program on a time-share computing system at work. Computing was pretty primitive back then—the computer itself had less computing power than the Palm Pilot I carry around today.

In the simulations, the method really did seem to work—it didn't produce the 20 percent you often cite as a goal, but it did yield about 16 to 17 percent. I experimented with different averaging intervals—from 13 to 52 weeks. Eventually, I settled on the 39 weeks that you use. I set a goal of doubling my money every 5 years—that's the same as 14.9 percent per year. With the plan it looked like I could do it, and in the past 20 years, I actually have.

I started with about $20,000—pretty much all I had, sometime in early 1981. I became a subscriber to the *Telephone Switch Newsletter* in November of 1981. (My subscriber number back then was L7338). I still have my original newsletter issues and investment manual—in fact I've saved them all.)

I added more money over the years, and when you pointed out their advantages, I moved my money into Variable Annuities. After 20 years I have the $2.5 million pre-tax I mentioned above. Most of that money comes from growth. I've realized somewhere between 15 percent and 16 percent equivalent annualized yield.

Though my grandmother would say "Everyone should have such problems," the only "downer" now is taxes—especially if my annuities and IRAs end up getting hit by estate and income taxes. I'm protecting against that with an irrevocable life insurance trust, gifting the premiums to my kids. I'm also putting future cash into an Ameritas VUL account so that I can get at some of it before age 59 without penalty, and I'm following your lead by transferring my largest annuity (with Nationwide) into American Skandia.

On the personal side, I've been married 28 years and we have two great kids, ages 16 and 11, both at the top of their school classes and both of whom we can comfortably send to college. I'm teaching both of our children about investing with an UTMA account that we're managing via the Fabian plan. I have a good job now, but thanks to the plan, I am also thinking about early retirement, other kinds of jobs (like teaching), or even starting a small company of my own.

Again, my thanks, compliments, and best regards to you both. I hope I'll get to meet you in person one day.

Dave L.
Scottsdale, AZ

FINIS

I love these two stories! First, they give me the opportunity to acknowledge once again the huge debt that I owe to my dad—a debt that lots of people out there seem to share with me. Second, they are great examples of how real people have used the maverick principles to empower themselves to build the wealth they desire.

I hope you found them at least a little bit inspirational. And I hope you noticed how *similar* they were, once you got past the specific details. Believe me when I say that they are also similar to many of the other maverick stories that come over my transom. Collectively, they reassure me that there really are maverick principles that can be applied to a wide range of individual styles and circumstances. They reassure me that these maverick principles can lead all kinds of people to financial success.

I want you to imagine your future success story. (Think about the letter you want to write me, in 20 years.) Think about how you and your family could benefit from the power of compounded growth. Think about that feeling of being *in control,* knowing how to react in every situation that comes up when investing. That's what the principles of maverick investing can do for you.

I want *you* to become an extraordinary investor. "Ordinary" is not for you and me. We will not settle for second-place. We will not place our future in the hands of others and hope that things work out. We will not allow others to use our hard-earned money so they can get rich.

Let's agree to set our goals high. Let's agree to focus on the most important priority in our lives, and get all of our assets working toward that priority. Let's agree to assume the responsibility for managing risk, and building wealth.

Let's agree to be *mavericks.*

Index

About the Author

Doug Fabian is the host of the popular syndicated radio program *Maverick Investing with Doug Fabian,* which airs on major markets in Los Angeles, Chicago, Las Vegas, and Phoenix. As president of Fabian Investment Resources, he has advised individual investors for more than 20 years and has made frequent appearances at investing seminars across the country. *Smart Money* magazine named him one of the 30 most influential people in the mutual fund industry, and he is regularly quoted on television (including CNBC, CNN, and the Fox News channel) and in newspapers (including *The New York Times, The Wall Street Journal,* and the *Los Angeles Times*).